Being Anglican in the Third Millennium

Panama 1996

THE OFFICIAL REPORT OF THE
10th MEETING OF THE
ANGLICAN CONSULTATIVE COUNCIL

Editors: James Rosenthal and Nicola Currie

Published for the Anglican Communion by

MOREHOUSE PUBLISHING
Harrisburg, Pennsylvania, USA

Acknowledgements

The official documentation of the 10th meeting of the Anglican Consultative Council, October 1996, Hotel Continental de Riande, Panama City, Panama. Hosted by the Diocese of Panama.

The Most Revd and Rt Hon. George L. Carey, *President*
The Revd Canon Colin Craston, *Chairman*
The Rt Revd Simon Chiwanga, *Vice Chairman*
The Revd Canon John L. Peterson, *Secretary General*

Those who made this report possible

James Rosenthal, Director of Communications
Nicola Currie, Assistant Editor *Anglican World*
Photographs: Lynn Ross, *Anglican World*/Rosenthal
Secretariat Co-ordinator: Christine Codner

ISBN 0-8192-1729-8

Published 1997 for the Anglican Communion Office,
Partnership House, 157 Waterloo Road, London SE1 8UT, UK

by Morehouse Publishing
P.O. Box 1321
Harrisburg, PA 17105

Contents

Member Churches
of the Anglican Consultative Council

The Anglican Church in Aotearoa, New Zealand and Polynesia

The Anglican Church of Australia

The Church of Bangladesh

The Episcopal Church of Brazil

The Church of the Province of Burundi

The Anglican Church of Canada

The Church of the Province of Central Africa

The Church of Ceylon (Sri Lanka)

The Church of England

The Church of the Province of the Indian Ocean

The Church of Ireland

The Holy Catholic Church in Japan (Nippon Sei Ko Kai)

The Episcopal Church in Jerusalem and the Middle East

The Church of the Province of Kenya

The Anglican Church of Korea

The Church of the Province of Melanesia

The Church of the Province of Mexico

The Church of the Province of Myanmar (Burma)

The Church of the Province of Nigeria

The Church of North India

The Church of Pakistan

The Anglican Church of Papua New Guinea

The Episcopal Church in the Philippines

The Province of the Episcopal Church of Rwanda

The Scottish Episcopal Church

The Church of the Province of South East Asia

The Church of the Province of Southern Africa

The Anglican Church of the Southern Cone of South America
(Iglesia Anglicana del Cono Sur de América)

The Church of South India

The Episcopal Church of the Sudan

The Church of the Province of Tanzania

The Church of the Province of Uganda

The Episcopal Church in the United States of America

The Church in Wales

The Church of the Province of West Africa

The Church in the Province of the West Indies

The Anglican Church of Zaire

Preface

by the Rt Revd Dr Richard Harries, Bishop of Oxford

Being cooped up in a hotel conference room under chilly air condition-ing is not my idea of fun. The compensation was meeting other members of the Anglican Communion and hearing their stories. We were strength-ened and encouraged by one another's faith.

The variety and cultural richness of the Anglican Communion is very marked. We needed to have simultaneous translations into Spanish and French. Sometimes Arabic could be heard creating a bridge across conti-nents. Round my table, apart from the two Observers, a French Jesuit and a Canadian Lutheran, I was the only pale face. This was pretty typical of the other tables also. Panama itself must be one of the most multi-coloured countries in the world, with every shade of tan, brown and black. People were warm and friendly and the small but vibrant Anglican Church in Panama gave us a wonderful welcome. On the first Sunday in the indoor sports stadium we celebrated the Liturgy before thousands. A highlight was the liturgical dance, with girls dressed in attractive red and white Spanish style dresses. The dancing combined the dignity of old world Spain with the vivacity of Latin America. For the Offertory proces-sion instead of the swinging Thurifer, the dancers came down the aisle with censors on their heads, smoke billowing forth. There were a number of other examples of attempts to relate the Christian faith to different cul-tures, always to our enrichment. Lenore Parker from Australia, for exam-ple, shared her conviction that God had been with her aboriginal people for many thousands of years before Christianity arrived. For her Jesus was "God's holy dreaming" and a lovely prayer of hers stays with me:

> God of holy dreaming
> Great creator spirit
> From the dawn of creation
> You have given your children
> The good things of mother earth
> You spoke and the gum tree grew.

Another good moment was the use of a Korean song in one of our week-day liturgies: O *so* O *so so* (Come now, O Prince of Peace).

We began every day with a Eucharist and for the first time at an ACC meet-ing a woman priest celebrated.

Anglicans in many parts of the world are seeking to be faithful in the most difficult circumstances. We were particularly conscious of the Sudan where Christians have been suffering oppression for many years, the struggle for a lasting peace in the Middle East and the terrible tragedy of Central Africa, especially Rwanda. But from these dire situations came some encouraging stories. Every day we got off to a wonderful start with the Bible Study led by Dinis Sengulane, the Bishop of Lebombo giving us faith and humour in equal measure. He told us about all-night vigils of prayer and somehow seemed to find a place within the divine providence even for mosquitoes. Prayer emerged as a vital necessity for so many. In my group for example Maureen Sithole described how after 20 women had been raped and murdered and the perpetrators not caught, cells of women came together to pray for a new awareness of women's dignity in the country. In Uganda also a network of intercessors has started.

It is clear that in many countries the main challenge which Anglicans face comes from Islam. Alexander Malik the Bishop of Lahore gave ACC members a global perspective which was reinforced by many members present, who were conscious that in many contexts Muslims were gaining influence, with substantial resources behind them. But the testimony was not all negative. Samir Kafity, the Presiding Bishop of Jerusalem recounted how Yasser Arafat began a Christmas sermon at Bethlehem with the words "You Christians do not have a monopoly of Jesus. I as a Muslim, worship him too." Bishop Samir also pointed out that a Christian Church in Oman had been built with the help of 90% of Muslim Arab money. He strongly resisted the attempt by some, as he perceived it, to look for a new global enemy in the wake of the Cold War. Bishop Samir also gave a powerful presentation on Jerusalem, highlighting its spiritual importance for Christians. Bishop Alexander recounted how he met a Muslim going into the Cathedral in Lahore who said, "I'm not a formal Christian but I love Christ." The challenge of Islam however is not confined to the East. It was pointed out by Bishop Mark Dyer that Islam is the fastest growing religion in the deprived areas of American cities, with the power to wean young blacks away from drugs and crime.

Another challenge faced by some Anglican Churches, was the loss of members to new evangelical and pentecostal groups. How are we failing? In other countries the challenge is provided by an all-pervading secularism. One bishop recounted how his son, previously devout, spent three years in the West and came back an anarchist. In the early stages of his period abroad he had been invited to a business breakfast. As was his custom he said Grace. When asked what he was doing he received the reply, "The Bank of Montreal provides this breakfast!" This secular outlook is now encompassing the globe. We were reminded for example that a recent survey revealed that the best known sign in the world was the

MacDonalds sign, the second best known was the Shell logo. The Cross was the third most recognisable symbol.

There was a particularly sombre mood when we spent two hours hearing about the failure of the Churches in Rwanda and some of the historical factors which brought this about. Since then, of course, the tragedy has spread to Eastern Zaire. During the sombre discussion on Rwanda the ACC was presented with a particularly difficult resolution. The bishops of a number of dioceses have been out of the country now for two years and despite invitations have not been willing to return. Those dioceses would like to declare their sees vacant and elect new bishops. But would they have the authority to do this? They looked to the ACC to give them moral and spiritual backing which, despite some very proper hesitations, was indeed given in the form of an appropriate resolution. It is good that we have the ACC, together with the Archbishop of Canterbury, the Primates' meetings and the Lambeth Conference, as instruments of Anglican unity and authority, able to offer some help to a local Church when internal problems seem intractable. Nobody in the Anglican Communion has the authority to order anyone else about. But within the Body of Christ we can listen to one another's pain and offer godly counsel.

Business at ACC-10 was conducted briskly and efficiently, with the aid of some wonderful Panamanian interpreters. At the beginning there was a suggestion that we might go in for mango tree democracy, defined as talking on and on until everyone agrees. It was pointed out however that whereas the Africans have the time, Europeans keep the watch. And we did keep to time, enabling us to get through a fair amount of business which included major addresses from the Archbishop of Canterbury and the Secretary General of the ACC, a discussion on whether we should have a major Anglican Congress in a few years time, a scheme for the Anglican Church to help rebuild Bethlehem, a presentation from Bishop James Ottley, the Anglican representative at the United Nations, a session on mission and evangelism and an important report from the Inter-Anglican Theological and Doctrinal Commission chaired by Robin Eames, the Archbishop of Armagh. This last poses a number of tricky questions with potentially controversial answers, which will need to be taken up at the next Lambeth Conference.

One morning was spent on discussing the networks, which are a vital way for Anglicans in key areas to keep in touch with one another and fertilize the thinking and work in their Churches. Reports were heard from networks on youth, peace and justice, NIFCON (inter-faith), migrant and refugee issues, indigenous peoples, the family with reference also to a possible Anglican women's network. In addition to the small group for Bible Study, there were larger sections set up to produce four statements on aspects of our life and mission.

It was encouraging to learn of steady progress being made on the ecumenical front in relation to a number of other Christian denominations and it was good also to hear something of the women's conference in Beijing and to learn of exciting developments on the communications front as well as consultations going on in relation to the family of Anglican liturgies. The plans for the Lambeth Conference were outlined, as was the existing possibility of an Anglican investment agency, the result of a lay initiative from the Episcopal Church in the United States. Michael Peers, the Primate of the Anglican Church of Canada, helped people to see that planning a budget was not simply a question of financial crisis but a real ministry.

Farewells were said to some long standing members of the ACC, especially to Colin Craston, the Chairman, who has been held in such affection and the Revd Dr Donald Anderson the Director for Ecumenical Relations and Studies. But there is an excellent team for the future. Simon Chiwanga, the Bishop of Mpwapwa in Tanzania was elected Chairman and John Paterson, the Bishop of Auckland, Vice-Chairman. The Committee which was elected is a very well balanced group from a number of different continents, representing both clergy and lay people. Real thought was put into the elections and it is good that the result is such a representative body.

Inevitably at a gathering like ACC, there are cultural differences, some funny and some serious. We were told for example that in an aboriginal account of the Garden of Eden, Adam and Eve could not have been black. If they had been they would have eaten the snake and thrown the apple away. Similarly, when faced with the Gospel saying, *"Is there a man among you who will offer his son a stone when he asks for bread, or a snake when he asks for a fish?"*, a Ugandan replied, "But I eat snake and I have never seen a fish." More divisive is the subject of homosexuality. In some cultures this is a burning issue. In others it is never discussed, indeed it is alleged that there are cultures in which there is no word for this kind of sexual orientation. So my presentation on the subject aroused strong reactions. Interestingly, some people came up to me privately afterwards and said that, despite what might be said in public, there is a problem in their country and they don't know how to handle it.

After some long days of hard work we were allowed a break! We went on a trip to see the Panama Canal and heard a lecture on its building and workings. We also visited the old Panama city, now in ruins as a result of the pirate, Henry Morgan, who in 1671 burnt and destroyed it totally. I understand that he was rewarded with a Knighthood by the British Crown. A highlight for some was the wonderful Panamanian evening, where we not only enjoyed the local fare but experience some wonderful dancing by a group of young Panamanian girls and boys. It was an electric performance which encouraged even some of the older ACC delegates to get on to the dance floor afterwards. They were joined there by the British Ambassador to Panama and his beautiful Ghanian wife, who had kindly entertained the delegates with a reception at the Embassy a few nights before.

There was a very good atmosphere at ACC-10, friendly and constructive. We were conscious of the difficulties and challenges facing so many Churches. We were aware of those who could not be with us because of what was happening in their own country especially Chief G. O. K. Ajayi from Nigeria and the Revd Bernard Ntahoturi from Burundi. We were aware of the frailty of our own human nature. But we were told about a press conference after the Ascension. Jesus was asked, "Didn't your mission fail? "No," he replied. "What about Peter? How can your mission possibly go forward?" "The Church, that's all." But we can do so much more together than we can on our own. We were given the lovely image of birds flying in formation. When a bird flaps its wings it creates a thrust of air which helps other birds to fly. The result is that a formation of birds adds 71% to their flying distance. The Anglican Communion is flying in formation, not always a very tidy formation for our birds each have their own individual character, but a formation none the less. ACC-10 has, I believe, helped that formation and therefore helped us to fly further and stronger in faithful worship and witness.

Introduction

by Canon James M. Rosenthal

ACC-10 will be memorable for many reasons, not only because of the excellent meeting itself, with people speaking freely and with confidence from all parts of the Communion, but because we were in the context of such a wonderful place as Panama.

The Episcopal Church in Panama, living with the ecumenical reality of our sister Church, the Roman Catholics, finds itself in a unique situation in its various ministries, most notably in the area of education. The Grand Misa was one of the true highlights of the communal life of the Anglican Consultative Council meeting. Vibrant music, exquisite dance, and the chance to gather at the table of the Lord together as an international family made this celebration of the Eucharist a unique experience for the thousands who gathered there.

Both Panama as a country and Panama as the diocese face challenges in their relationships with the United States and the world community especially regarding the important resource of the famous Panama Canal. Our host Bishop, the Rt Revd Clarence Hayes, and his assistant, Mr Biron Daniels, did everything possible to make our brief time in Panama one of comfort as well as an opportunity to learn about the various cultures within the Panamanian community. For the people of Panama, for the Church of Panama, we say, "Thanks be to God".

SERMONS AND ADDRESSES

The diversity of those who gather for an Anglican Consultative Council meeting dictates that there be various points in the proceedings that draw us together as a world-wide family. This was done most vividly in the sermons and addresses that were presented at various stages in the programme by ACC leaders. The challenge of Bishop Kafity, the vision of Archbishop Carey, the warmth of Canon Craston, the new direction offered by Bishop Chiwanga, and the provocative look to the future given by Canon Peterson all provided a well-rounded experience as members listened attentively to the various preachers and speakers.

Sermon by the Most Revd Samir Kafity

Thursday, 10 October 1996, at the Cathedral of St Luke, Panama City

St Augustine devised a new version of the 10 commandments, and also a pragmatic translation of Christ's new summary of the commandments, which we find in John 13:34: *"A new commandment I give unto you, love one another as I have loved you."* Augustine's version is "Love God and do as you please." No limits! But very wide open possibilities are available should you first love God. The Gospel for today says, *"thou shalt love the Lord your God, with all thy heart, with all thy mind, with all thy soul and with all thy strength and thou shall love thy neighbour as thyself." "I am the Lord your God. You shall have no other gods, but me."* You shall love the Lord your God with all your heart, all your mind, all your soul, and all your strength, not with part of it, not part-time, not partial love, but with all.

"You shall not make for yourself any other idol," for God is spirit and the ground of all being, which is love. The creation is an expression of his great spirit of love. We live in a world of love. Therefore you shall not dishonour the name of the Lord your God. God is the ground of our being. Our being is grounded in love. God is love and love is God.

You shall worship him. Worship God. Give thanks to Islam, to the Muslims who remind us five times a day that God is great, that God is love. And they pray five times a day, wherever they may be, for God expects worship and praise for God. In the 1960s some theologians declared the death of God in the streets of London. Now, near the beginning of a new millennium, the very heart of this Communion being a living Communion is to declare to the next millennium that God lives, that God loves. He lives. He loves. He is love. The basis of the commandments is love. St Paul, in the 13th chapter of Corinthians, describes this as the greatest thing in the world. We need to trust the love of God in order to join it, and he is love, because it is in his love that we live, move and have our being. It's not automatic, it's not part of the future, it is the love of God, which is real.

I will place before you two definitions of love. One is very simple. It is given by the Lebanese professor, poet and philosopher, Khalil Ghibran, who wrote a great book with poems called "The Prophet." He says love is that spontaneous energy which gives itself and only draws from itself, not from somewhere else. This is real spontaneous love. An American hymnologist,

John Oxenham, added more clarity to this definition when he said:

> "Love ever gives, forgives—outlives.
> And ever stands, with open hands.
> And while it lives—it gives.
> For this is love's prerogative to give—to give—to give."

And Paul ranks love as above all. It is even more important than to have faith in God, or belief, or doctrine. It is greater than belief. It is the background of hope and life. If we want to stay in the realm of belief and doctrine, we will arrive at what the ecumenical movement has arrived at after 50 years of academic debate in unity—we arrive in the season of winter. Now to experience Grace in God you don't need 50 years in Faith and Order to speak about the unity of humanity. In India, they just did it. They didn't speak about it, they did it and there is a united Church in India.

The other definition of love comes from music. Otis Skilling, the American who wrote it, composed a piece of music called "Love." He said:

> "The world is ablaze and burning with sin.
> Life is a maze of searching within.
> Amazing love can change all of this,
> For love, love is a man.
> The incarnate man. It is all man.
> He came to the earth two thousand years ago.
> He paid with his life sin's debt that we owe,
> He rose again and lives today here in Panama.
> For love, love is the incarnate man.
> This man fulfilled God's plan;
> When Jesus came true love began.
> Because he came, we all can claim
> A life of love today.
>
> Love can change attitudes
> No matter how hard these are
> No matter how superior, how academic people feel they are
> Love can change the attitudes
> Love can change the mind
> Love can make us likable
> Love can make us kind
> Love can make us break the barriers
> Love can set us free
> In other words, love can mould
> A new life for you and me."

If this is love, then this is how we should relate to God and the world, to God and each other. *"You shall love the Lord your God with all your heart, "*not only partially or on Sunday or on the great festivals. *"With all your soul, "* your spirituality, like our brothers and sisters in Islam who pray five times a day and proclaim God is great. They pray five times a day anywhere—indoors or outdoors. They are not ashamed to declare their love to God. That is perpetual worship. The way to love is to worship God, not with our lips, and not by making idols that only do service for him. Not only by just honouring his words by name. Love is an ongoing way of life and one that can change attitudes and prejudices. It is by loving God, only by loving God, that the peace of the world can become a reality. It is only by loving God that the Middle East can attain and achieve peace by changing attitudes to become more human. It is my hope that my people the Palestinians and my cousins the Israelis will love God in this way, when they do not politicise God and make him an object of controversy that peace will become a reality.

We, in the Anglican Communion, recognise the depth, the breadth, the height and the width of this love. *"Love your neighbour. "* Do you know who is your neighbour? Do we recognise, as an Anglican Communion throughout the world, about 70 million adherents? Do we recognise our neighbours, or are we living in a vacuum? Do we need to rehearse the story of the good Samaritan? It was not the priest, not the organised Church, the highly structured Church, it was not the Church who made new doctrine. It was not the Church with great and high degrees from academic institution, nor was it the Church that is hierarchical—it was a non-believer that became the neighbour to the man who fell among thieves. The Church was busy, maybe with the Mothers' Union, or with its other issues and concerns and forgot that its true purpose was as a servant of humanity. Let us remember 80% of the population of the world is living on 20% of the resources of the world, and 20% of the population of the world is living on the other 80% of the resources of the world. What is our response? How can we say love God with all your heart and love your neighbour, exactly in the same manner and degree that you love yourself? The motto of the priest in the organised, highly academic Church in the story of the Good Samaritan was—"what is mine is mine. Mind my own business—my own agenda. What is mine is mine and I will keep it."

The motto of the Good Samaritan was "what is mine is yours," no matter what kind you are or what nationality, or what degree you hold, or how little you have, you are the child of God, "whatever is mine is yours, let us share it." Sharing, sharing and again I say sharing.

And now I want to come to the centre—Jerusalem. Bishop Kenneth Cragg of the United Kingdom and an assistant bishop in my Province wrote:

"The road to Jerusalem is in the heart; and whether present or absent, its passionate history absorbs the spirit."

It certainly does absorb the spirit, of all its past people, current residents, and all the pilgrims of all three monotheistic Abrahamic faiths. It is a peculiar spiritual focus, a symbol that could perhaps change the course of the present world. One cannot, and perhaps should not, forget Jerusalem. At 2,500 feet above sea-level, the psalmist viewed this city as a unity in itself, as the abode of God, the abode of God, as the house of peace. When speaking on Jerusalem, the language of the heart supersedes the mind. The religious significance overrules its secular significance, the universal, local, multi-lateral, multi-cultural cannot be sacrificed for only one local ordinational rule. Perhaps this is what was conveyed by John when he spoke of a new Jerusalem. Paul in Galatians calls it the mother of us all, Jerusalem which is above, which is free. It is the motherhood of Jerusalem that reminds us of the religion of God. It's not the old Jerusalem, that city which was ignorant, and sometimes we feel it is still ignorant of the things that belonged to its peace. It was our goal, it was Jesus, the incarnate son of God, who wept over that kind of Jerusalem and he still lives. Perhaps to us it must become the symbol of God.

I always remind pilgrims who come to see us in Jerusalem that this is the eighth sacrament. Jerusalem declares there are eight sacraments. The eighth is to come and say your prayers in the footsteps of the land that God has chosen to enact the drama of salvation. It's not just another piece of geography. It's not just another country. It's the place of the incarnation and the resurrection of a new hope, a new providence, a new testament, a new relationship, a new world. The significance of the motherhood of Jerusalem, to Judaism, Christianity and Islam is that motherhood does not discriminate. Motherhood does not have preference. It will not prefer a Jew, or a Christian or a Muslim. It will cease to be central, it will cease to be a mother if it makes preferences. Yes, and all the children must attribute this marvellous love to their mother who does not compromise the rights of the other two children.

This symbol of motherhood, of love, and of peace is what Jerusalem offers to humanity. A translation of God's humanity. We pray that it may regain this eternal symbolism and may once again be the answer to the quest for peace, not to be negotiated as the substance of an agenda, but an answer to peace.

Christianity strongly affirms equality between people without discrimination. Therefore, we of the Holy Land, which is holy to our Jewish and Muslim and Christian brethren, plead in the name of the three key principles of love, of equality, of peace, will contribute to a new situation not only in the Middle East, but in our world. This is what we mean when we say we love God and we must and should love our neighbour exactly as we love ourselves, and we call on the Anglican Communion to continue to become not only a liturgical Communion, and not just an academic Communion, but also a diakonal Communion, a Communion that gives and gives and gives until all our lives are reconciled and healed. Amen.

"Looking to the Future": Presidential Address by the Archbishop of Canterbury

Friday, 11 October 1996

Welcome to ACC-10. Together with Canon Colin Craston, Chairman of ACC, I greet you all in the name of our Lord and pray that this time together will be a time of blessing as surely as it will be a time of hard work!

I want to begin this Presidential Address by thanking the Secretary General and his staff for all the preparation that has gone into this Assembly. We are most grateful to them.

But let us also acclaim the warm welcome of the Bishop of Panama, Bishop Clarence Hayes, and his wife Connie and colleagues who have already made us feel very much at home. This is a picturesque part of our common world and we are glad to be here.

We have before us a very full agenda which could keep us going for many weeks! Doctrine, ecumenism, liturgy, mission, social and political issues— to say nothing of finance which, like the weather, is always with us.

Few of us would deny that the context in which we meet is most appropriate. The Diocese of Panama is a small and somewhat isolated diocese and perhaps similar to the one you have come from. It is a tiny Anglican community in the enormous ECUSA and a tiny church in a predominantly Catholic country. The culture of the country may not seem obviously sympathetic to Anglicanism, but as in many other cultures is welcomed for the contribution it is making and is steadily growing as a Church and as a religious tradition. Central to its mission in this land is the excellent work it is doing in the field of education and I hope that we shall learn more about this during our time here. But also significant is the warm ecumenical relationships it has built up, particularly with the more dominant Roman Catholic Church.

It is, as I said, typical of many Anglican dioceses throughout the world— small, seemingly isolated, struggling to express its distinctiveness and faithfully serving our Lord where he has placed it.

Such a context as this will make it very hard for us to do our work unrelated to the real world in which we live. It provides us with the background against which we can ask: How can the ACC serve the Anglican Diocese of Panama? How may the Anglicans in Panama utilise the resources which ACC, the Lambeth Conference, the Primates' Meeting and the Archbishop of Canterbury represent? How may we, the wider Church, hear the concerns of Panama and respond to them in the deliberations of our Councils?

The title of my Address is LOOKING TO THE FUTURE, and I want to begin with two passages. The first comes from that well known verse of W.B.Yeats:

> "Things fall apart; the centre cannot hold,
> Mere anarchy is loosed upon the world,
> The blood-dimmed tide is loosed,
> and everywhere
> The ceremony of innocence is drowned."

My second passage comes from the book of Revelation where, from the reality of persecution in the early Church, the risen Christ proclaims: *"Behold I make all things new."*

The first passage is a bleak and vivid picture of the world we live in. Wherever we look things appear to be "falling apart." To be sure there is much in our world that is good. In many parts of the world people prosper and make plans for a better world. It would be plainly stupid and against direct experience to universalise Yeats' verse, as if Armageddon was around the corner. Nevertheless, there are enough worrying signs to make us pause if we are tempted to assume that the world is getting better and better. In brief, the world's population continues to mount steadily; the gap between rich and poor continues to widen; corruption and crime infect modern life at all levels of society. When we add to that list the confusion in all our countries about the nature of morality, and what models of human living and dignity we are offering our young, to say nothing of the damage we are doing to our fragile and enfeebled mother earth, we do well to ask whether Yeats' cry was actually quite prophetic.

Things may seem to be "falling apart" in the Church too. We are not alone as a world communion in feeling the exhaustion, straining as we seek to care for those parts of the world where our brothers and sisters suffer— in Rwanda, Sudan, Burundi, Northern Ireland, Palestine and elsewhere. Even in those parts of the world where Christianity rooted itself many centuries ago—Europe and elsewhere—the Church struggles to come to terms with modernity. If it does not face persecution, it experiences the debilitating wounds of apathy, cynicism and sometimes amused contempt. Yes, the experience of things "falling apart" may not simply be a Third World Church problem.

If that quotation from Yeats is a reminder of the context in which we live and work, my second text is a statement of the way God considers the future *"Behold I make all things new."* The Christian faith always faces the future with optimism, because the hope is Resurrection hope.

Let me attempt to relate this great Resurrection hope to our task over the next 10 days.

I believe that our Lord is calling us towards a threefold calling:

1.   To be a people committed to God's mission in the world

How does Anglicanism fit into this ever-changing kaleidoscope of human community and experience? We know about the disparity between rich and poor, powerful and weak, the educated and the uneducated, the corporate and the individual. We know from our own experience about the disruption of family life, of traditional structures of community. We know that many individuals are on the one hand bewildered by the speed of change, bewildered by the many competing demands and seductions which appear to point the way to success and happiness. We know that many are seeking security and affirmation that they count, and that there is meaning in their lives.

We know too—and this is one more challenge to us—that there are a multiplicity of religious traditions and communities that are seeking to offer some of the answers. With the mass migration of people—both forced and by choice—the reality of other faith traditions has been opened up for many people in an unexpected way.

How does Anglicanism meet this challenge?

We cannot ignore the reality of people's experience. Evangelism which fails to address the physical situation which people are in borders on escapism. True evangelism is always holistic and addresses the whole of life.

We must, therefore, begin with the basic assumption that "Christ has called each of us by name to follow his way." We are not in the business of institutionalising mission; we are in the business of liberating the people of God for mission.

That is where our understanding of authority must begin as well—with the whole people of God. As *Lumen Gentium* says so splendidly of the work of the Spirit: He "allots his gifts at will to each individual and also distributes special graces among the faithful of every rank" (*Lumen Gentium* 12). "All women

and men are called to belong to the new people of God" (*Lumen Gentium* 13).
Any authority structure which we develop—whether at local, national,
regional or international level—must always hold at its centre the sense of
the people of God, the Body of Christ. I'm glad that the *Porvöo Common
Statement* recognises that very clearly, and develops its view of authority
from these. It states "We believe that all members of the Church are called
to participate in its apostolic mission… This is the corporate priesthood
of the whole people of God and the calling to ministry and service"
(*Porvöo Common Statement*, para 32i).

All structures are there to serve the mission of the people of God.

This, in turn, is a reassurance as well as a challenge to Anglican structures.
The reassurance is that we are on the right lines! We gather together as
members of the one body with different gifts and different offices. We are
called together to serve the Gospel. As soon as we recognise the need to
work together we begin to see the need for structures, which run the risk
of creating bureaucracy and institutionalising mission. The image of the
body in Paul is central. Each part of the body is vital and valued, under
Christ as head. But each part must be free to carry out its task. It is no
good asking a hand to do a foot's job, or an ear to do a nose's job. Each
of us is called to a particular task, and to utilise our God-given gifts and
skills in the pursuit of that task—but to do it in harmony with others.

The challenge however comes from the temptation—sometimes unwitting-
ly encouraged by our tradition—to give greater value and importance to
particular callings, especially the ordained ministry and the episcopate.
Even worse to see this as a career structure! The gift of leadership may
indeed be a particular charism, but it does not imply total authority in all
fields.

The sometimes uneasy tension between synodical government and episcopal leadership which is peculiar to Anglicanism is a significant attempt to
express this, and ACC derives from that tradition. If we are still some way
from perfecting it, the idea is not to be sneezed at! The danger is over-heavy
bureaucracy. Synods become weighed down with minutiae of legislation
and fail in their primary task of liberating the people of God for mission.

Individuals engaged in innovative mission work often feel just that—individuals, isolated from the mainstream of Church life, because they feel
unable to claim the name of the Church for their work, and the Church
appears unwilling to authenticate their activity.

We need a model of the Church which is missionary in essence. *"You are a
chosen people… that you may declare the wonderful deeds…"* (1 Peter 2:9).

It is my great hope that the Decade of Evangelism, which we as a Communion have taken up as a central *'leitmotiv'* of the 1990s, will infuse our structures so that everything we do is permeated by a sense of being "called to mission." I believe we are capturing a sense of David Bosch's statement that "Mission is not a fringe activity of a strongly established Church, a pious cause that may be attended to when the home fires are first brightly burning... Missionary work is not so much the work of the Church as simply the Church at work" (quoted in D. Bosch: *Transforming Mission*, p.372).

Thus, time will be given during this Council to review the progress we are making and how to develop our structures so that this missionary task is at the heart of what we are. In turn, these will give new direction, new substance to everything else in which we are engaged as the Body of Christ— worship, ecumenism and pastoral care. Indeed, we shall receive the results of an important liturgical consultation, "Renewing the Anglican Eucharist," which we will examine closely. It is a detailed examination of the theology and the liturgy, but also includes a reminder that the Eucharist is, or should be, in itself a missionary event. "The missionary power of the sacrament lies in this demonstration of the free grace of God offered to all people." (p. 18)

This being called to be engaged in mission is to engage in God's future. The *"One who makes all things new"* is not the Lord of dying congregations. He gives us courage to believe that all things are possible; that with vigorous leadership and committed lay people the Body of Christ will continue to grow and develop in unexpected and God-given ways.

2.   To be a people committed to reconciliation

When "things fall apart" there is the tendency to huddle together with like-minded people for warmth. It is the instinct for survival and self preservation. When things fall apart the last thing we want to do is to open our hearts to others. But this is not true of authentic Christianity or Anglicanism at its best. I truly believe that the openness of Anglicanism is a great gift to world-wide Christianity. The tolerance and breadth that has characterised our tradition has nothing to do with vagueness, wishy-washy faith or lack of commitment. It is characteristic of a faith which welcomes others and wishes there to be as few barriers to Eucharistic sharing as possible.

As I look back over the last seven or so years I realise with great joy that the prophesied demise of the Communion over the ordination of women to the priesthood and episcopate has not happened. This is due in no small measure to the Eames Commission, chaired by Archbishop Robin Eames, but also to the determination of so many of us to stay together in spite of strongly held views and theologies. No doubt we shall be faced with many more difficult issues in the future, which will threaten to split asunder our fellowship and destroy the Communion. I am confident, however, that that will not happen so long as we carry on listening to others and maintaining the bonds of fellowship with all the generosity we see in the Gospel.

The same applies to our ecumenical relationships too. I believe our Communion has a special ecumenical vocation. Our historic claim is that we are both "Catholic" and "Reformed" and we attempt to give equal weight to those terms. "Catholic" in our conformity with the faith of the Church, expressed quintessentially in the Four Ecumenical Councils. "Reformed" because of our commitment to scripture as our primary authority.

If, then, we are partners with God in his task of *"making all things new,"* we should unite in challenging phrases like "this is the winter of ecumenism." They do not reflect today's reality. The presence of ecumenical guests during this conference demonstrates the continuing commitment to unity. We have seen real achievements. Let us be unwavering in our commitment to build on them.

But here again mission must fuel that desire for unity. Our ecumenical endeavours, too, can be transformed if mission is given a central place. During our time together we shall be considering a number of extremely hopeful reports on dialogue with our sister Churches. I want to applaud these, all who have participated in them, and the progress which has been made.

But let me also be clear about one thing. Real unity among Christians will only come when people at local level see the urgency of engaging together in our common mission. Of course it is happening in some parts of the world, where the crisis facing humanity is so severe that a divided Christian witness and ministry really would be a scandal. Talk to brothers and sisters from Southern Sudan. There you will find Christian unity in action. We see it in very concrete terms in India, Pakistan and Bangladesh where, despite many institutional difficulties, Christians are determined to witness together, and have been a shining example to the rest of us. Now, all the possibilities of Porvöo and the Concordat in the USA are opening up—if the theological and structural agreements can be turned into real enthusiasm at local level for common witness.

Once again, the primary concern must be to enable the mission of the people of God and in all our ecumenical negotiation that must be the heart of it. We must ensure a symmetry between the great conversations which continue to make progress on ecclesiastical unity and the vital task of encouraging and resourcing united Christian Witness among local congregations.

3.   To be a people committed to renewal

At this point it would be easy for a sense of complacency to invade our Council. It may seem as if I am saying that, as we are heading in the right direction, all is well.

No. Yeats' poem talks about the "centre cannot hold." Yeats, of course, did not have the centre of the Anglican Communion in mind. But that is where my concern is. We are here for these 10 days to pay attention to our structures and the way they either serve or hinder our common mission.

I detect with some joy that there is a growing perception that to enable the Communion to develop further, and to meet both the needs of the Church and the profound challenges of the world, we must review how the instruments of unity are operating, and whether there are ways in which we can make them more effective. The Virginia Report raises some significant questions which we here at ACC and the Lambeth Conference—now less than two years away—must seriously address.

Bearing in mind the basic thrust of this address that the Church is the whole people of God, that it is with these that fundamental authority in the Church lies, and any other structures, hierarchies or bureaucracies we choose to put in place are there to service the apostolic mission of the people of God, let me outline some examples of the issues which challenge us.

Rwanda: I think of our Church there, whose mission has been radically undermined, in a context which is almost impossible to imagine. A Church deeply divided, physically—refugees, bishops out of the country—and spiritually—a climate of suspicion, accusation and counter-accusation. A Church facing financial crisis, and with little potential for raising its own monies in the foreseeable future. It was my experience, shared by several Primates, particularly Michael Peers, that the terrible genocide in Rwanda revealed terribly and starkly the lack of resources we have in the Communion to respond swiftly, effectively, and generously to such a crisis.

The Holy Land: We have watched with horror the latest outbreaks of violence in Palestine. We are deeply concerned at the continuing inability of political leaders to find the right formula for peace, compounded by the new Israeli Government's apparent intransigence. The tiny Anglican Church is making a significant contribution alongside much larger Roman Catholic and Orthodox communities, but feeling very isolated and oppressed. I pay tribute to Bishop Samir Kafity and others for their determination to continue the struggle for basic human rights and recognition in a largely non-Christian population, which appears increasingly hostile to the Churches.

New Provinces: Faced with particular circumstances in different areas, a number of proposals for new Provinces are being explored or formulated. Sometimes it is unclear to those outside the situation exactly why these proposals are coming forward. The ACC has offered support and advice, and indeed new Provinces have to apply to join ACC. Questions inevitably arise about the balance between autonomy and membership of a wider communion. We want to support structural changes which will genuinely aid the mission of the Church, but we also hope that the value of consultation with ACC will be recognised. That is what it is to be part of a family.

Finance: We cannot escape the fact that much of the financial wealth of the Communion is focused in a relatively small number of Provinces. We also notice the extreme poverty of many resources. How much longer can we limp along with so many Provinces not paying their full contribution to the budget? Is it fair to expect the Secretary General assisted by the Archbishop of Canterbury to spend an increasing proportion of their time on supplementing the budget? Is there not a challenge for all ACC representatives to take the message back to our Provinces that each Province has a moral responsibility to pay the proportion that has been agreed? The Virginia Document rightly observes that "It is urgent that ways be found to strengthen the resourcing of the ACC Secretariat if it is to serve effectively the world-wide structures of Anglican belonging"(6.34). That will remain a pious hope if we leave it to others to find the solution. Belonging to the Communion means sharing in that common responsibility to resource the structures that resource us all.

Having said that, new initiatives will be before us that offer great hope for the renewal of our life. We shall consider the exciting opportunities offered by the Anglican Investment Agency together with other possibilities. I hope that the initiative being shown by a number of very generous individuals will inspire us all to work harder at this.

Let me turn to another possible development. I do not believe we exploit Primates enough! We are a college of leaders, who together have key responsibilities in the leadership of the Communion; and because we are smaller in number and meet more frequently, we should have the facility for initiating action. The "mutual counsel and pastoral care and support of one another and the Archbishop of Canterbury" expressed in the *Virginia Report* is vital, and certainly I deeply appreciate it. But it is also significant for consultation on major issues which may arise between Lambeth

Conferences, and between ACC's; and because it is a manageable number, we find ourselves consulting each other by post and fax between meetings on quite a regular basis.

I hope this collegiality can be further developed. I believe that, whilst retaining a central symbolic role for the Archbishop of Canterbury, my brother Primates should have a higher profile in the Communion. It is happening here and there. The Presiding Bishop of the United States has played a significant role in the Middle East, as well as in Central and South America. Archbishop Keith Rayner plays a very important role in the plans for the Lambeth Conference. Archbishop Brian Davis of New Zealand's role in the ACC and again, nothing but praise can be uttered when one thinks of Archbishop Robin Eames' and Presiding Bishop Samir Kafity's roles in Northern Ireland and Palestine, respectively. My recent visit to Mozambique brought home to me the major role Bishop Dinis Sengulane has played in bringing peace to his country, a role which has been recognised all over the world. In many ways leaders such as those mentioned, act for the rest of the Communion and need our prayers and our support.

Is it time to share and develop the representative role inherent in shared leadership? I was glad to meet the Archbishop of the Indian Ocean at Desmond Tutu's retirement celebrations. This representative role can be played by more. Should this be done regionally? Should we always seek to invite a Primate from a totally different Province and culture to represent the Communion at our major events? It was so good to have the Archbishop of Uganda, as well as a number of other bishops from around the Communion, at a recent consecration service in London. There was a real sense of the presence of the Communion in its great diversity—and that is a vital message to convey in our mission.

"The road to the future is always under construction."
(Graffiti in a South African township)

I like that image! We are on a journey together; we cannot see into the future, but we move on in faith and hope, rejoicing in what has past. We live in a rapidly changing world which presents us with huge challenges. Faith is certainly under fire in many different ways and in many different places. We must travel light. We must seek to build up the Church, but always remembering that the Church is not an end in itself. We seek to liberate Christian people to fulfil their calling as apostolic missioners for Christ.

Yes, it may seem at times that "things are falling apart," but the eye of faith looks ahead to God's future. We are constructing the road to the future, we pray with God's guidance. The millennium is clearly becoming a land-mark of great significance in the world. Let it be a time when we, the Anglican Communion, alongside all Christian people, proclaim together the Gospel of Christ crucified and risen, that our world may be trans-formed; and let us ensure that our Communion in all its untidy and glo-rious diversity, with all its struggles and sufferings, offers in all its councils and all its leaders a transparent commitment to the service of that Gospel.

Opening Remarks by the Revd Canon Colin Craston, Chairman of the ACC

Friday, 11 October 1996

It has been suggested that I might speak for a few minutes about the role of the ACC in relationship to the other instruments of unity'—the Lambeth Conference and the Primates' Meeting. The first Lambeth Conference met in 1867 convened by the then Archbishop of Canterbury in the interests of preserving the unity of the Anglican Communion. The ACC was proposed by the Lambeth Fathers in 1968, and approved by all Provinces the following year. Its first meeting was 1971. The Primates' Meeting emanated from the Lambeth Conference of 1978.

Basic to appreciating the roles and inter-relationships of those three 'instruments of unity' are two principles in the Anglican understanding of the Church.

1.   We believe Christ has given authority in the government of the Church to the whole body of his people—the whole *laos* of God. So, while we are episcopal Churches, inheriting and cherishing the historic episcopate, and so recognising Episcopal leadership, we also hold in balance with that the need for bishops (personally and collegially) to act in council with laity and other clergy through their representatives. The twin concepts of episcopal leadership and bishops in council are to be held in creative relationship. Hence, the right, proper decision of Lambeth 1968 that consultation between the autonomous member Churches and Provinces of the Communion should not be confined to bishops alone, meeting in a Lambeth Conference. As well as a Lambeth Conference there should be the ACC bringing together the three Orders in the Church (bishops, laity, clergy).

2.   The second principle is that of dispersed authority. That means that there should not be concentration of all authority in a monolithic structure with legislative powers. But authority should be dispersed at Communion level through 'instruments of unity.' This system provides checks and balances necessary in any company of fallible and sinful human beings. A heavy responsibility rests on the 'instruments of unity' to work in harmony, while contributing their own experience and insights, in order to coordinate their guidance to the Communion. Exercise of authority, therefore, is a process, not a passing down of decisions from a

single source. It is for this reason that now the ACC Standing Committee and the Standing Committee of the Primates meet together and the latter attends the full Council of the ACC. We are delighted to have these Primates with full voice but not voting rights on business matters in the Council.

The existence of the three bodies—the Lambeth Conference plus the other two—has come about in the last 30 years. Their relationship is not static, fixed in stone, but is developing and should continue to develop. Why? Because we are committed to Unity in Diversity, and Unity in Diversity has to react to the changing contexts of the times and all the cultures in which the Church is set in its mission.

I turn lastly to two concerns for our own instrument, the ACC.

a.   We have now a tradition in the ACC, developing over nearly 30 years. There is much of value, work and output from the previous nine meetings, as of course with the Lambeth Conference. Not all in the past is of equal value, but there is much of value. As we meet we need to have in mind what is good in the past and build on it. And the fact that normally members serve for three meetings enables the memory of the way we think God has led us in the past to help us in the present.

b.   We need to improve our effectiveness as a consultative body in three respects:

>   i.   In the way our Provinces are represented on the ACC through us. We need to work towards a better balance of bishops, laity and clergy, men and women, younger and older.

>   ii.   Communication. All representatives need to have a voice in their own Province where policy and finance decisions happen. It is a two-way basis—before and after meetings.

>   iii.   The way we conduct our business, given the many cultures and languages we come from.

Opening Remarks by the Rt Revd Simon Chiwanga, Vice Chairman of the Anglican Consultative Council

Friday, 11 October 1996

Your Grace, the Archbishop of Canterbury, Mr Chairman, Brothers and Sisters. The Design Group has worked out a very helpful pattern of introducing us to our work here in Panama. After the warm welcome by our President, His Grace, the Archbishop of Canterbury, to whom we are all grateful, followed the Chairman of ACC, Canon Colin Craston, who directed our attention to the role and place of the ACC in the Anglican Communion, I have been asked to focus on our life together, both outside and inside the business sessions here in Panama. After me, Dr Diane Maybee, the Chairperson of the Design Group, will take us through the agenda of our meeting. I am going to briefly highlight two areas of our being together here, based on the following two words:

Sharing and Communication

Sharing

A late-19th century book entitled, *"Correct Manners—a Complete Handbook of Etiquette,"* contains a list of rules on some of the day-to-day obligations that allow people to get along with one another. One of the rules for example says, "Be punctual as to time, precise as to payment, honest and thoughtful in all your transactions." But here is one rule that I did not like: "Ask no questions about the affairs of your friend unless he wants your advice. Then he will tell you all he desires to have you know." I did not like this one, certainly not at a meeting of the ACC, because we have come together here to share stories about the mission of the Church. Our Communion is engaged in a most exciting agenda of mission and evangelism, among other things. The Decade of Evangelism is uppermost in our minds. Every Province and Diocese is committed to this agenda and it is fulfilling it in various ways. We need to share our experience and insights.

Some are able to share readily, while others need some encouragement. If we do not ask them questions about the affairs of the Church in their place, some may be missed out. We should not wait until they decide to tell us what they desire to have us know. Some may not share with us some of their stories which can be of great benefit to the rest of the

Communion, not because they do not want to, but because they have become so used to the stories that they feel the stories may not interest anybody. Asking questions in the right way, if there is a right way, will encourage some to share their stories. Some member Churches of our Communion are going through an extremely trying period. While others, and even the suffering ones, are experiencing very rich blessings from God. As St Paul reminds us, *"Where sin increased, grace abounded all the more."*

Let us therefore encourage each other to share stories—the happy ones and the painful ones. Let me quote from the Report of the Inter-Anglican Theological and Doctrinal Commission, p 24: "The mutual attentiveness required when members from various parts of the Communion share the richness of their experiences also helps to form the mind of the Communion and is a reminder of the rich diversity of gifts which God has given us. The sharing of stories enhances and deepens the Communion's experience of interdependence at all levels."

Communication

Here I would like to ask everyone of us to strive to make communication to be absolutely open and two-way during this entire ACC meeting. The various reports which will be brought before us should be considered with care, and if anything needs clarification—please, raise it sooner rather than later.

It has been pointed out at times, that one factor which inhibits communication at our ACC Meetings is the use of Western based parliamentary rules of procedure. It may be so; but I want to say two things here. First, until we change our Canons, we are bound to follow them. Second, I personally think that sometimes it may be an oversimplification to claim that the rules of procedure of what is called "Democracy under the Mango Tree," i.e. "Talk until you Agree," are easier to follow. Like many of you, I also have sat at a few of traditional assemblies that lasted for 24 hours. When later I went into Parliament, I found it easier to follow parliamentary rules of procedure than those of the traditional assemblies which can be quite elaborate. I believe the two sets of rules (one written, the other oral) have one thing in common: that is they have got to be learnt; they cannot be taken for granted. I wonder, therefore, if I may remind myself and a few of those who come from a background like mine, to be familiar with, and to have in front of them, the Bye-Laws found under section 4, page 11 of our Handbook, which I believe every member of the Council has.

Secondly on communication, I want to thank the Secretary General and his Communication staff for providing simultaneous translations to some languages at this meeting. I am sure this will greatly boost our communication. I want to appeal to the fluent English speakers. Most of them do speak deliberately slowly to allow some of us to follow. Therefore I am appealing to the remaining few to do so as well, and to, please try to minimise the use of difficult idioms and jargon unless they are immediately explained. We are all familiar of how a mistake or misunderstanding of just one word can change the whole meaning of a statement. Their patience with us as we struggle with English will be very much appreciated. The *Virginia Report* is again helpful on this when it says: "Christian attentiveness should mean giving special heed to those whose first language is not English, and to those who do not come from politically, culturally and economically powerful Provinces in the Communion. Attentiveness becomes distinctively Christian when those assembled give ear to, and make space for, the voices of those Christians who are seldom, if ever, heard."

Finally, a word on communicating the proceedings of our Council to our constituencies. I would ask every member of the Council to find every possible and effective way of sharing the experiences of our Council with our Provinces and Churches. I cannot put it any better than the way it has been expressed, once again, by the *Virginia Report:* "Important to this process (of sharing) are representatives who are able not only to bring the concerns and stories of their Provinces with them but carry the proceedings of the Council back to their communities, at the Provincial, national and diocesan levels. Only this constant interchange will provide the basis on which member Churches are able to develop and maintain constant relations and full communion with their sisters and brothers around the world. Each Provincial Church has a responsibility to assist their representatives to carry out this task."

I wish you all a most rewarding time at this Tenth Meeting of our Council.

Address by the Revd Canon Dr John L. Peterson, Secretary General of the ACC

Saturday , 12 October 1996

The Grace of our Lord Jesus Christ, the Love of God and the Fellowship of the Holy Spirit be with you all.

What a great joy it is for me finally to stand before you after being in office for almost two years. What a great privilege it is to meet the appointed members of the Anglican Consultative Council from around the Anglican Communion. I have been waiting a long time for this day and I am thrilled it has finally come.

I am ready, willing and eager to stand with you as we explore together the significant ministry and witness of the ACC as one of the four instruments of unity' in the Anglican Communion. Already I have had in my first two years as your Secretary General the special privilege to get to know and work with two of the instruments of unity' of the Communion quite well.

One, the Primates. The Primates had a very successful and encouraging meeting in England this last year. The theme of that meeting was leadership and in the context of prayer and Bible study, led by the Revd Canon Kenneth Bailey, the Primates discussed different forms of leadership in the Church today. In addition, time was given by the Primates to the International Debt, Islam, and the continuing crisis in Rwanda.

The second Instrument of Unity with whom I have had the great privilege of working is the Archbishop of Canterbury. As some of you who are old timers know, the relationship between the Anglican Communion Office and Lambeth Palace has not always been smooth. Let me tell you today, that has dramatically changed. I am always greatly appreciative of his Grace's ability to bring our combined efforts together for the good of every single Province in the Communion. I give thanks for the time which he so generously gives to me and to the other members of my staff. The visits I have made with him, and the experiences I have shared with him in our regular meetings, tell me that our Communion is well represented and served in the person of the Archbishop of Canterbury in his ministry of presence and proclamation.

One Instrument of Unity I will not encounter until 1998 is the Lambeth

Conference when the Bishops of the Anglican Communion, along with the laity and clergy of the Anglican Consultative Council, gather in Canterbury for the 1998 Lambeth Conference. The planning for the Lambeth Conference is well under way. I am becoming more and more familiar with the working of the Conference, thanks to the help of David Long who is the Lambeth Conference Manager. I might also add that it has been David who has been instrumental in the planning and the implementation of this meeting here in Panama.

The fourth Instrument of Unity I have the great privilege to address today. You cannot imagine how much I am looking forward to working with you. This Instrument of Unity is the only instrument in the Anglican Communion which represents all four orders in the Church, laity, bishops, priests and deacons. You have a unique role in the life of this Communion, one which has been greatly appreciated by the report we will be given by the Inter-Anglican Theological and Doctrinal Commission. In this meeting you are going to be called upon to set the priorities for the work of our Communion in the next millennium.

It also gives me pleasure to greet the Bishop of Panama, Clarence Hayes, and on behalf of the Secretariat I want to thank Biron Daniels and his entire team for the enormous amount of work they have done to make this meeting of the ACC possible here in Panama. It is not an easy task to host people from all over the world. There are visas, there are dietary requirements, there are all sorts of things which make preparations rather difficult, so for all that you have done, Biron, and for the outstanding support of Bishop Hayes, I thank you. You will be experiencing and hearing more about the arrangements that Panama have made for us in the days ahead.

The Secretary General is only as good as his staff. I am thankful for those on the staff who are supportive and who are eager to see the Communion respond to the needs of the Provinces throughout the world. I would like to take this opportunity to thank Dr Donald Anderson who at the end of this meeting is retiring as the Director of Ecumenical Relations and Studies of the Anglican Communion. Don, for your work over the years I want to say a special word of thanks for all that you have done so that we might share and participate more fully and intelligently with our brothers and sisters in Jesus Christ who represent many different denominations and traditions in the Body of Christ. It is also important to know that one of our staff, Mrs Deirdre Martin, who unfortunately cannot be with us in Panama due to health problems, has reached a milestone in her work at the ACC by celebrating her 20th year a couple of months ago.

However, practical problems haunt us. The Secretariat Office faces some serious physical challenges. We have outgrown our space at Partnership

House. We have no storage space, no closets, two people have to share office space and sometimes three people are at one desk. Our present existence is very difficult and we must find a new facility and we need to find it soon. We have been blessed over the last couple of years by the presence of volunteers who give substantial help to our overburdened staff. The least we can give to these volunteers is a desk. To be honest, with the Lambeth Conference approaching, I do not know what we are going to do if we do not find a new home soon.

I would like to take this opportunity to welcome two new staff members who will be joining the Anglican Communion team at the end of this year. The Revd Dr Joan Butler Ford of the Diocese of California who will be the new Director of Telecommunications for the Anglican Communion. Joan will help to expand telecommunications within our Communion, something that is a growing need. Although Joan has been involved with telecommunications for nearly two decades, recently she has been involved in developing an online theological education program for the Church Divinity School of the Pacific, in Berkeley, California.

Our new Director of Ecumenical Relations and Studies, the Revd Canon David Hamid, comes to us from the Church of Canada. For the last nine and a half years he has been the Mission Co-ordinator for the Caribbean and Latin America Region for the Church of Canada. He brings many new talents to his new ministry including an understanding of mission and local praxis. He also brings to his office a keen interest and sensitivity for interfaith issues.

I also want to thank the Revd Canon Andrew Deuchar for all he does for the Anglican Communion Office in his capacity as the Archbishop of Canterbury's Secretary for Anglican Communion Affairs. His is an awesome task. He is an excellent colleague and I thank him for his patience and his expertise which he so freely gives to us.

Where does all this lead us as a Communion?

My vision for our work stems from what we are commanded to do by our Lord Jesus Christ. That work centres on the call to be disciples of the one who came among us as the Prince of Peace. But in saying that I also realise that if we take this call seriously, we are going to have to face the reality that all of us will be called upon to "turn around," to repent, for the Gospel of Jesus Christ calls us to a radical discipleship. For the Prince of Peace did not wear a crown of gold or silver, adorned by diamonds and rubies; instead He wore a crown of thorns. Jesus turns our values upside down. I call this the divine reversal. All the things we hold so dear are turned upside down when we are confronted with the compelling gospel of Jesus Christ. For Jesus commands not only a change of life, but a change of attitude. Jesus challenges us to change the way in which we live. Jesus calls us to learn a new respect and honour for God's creation. Christ is in us. We are God's instruments. In 1 Corinthians, St. Paul talks about the Church being one body with many members. Today we are God's hands, we are God's feet, we are God's eyes. Whatever we do here at ACC-10 we must centre our deliberations in prayer, asking for God's guidance so we will always reflect the radical vision of the Kingdom of God. *"On earth as it is in heaven."*

So on earth we must ask the question, "What will Anglicanism look like in the next millennium?" First of all, I believe Anglicanism will be alive and well in the next millennium. I believe this because of people like you who are dedicated to represent your Province on the Anglican Consultative Council and show concern for our future. But as we prepare for the new millennium, are we ready as a Communion to be God's hands, feet and eyes in our global family to help others? Are we willing to take those risks? Are we prepared to pay that price? Are we willing to wear that crown of thorns?

I know each Anglican Province is an autonomous unit. We like being independent and, of course, there are serious theological and historical reasons for that independence. But the Scriptures call us to be a part of a whole body. St. Paul's beautiful analogy again comes to mind.

"Indeed, the body does not consist of one member but of many. But as it is, God arranged the members in the body, each one of them, as he chose. If all were a single member, where would the body be? As it is there are many members, yet one body. The eye cannot say to the hand, 'I have no need of you,' nor again the head to the feet, 'I have no need of you.'" Then he says *"if one member suffers, all suffer together with it; if one member is honoured, all rejoice together with it."*

Without a doubt we are entering into an age when our sense of interdependence and our sense of co-operation has never been needed more. We need each other. It may sound trite, it may sound simple, but it is a fact that we need a strong base to enable the work that supports the Provinces which we represent. This must be the primary work of the Secretariat.

The Communion faces challenges, joys, sorrows and many opportunities day by day. I am gratified, yet often perplexed, by the number of requests which we receive from Provinces for help. Help on every level, help with ecclesiological problems, help with bishops, help with disciplinary problems, help with government problems, help with practical needs such as food and supplies, help with educational materials, help with providing expertise in various areas such as ecumenical affairs or communication. Help in every possible way.

The challenges which we face as an Anglican Communion are at all levels. This often makes things more difficult because if one aspect of the life in the Communion is intact, then it is easy to concentrate on another one. However, we are finding right now that there is a state of flux in almost every aspect of our work. This makes life more challenging, but we also have to remember that we are not the only denomination feeling this kind of crunch. But we must be honest about it and face the realities of the situation.

The millennium also challenges us in direct and indirect ways. Firstly, it calls us to get our house in order, to move forward with confidence and to look to the future with great expectations. Indirectly, we can assist in various projects and programmes that will be introduced at this unique moment in time. At this meeting I will be asking you to give your full support, prayerful and financial, to what we are calling Bethlehem 2000, a project which will be done by Anglicans for the people of Bethlehem. We, as Anglicans, will have a chance to make a difference at this great holy place of our Christian faith.

Our commitment needs to be considered in light of our mission. The question we must ask is what is our mission today as we look forward to the new millennium. What is the mission that only the ACC can do for the Church, that the local Church, the diocese or the Province cannot do for itself? Today we have to face the reality that 12 of the Provinces of the Communion do not pay their full share to the Anglican Communion budget. We are definitely living by faith, but the reality is that our faith is being tested.

At ACC-10 there are going to be two major funding initiatives brought before you, and a third opportunity which is still on the drawing boards. This project will generate and provide development funds for dioceses and Provinces of the Communion. The development funds will help Provinces and dioceses to be more self-sufficient and at the same time to have outreach programmes in local communities. They will also help meet crisis situations.

The two programmes we hope to launch at ACC-10 will have a significant potential for non-core items in the Anglican Communion budget. Both programmes have been set in motion by lay members of the Communion, and for that I am particularly grateful.

The Anglican Investment Agency, which is already well underway with the backing of our Standing Committee, and the proposed Anglican Communion Friends programme, again already in its first stages of development in the United States, are two major fund-raising programmes which are important for ACC-10 to support. We will want to look at these programmes in detail as our days together unfold.

It might still be fashionable in some circles to talk about the provisionality of Anglicanism. I believe our need for a confident Anglicanism is essential. Indeed, I am firmly committed to the ecumenical movement. Why? I am committed to it because it is the command of our Lord himself that we all may be one. I am also committed to the ecumenical movement because we as Anglicans or Episcopalians have something significant to offer to the ecumenical process. Thus, all the money and energy that we spend on ecumenical endeavours helps us to realise and appreciate the great tradition which we have. Ours is an inclusive tradition. Ours is a gospel tradition. Ours is a liturgical tradition. Ours is a Christ-centred tradition which allows Christians to think, pray and work in an atmosphere of discovering what our minds and hearts tell us as we listen for God's word in our age. Scripture, tradition, reason and experience prove to be excellent guides for us as a faith community.

Our ecumenical work has its ups and downs, but we all rejoice with the recent exciting developments with our sisters and brothers of the Lutheran confession in several parts of the Communion, most notably, in England, Scotland, Wales, Ireland and the USA. The Anglican/Roman Catholic work (ARCIC) continues, following an excellent celebration in Belgium where the 75th anniversary of the Anglican/Roman Catholic Malines Conversations were observed in the presence of the Archbishop of Canterbury and the Cardinal Archbishop of Malines. There was a spirit of co-operation and friendship evident that was most encouraging. Throughout ACC-10 we are going to be welcoming many ecumenical observers who will be coming to join us.

I believe the Anglican Communion has a vocation and ministry in the Body of Christ. I not only believe it, I know it from what I have seen in the Provinces that I have visited. Indeed, I have been in almost 20 Provinces in my first two years as Secretary General. I must say, it is a bit physically exhausting, but I also have to say, it is rewarding and refreshing spiritually to see even under the most dire circumstances what our Communion has done and is able to do.

Is there more we can do? Of course, there is always more and we need to have more support and a better way of approaching the challenges which confront us. I ask you therefore, as members of the ACC, to take seriously your role, because your role is fundamental in the Anglican Communion structures. I would ask you to look deeply into your hearts and minds to see what it is that you can offer to the Communion over these next few days. For what is decided here, and the commitment you make to those decisions, will determine the effectiveness of the ACC as we look to the new millennium. ACC meetings, Primates meetings or Lambeth Conferences are not meant to be one time events. They are meant to be the source from which the energy and work flows for the years ahead.

There are problems. The confusion about the ACC networks, the confusion about the role of ACC in the structures, are things that need to be discussed. There is no one who has worked harder or more diligently to help define the role of the ACC in the Anglican Communion than our Chair, Colin Craston. As you will see in the different papers you receive, Colin has been instrumental in developing how the ACC can be a more effective instrument for the Anglican Communion. The greatest tribute we will be able to pay Colin for his 15 years of service to the ACC is that when ACC-10 is over, we will have a fresh vision. When ACC-10 is over we will have a new way of working together.

As you well know from letters and articles which I have written, I believe communication deserves our greatest attention.

I marvel at the work that has been done in communications with the limited resources which we have had over the years. When I became Secretary General I was confronted with the fact that our excellent publication, *Anglican World*, reached only a very few people and indeed, received almost no support. When I arrived, there were only 250 paid subscribers out of the thousands distributed. I rejoice that the paid subscribers have now reached into the thousands and we receive more paid subscriptions every day. I firmly believe that the printed word is still the most important way of communication in a Communion as global as ours.

I continue to pledge my support to Canon Jim Rosenthal and those who assist him to make their job more feasible as they continue their excellent work. Everything costs money and we have to remember that a good two thirds of our Communion cannot afford to pay for *Anglican World*. Indeed, in Provinces like Zaire, one year's subscription to *Anglican World* would be the equivalent of a month's salary. So therefore, I call upon those who can, to do all in their power to enlist subscriptions so that every time we receive a paid subscription we can send a free subscription to someone in a part of the world who cannot afford it.

Let me share with you what an impact this can have. The Parish of St. Mary's-in-the-Highland, Birmingham AL, ordered 400 copies of *Anglican World* for every member in their parish. They then designated 400 copies to be given to the Province of Brazil. Christ Cathedral in Eau Claire, Wisconsin, just ordered 43 subscriptions of *Anglican World* for the leadership in the Cathedral and they designated 43 copies to be sent to Myanmar. Hopefully, more parishes and dioceses will do this around the world. I challenge you to participate in this programme.

Communication is a two-way street. We must receive information from the Provinces and from every diocese. Every newsletter we receive in the Secretariat is read by someone on the communications team. So, therefore, please make sure that we are informed of what is happening in your Province. There is so much good news happening in the Anglican Communion that Jim predicts we could double the size of *Anglican World*. Well, we cannot do that financially, but praise God there is a reality, that we could, if we were able.

I see the goal with regard to evangelism, while building on what has been achieved so far in the Decade of Evangelism, is to see evangelism integrated increasingly into all the aspects of total mission—all that Christ sends his Church into the world to do as his hands, eyes and feet. It is when Mission is seen and pursued as a whole that true converts and conversion come, thus the report, edited by Cyril Okorocha, *The Cutting Edge of Mission*, must be carefully examined and studied and I encourage you to do that.

Indeed the proclamation of the Good News in Christ—in Burundi, Korea, Papua New Guinea, South East Asia, and not least the First World—must have priorities of witness and action for justice, relief of oppression and suffering. Without these priorities, proclamation of "spiritual" benefits of salvation will lack credibility.

I trust that a new video that will premier during this meeting, *The Many Faces of Anglicanism*, will be a vehicle to bring before your eyes the realities of our Communion and help in our outreach.

As I have already mentioned, finances are a major problem and seem to control our hopes and dreams for the work set before us. Or do they?

The situation I faced when I was appointed to this office spoke for the need for extensive fund-raising to make programmes possible. I have committed myself to that task. There has been some success, for which I thank God. However the challenge for this year, the 1996 budget, has met some obstacles, even just as recent as last week when a promised large gift I learned was going to be "held over" to a future date. However, on the same day I learned of a potential donor who was interested in our work. So there are disappointments as well as successes and indeed we learn from both.

However, I do need your help in identifying possible sources of financial support in your Province. Our budget can not meet the demands which we are called upon to do in this 1996 world in which we live. Because of the shortfalls we experience from some of the Provinces, I will have a strategy in place by the Meeting of the Joint Standing Committees in early 1997, but I cannot do it alone. When a Province does not meet its asking, that poses difficulties for all the other Provinces. Therefore, we need to look to foundations and individuals who can be brought on board with our communion-wide vision. Please share with me your ideas over the next few days.

Just recently I represented the Anglican Communion at a meeting of the Seventh-Day Adventists with 30,000 in attendance. Each person paid their own expenses and huge amounts of monies were raised by the people there who are strong believers in what their Church represents. Can we show such strength as the millennium approaches? I pray the answer is yes.

Our commitment must be to each other and our world-wide Church must be strengthened. There is an old saying that goes, "life is a banquet and the world is starving." Indeed that is true and our banquet symbolised in the Holy Eucharist is a banquet for the starving world. The time has come for us to be a Church that welcomes people from all walks of life, people who can share with us their experience, and we can broaden our horizons and live a fuller life. The banquet is ready, the scripture tells us and we must be open to receiving our guests as we would receive Christ himself. The world is starving, some places have literally no food, no medicine, no nothing. But the world is also starving spiritually and we all know this from what we read and hear happening around us. You know that New Age religions and fundamentalism of many kinds are staking their claims in many societies today. I saw it in Accra, I saw it in Sydney, I saw it in Cape Town, I saw it in New York, I see it in London. In his address to the Malines Conference, Professor John A. Dick argued:

> "In an age when more men and women look for signs of transcendence in fossils from Mars, mysteriously unexplained geometric problems in wheat fields or in neo pagan feminist rituals, more than they do in traditional Word and Sacrament, the credibility problem for the Church is real. Our Christian dreams and visions must lead to transformative action—action which helps people better see God. Action which helps a secularised culture re-discover signs of Incarnation. Action which flows from and forms Gospel values. Action which builds—not disrupts—the Reign of God."

But I want to say New Age advocates and fundamentalists do not have anything over us as Anglican Christians. Ours is a timely and vibrant faith, ours is a living God, ours is a powerful testimony, ours is a global family. We have something to offer to a starving world. We have hands of compassion, we have feet of action, we have eyes of love, we have the banquet feast of the Eucharist which binds us all together. Wherever we go around the Anglican Communion the Eucharist is faithfully celebrated in parish after parish, day by day, week by week. Today more than ever before, the Eucharist is being celebrated in our own languages in our own national prayer books. Wonderful examples of that are the Prayer Books of Australia, Kenya and Aotearoa, New Zealand and Polynesia.

Now all we have to do is learn how to bring more people to this great banquet table. To welcome more people to baptism, to incorporate them into the family of Christ where one receives freedom, liberation and salvation. People are bound by fears, distrust and compromise, but what we have to share is a faith that broadens the horizons, opens the heart and mends the wounded soul. The world struggles with the reality of AIDS, famine, natural disasters, marriage breakdown and the horrors of violence.

I know that many of you face persecution for your faith in Jesus Christ. The stories that the Archbishop of Canterbury has told of his visits to Sudan are compelling. The horror which we have seen on our televisions these last two weeks as the peace process fails in Israel/Palestine brings back to mind the courageous ministry of President Bishop Samir Kafity and the Church in Jerusalem and the Middle East during the Intifada. The renewed bombings in London and in Northern Ireland bring to our attention the extreme pressures under which Archbishop Robin Eames works for his people so that a true peace can be established. All of us know the outstanding work that Bishop Dinis Sengulane has done in Mozambique, South Africa and Burundi.

One of the most significant opportunities that we have as Anglicans is our presence at the United Nations. We are all grateful for the work that Bishop James Ottley does in this regard, and I know that the Diocese of Panama rejoices with us that he is in this position, after serving this Diocese so well. Like many of the important programmes of the Anglican Communion, the needs surrounding the UN Office are multitudinous. You will hear much about the UN Office later, but I hold it up as a programme that is of primary importance if we are to have influence in the councils of the world.

All I can say to you is thanks be to God for your witness, your ability to stand firmly in your faith. I also know in some places in our Communion where there is persecution, trial and tribulations, it is also there that the Church is growing the fastest. Nigeria immediately comes to mind. Here in a country where basic human rights are being denied daily, the Church is growing at an incredible speed. This has something to teach all of us. Therefore, all of us are called to a firm commitment and love of our Christian faith. We have nothing about which to be ashamed. In the Churches and Province of Southern Africa they have little posters that go like this: "I love being an Anglican" and in the Episcopal Church in the United States they have posters saying "I am proud to be Episcopalian." May this be so for all of us. If we are not proud, and if there are things within the Church that inhibit our sense of will to proclaim the Gospel message, let us seek ways within our structures to open up new dialogue.

Let us find ways to address the often difficult issues of our time. We will talk about some of them at this meeting: Sexuality, Islam, Fundamentalism and many more. Let us not be afraid of them—these are the issues which Jesus challenges us with today. We will hear about the situations that our brothers and sisters face in their own lives. Problems continue to plague our Church and we will hear the continuing struggle of our fellow Anglicans in Rwanda. We will hear about the devastation of AIDS in Uganda, but we will also hear about their excellent AIDS education programme. We will hear about Indian rights in the Southern Cone and then call there for justice for the indigenous peoples. We will hear about the courageous stand that the Church in Japan took last year when they were able to say "We're sorry" and the great healing which takes place when we can ask for forgiveness.

In a way, what I have been saying is in the form of a testimony. I believe in what I have said. I believe our Communion is a wonderful family. I believe it because I have seen it. I believe in the power of the living Christ. As many of you know, I have come to this post nominated by the Province of Jerusalem in the Middle East. Having had the great opportunity to live in Jerusalem for 12 years, I not only saw the faithfulness of the Palestinian Christians, but I saw the faithfulness of the pilgrims who came to that holy city from around the Anglican Communion. I saw their faith being lived out in the living Christ. I saw people experience the wonder, the awe of the empty tomb. I know that Christ is living.

> I have seen the living Christ in the Philippines
> I have seen the living Christ in Mexico
> I have seen the living Christ in Wales
> I have seen the living Christ in the West Indies

I know that Jesus' message is clear. I know that Christ is calling us to a unique vocation today as Christians. Remember, Christians are ordinary people who make extraordinary claims.

I believe that Christ is challenging us as Anglicans to touch the lives of the people to whom we are called to serve. There is no task too big, had there been, Jesus would not have been crucified. Jesus had that option. Instead, Jesus called upon God's strength, *"thy will be done."* We are challenged to do the same. Jesus calls us to a new unity, a unity that will give an opportunity for laity, bishops, priests and deacons to be part of the process, men and women, young and old, people from all walks of life. I believe once we start isolating and marginalising people for whatever reasons, once we humanly choose to separate people one from another, then we have lost the essence of the message which Jesus proclaims.

We all have a gift to bring to our Lord's Table. We all have something to present at the altar. I do not want anyone to leave this ACC-10 meeting feeling that they have not had a chance to be heard. I do not want anyone to leave this ACC-10 meeting feeling intimidated, that what I might say might not be as articulate as someone else. Everyone's voice must be heard and the ACC-10 Design Group under the leadership of Dr Diane Maybee and Archbishop Brian Davis has worked hard to make sure that this would happen especially in our small groups and in our regional work. We must be sensitive to each other's needs over the next few days. We are here to learn from each other and to share what we say as a family. Let us listen to each other.

Let us address these issues and ask, "Can the Anglican Communion make a difference?" All the issues are important, but let us resolve that nothing should separate us from the message that a child was born of Mary, that this child was crucified under Pontius Pilate, and on the third day, broke the chains of death for our salvation. Might we worship him as Saviour and Lord.

Once again, I appreciate your presence here, your taking time from your work and from your Church to be part of the important deliberations of ACC-10. I trust that the days ahead will enlighten and enliven us all. It is my prayer that as a result of these meetings we will be more fit and more able to fulfil our own ministries as individuals, as congregations, as dioceses, and as Provinces. It is my prayer that you will join me and work for the openness which will allow us to speak freely, lovingly and carefully. Might we always remember the reason why we are here, why we have been called together, and why we accept the challenge of the Gospel that was given to all of us at our baptism. Therefore, I would like to close my testimony today by asking you to join with me in affirming our faith—may this be our communal testimony as we proclaim the mystery of our faith together. Therefore let us proclaim the mystery of our faith in the familiar words used at the Eucharist so often:

Christ has died, Christ is risen, Christ will come again.

Sermon by the Archbishop of Canterbury

Sunday, 13 October 1996, at the Gimnasio Nuevo, Panama City

Those of us who are members attending the ACC-10 are so grateful to the Diocese of Panama for your warm and generous welcome. We are delighted to be here with you and over the next week look forward to sharing your life.

It is astonishing to think that it was only three years ago that members of ACC-9 met in Cape Town. Those who were there will remember it well. We assembled in the University of the Western Cape. Apartheid was still the order of the day and clouded the Conference. There seemed very little chance of a solution to the political and social injustice that had excluded South Africa from the rest of the world. During that time we met the three leaders who played significant roles in the historic breakthrough that brought Apartheid to an end peacefully. Desmond Tutu, our own Anglican Archbishop of Cape Town, whose prophetic ministry was so important; President De Klerk, who was wise enough to realise that white supremacy had come to an end; and Nelson Mandela, who visited us and whose dignity, compassion, forgiveness and stature made such a deep impression on us all. All three men were people deeply inspired and influenced by the Christian faith and whose styles of leadership, though very different, were shaped by the Gospel.

Today's theme focuses on leadership. We gather leaders from many different nations and Provinces. It is not a bad thing to ask: What is the context, calling and cost of leadership today?

The *context* in which we exercise our leadership will of course vary from place to place. For some, leadership is exercised in the midst of privation, poverty, suffering and perhaps persecution. For others, the context may be that of apathy and indifference. For others still, it may consist of exercising our leadership as clergy or lay people in a minority Church where there seems little scope for evangelism, growth is slow and all our effort seems unrewarded. Whatever the differences in context, the first reading points to the similar conditions of human frailty and hardness that is true of every situation where leadership is put to work. Yahweh says through Ezekiel to the people of God: *"I shall give you a new heart and put a new spirit in you. I shall remove the heart of stone from your bodies and give you a heart of* _flesh instead. You shall be my people and I will be your God._ " The heart of stone. Have you noticed how so many newspapers have a limited view of sin? It is usually limited to sexual misdemeanours. How narrow that is when compared with the Bible. The Bible has a much wider perspective. It includes sexual sins, of course, but sin refers to the complex network of evil which destroys people. The _"heart of stone"_ says it all, because sin numbs, sin paralyses, sin distorts and sin imprisons. The _"heart of flesh"_ on the other hand, feels, understands and responds with tenderness and love. The context of our ministry is set between the reality of sin in its multi-layered forms and the promise that God is able to redeem any situation however hopeless, however evil, however bad—indeed as evil, hopeless and as bad as Apartheid looked just a mere three years ago.

But effective and visionary leadership is always a **calling**—the calling to follow a Lord whose majestic leadership was that of servanthood. There can be no effective Christian leadership worthy of the name that is not steeped in the calling to serve.

One of the great spiritual leaders of the Church of England at the end of the nineteenth century was Edward King. He became Bishop of Lincoln and seemed to be a very unlikely candidate. At the time, it was a very backward diocese. Such was the low standard of the clergy when he became bishop that he was told that "one third of the clergy were out of their minds, one third were going out of their minds—and one third had no minds to go out of!" Today King is rightly recognised to have been a wonderful example of true Christian leadership. In one of his famous spiritual letters he wrote, quite simply:

> "I long to see a real and simple imitation of the life we have
> shown to us in the Gospels. It seems to me that if people go on
> allowing themselves to shape their lives so much more by the
> circumstances of the world than by the Gospel, they will be in
> danger of disbelieving the truths of the Bible itself."

What prophetic words, and how much we need, each one of us, to read them and meditate upon them over and over again.

Listen to Edward King again: "While you keep up fresh and trembling all your old, nervous humility, just throw yourself back on the fact that God made you what you are, and, therefore, do not fear failure or want of power."

There are wonderful examples of Christian people standing out against the pressures of the world. In places of violence, in places of suffering, in places where Christians are oppressed for their faith, men and women are to be found living prophetic lives. We thank God for their witness and example.

But what is the **cost** of the calling that beckons us all?

Purity of life, willingness to go the extra mile, a willingness to face discouragement and work long hours—yes, this is part of the cost of leadership. But there is one insidious cost which belongs to our calling—and which is important for ACC to bear in mind—and that is for leadership to resist the seductive tones of bureaucratic power.

All of us here, whoever we are, have responsibility for the Church of which we are members. Whether lay people, clergy, bishops or archbishops, we are first of all part of the people of God, part of the Body of Christ, and we all—by what we say or don't say, by what we do or don't do—contribute to the way in which the Church is perceived. But those who are called to positions of leadership have a particular responsibility as we seek to nurture, to teach and to guide. How easy it is to be seduced by the lure of power, to allow the trappings which accompany our office to go to our heads.

There are plenty of examples in Christian history when the Church has become too bureaucratic, with the consequence that leadership is reduced to shoring up an institution rather than inspiring people for an adventure. When that happens the Church is in danger of being swamped by rules and regulations which stifle the pilgrimage of faith and makes Christianity a burden instead of a joy. As the great German theologian, Jürgen Moltmann writes, "A life which is worthy of the Gospel liberates us to be ourselves and fills us with the powers of the Spirit... The life worthy of the Gospel also has its discipline, but it is the discipline of love and joy, not the discipline of anxiety under the threat of the law."

At these times of temptation we need the support of a Church which has a clear vision of the nature of Gospel leadership: *"Anyone who wants to become great amongst you must be your servant, and anyone who wants to be first among you must be slave to all."* (Mark 1043-44)

The leadership which Jesus demonstrates in his life and in his death is of a person whose heart is always open to God, and whose arms are always open to humankind.

The Church must demonstrate to the world that our eyes and our heart, as well as our words, are set in the service of God, and our arms and our feet are set on serving the people of God. Again, we thank God for the many examples from around the world where the Church has stood firm in the face of **oppression**, and has been a beacon of light in an ocean of darkness. We have many parts of our Communion where that is a reality and we thank God for such costly ministry.

I referred to Edward King earlier; let me end with another anecdote from his ministry. It was said of King that he had a special ministry to railway boys. These were little urchins who did dirty and sometimes dangerous jobs to keep the railways going. King was often seen talking to them. One railway boy said one day: "Why, he must have been a railway boy himself to know so much about us and what we do." But, of course, the aristocratic King had never been a railway boy. He had never lived personally in such squalor and poverty. But such was his compassion, love and interest that his Christian faith bridged the cultural gulf and made his leadership accessible, giving hope and faith.

But, after all, isn't that the nature of true leadership, which works within the narrow context of ministry, accepting the wonderful call to serve God where he has placed us and accepting with it the cost to be servants of the One who came not to be served, but to serve and to give his life a ransom for many.

That is our mission—not merely to build up the Church, certainly not to build up ourselves, but to demonstrate and proclaim the reality of the one true God who can turn hearts of stone into hearts of flesh.

Sermon at the Closing Eucharist by the Revd Canon Colin Craston

Saturday, 19 October 1996

May I begin by saying again what a privilege and blessing it has been to be
involved in the ACC these past 15 years. It has been a life-changing experience.
Prior to 1981, I thought I knew something about the Anglican
Communion, through membership in the Council of an English missionary
society, but, in truth, actual experience of life in the Communion
through its multiplicity of cultures and nationalities, sharing in the worship
and fellowship of fellow Anglicans and observing their witness, has
brought enrichment beyond all expectations. It became like a "conversion
experience," for which I am deeply grateful to God.

Now, as I look forward to the next few years, I believe there are solid
grounds for hope of God's blessing and guidance of the Communion's
Churches in their partnership within the world-wide universal Church.

A Lambeth Conference, more thoroughly prepared for I think than any
previous Conference, is less than two years away. The ACC has enjoyed
here a good, successful meeting, better than some I have known. There is
a better framework for harmonious co-operation between the ACC and
the Primates' Meeting, through the Joint Standing Committees and the
participation of the members of the Primates' Standing Committee in the
meeting of the ACC. And, just beyond the dawn of the new millennium,
an Anglican Congress for the celebration of our faith could give widespread
encouragement across the Communion. So, hope is justified.
Hope, not basically because of human planning and effort, but because
God is with us. And all the signs are that he still has purposes for the
Communion. But, realistic hope cannot ignore heavy problems, even
threats to Anglican unity, in the way ahead.

The bishops at Lambeth will have a new experience of both male and
female members and have to find the way to turn that new thing into a
great blessing, to discover how divine grace can permeate human attitudes,
so that God's will is worked out. Issues of human sexuality, complicated
by different cultural perceptions as well as theological convictions,
will continue to threaten our unity. And the tensions between those who
claim to hold an orthodox, traditionalist understanding of the faith and
those who want to be open to new understandings, even in conjunction

with other faiths and new religious movements, could increase.

In all the seas ahead of us, be they troubled or even stormy, there is a unique role for the Instruments of Unity, of which the ACC is one. There has been a saying around for a long time that, "the family that prays together stays together." We have the framework for Communion-wide prayer. But we can also say, "the family that talks together, stays together— or, is most likely to do so."

Prayer for the Lambeth Conference, for the ACC, for the Primates, for the Congress, is increasingly needed, that in our talking together we are at the same time listening to God.

I have been convinced, however, more so in recent months, that it is not enough. In particular, it was the passage we had for the Epistle that has shaped my thinking. It is such a familiar passage, its challenge may so easily slide over us. But listen afresh to these exhortations of Paul to his readers.

They are not just pious thoughts given as a prelude to the great early Christian hymn that follows. "Consider others better than yourselves, look out for one another's interests, not just your own." That's one translation. Another is—"in humble mindedness each counting the other better than himself, each looking not only to his own interests but also to the interests of others." For "himself," also read "herself."

Now, let us put those injunctions in the context of the tensions and divisions we face in the Communion.

I can illustrate the sharpness of the challenge from my own personal history. For some 25 years I strongly supported the cause of women's ordination in writing, in planning with others. In the opposition ranks were men and women whose attitudes on this matter I disliked, whose arguments I regarded as fault-ridden, though I did not doubt their sincerity. But I have asked myself—"Did I meet this test of St. Paul?" "Did I count the others better than myself?" "Did I look to their interests as well as my own?" If these verses from Philippians 2 are about unity in the Church, then, at the heart of the matter is the creation of this humble-minded attitude, this spirit, mutually shared by Christian people.

The first four verses of the chapter, before we get to the Christian hymn on Christ's humiliation, are an exhortation to harmony and humility in the face of division and faction in the Church. St. Paul's stirring appeal is based on a four-fold incentive— *"If there is any encouragement in Christ, if any persuasive appeal springing from love, if any fellowship of the Spirit, if any tender mercy and compassion—then,"* (he continues the appeal—with a threefold directive)

> *"let there be oneness*
> *let there be lowliness of mind*
> *let there be mutual regard."*

"Oneness"—i.e. being of the same mind, having the same love, with souls united setting your minds on unity.

"Lowliness of mind"—doing nothing from selfish ambition or from empty conceit. Commentators tell us that the word translated "lowliness of mind" was frowned upon in the ancient world as denoting "abject cringing." It was through the life and teaching of Jesus that the word was rescued to be a virtue.

"Mutual regard"—in humble-mindedness each counting the other better than himself, herself. Now, I have concentrated somewhat on this verse as essential to true unity, but we might well ask—"is it practicable?"

We can point up that question in this way—"How can the industrious Church member, seeking to be conscientious, regard the rather lazy fellow member as better than himself or herself?" What St. Paul is advocating, surely, is not that one should consider every fellow Christian to be in every respect wiser, abler, and nobler than oneself. Rather, unless there is abundant evidence of consistent wrong-doing in others, we should ascribe good not evil motives to those we disagree with, remembering always one's own faults and failings and dependence at all times on God's grace. Knowing our own motives are not always good or unmixed, the good points and qualities in others should be honoured, looked for, and thus we will serve their interests to help them.

So, it has been borne upon me of late that the attitudes St. Paul earnestly pleads for here are at the heart of the unity we need as a family of Churches. Structures are very important, but without this spirit they can become areas of struggle, power politics, even though the struggle and politics are polite.

What is the secret, however, in getting to the mutual regard in humility and harmony? St. Paul finds no better way of answering that question than by turning to the hymn which begins— *"Let this mind be in you, or among you, as in Christ Jesus."* I am sure the *"mind"* there is not just your mental activity, but the whole set, mind-set of your inner being. For, the mind of Christ Jesus which Paul then describes is of total humiliation, self-chosen, leading to complete self-sacrifice.

Basic to the mutual regard and humility that must undergird our search for "unity in diversity" is the willingness to accept deep down within us that we do not possess the whole truth ourselves. However strong the convictions that "we have got it right", there is just the possibility we are forgetting, or ignorant of, something. We have not got the whole picture totally in focus.

I recently read an article by one of our most respected newscasters on British TV. Trevor McDonald is of Caribbean extraction. He is the main newscaster on Independent TV. Some years ago he had been to interview Nelson Mandela. He thought long and hard how he would interview him. He wanted Mr Mandela to talk about the pain and brutality of his prison experiences—but he refused to do so.

Disappointed, McDonald turned to political considerations and suggested there was really no possibility of a meeting of minds between the ANC and the National Party about South Africa's future. McDonald says, "Mr Mandela's response was unforgettable." He said, "when two parties begin serious negotiations you must be prepared to compromise on fundamental principles." McDonald thought he could not have heard right and Mandela could not have meant that, but Nelson Mandela said it again and again.

To Anglicans, to any Christians locked in disagreement over divisive issues—does Mandela's line sound like heresy? "Being prepared to compromise on fundamental principles." Apply it to any divisive issue we face! I do not suggest, of course, we have to accept ideas that seem quite wrong—to us dishonest! But I do suggest that if we can recognise that even in the convictions we feel most sure about, regarding contemporary divisive issues in our Communion, we may not possess the whole truth—we are getting to that humility which is essential to true harmony and unity.

Let us go back to the secret St. Paul presents. _"Let this mind be in you…"_

Four steps downward in Christ's humiliation are described with reverent awe.

> 1.   His essential glory laid aside—equality with the Father not selfishly hung on to or grasped (whichever meaning is given to the words).

> 2.   Incarnation as a helpless baby, and then growth into manhood.

> 3.   Service—epitomised by kneeling as a slave to wash the quarrelling disciples' feet.

> 4.   Crucifixion—death on a cross.

Four steps! Heaven's Glory, Bethlehem, Galilee and Gethsemane, Golgotha—four downward steps in humiliation self-chosen.

Let this mind be in you as in Christ Jesus. Some commentators think the "you" there is not singular, not just "you individually" but "you collectively" in the Church—all you who are in Christ Jesus.

I do not think Anglicans can do anything better as we look forward to the next few years, and beyond into the new millennium—as we worship, minister, communicate our belief in God and relate to society, than to pray earnestly for the mind of Christ Jesus to be in us.

> Father God, who gave your only begotten Son to take upon himself the form of a servant and to be obedient even to death on a cross, give us the same mind that was in Christ Jesus that, sharing his humility, we may come to be with him in his glory, who is alive and reigns with you and the Holy Spirit. One God, now and for ever. Amen

THE HEARINGS

Timely, forthright, visionary, and articulate were the hearings that were held on Jerusalem, human sexuality, and Islam, each with its own unique focus in the life of the Communion. The hearings themselves left each member with plenty to think about and, more importantly, plenty to pray about.

Presentation by the
Revd Canon John L. Peterson
Millennium - Dateline Bethlehem 1999-2000

Sunday, 13 October 1996

The Anglican Consultative Council in corporation with Anglicans throughout the world have been invited by the Palestinian National Authority to be part of a unique opportunity for Christian witness. This challenge, this opportunity, is Bethlehem.

The phrase "whose birthday is it?" reflects the need for all of us to return to Bethlehem to see this thing which has come to pass, the birth of the Prince of Peace, the Holy Child Jesus. Bethlehem sits in a land that has suffered greatly and is suffering greatly. The Christian population in Bethlehem dwindles day by day because of persecution and the lack of a strong economic structure. It has been my privilege along with other staff members, including the Revd Canon Andrew Deuchar and the Right Reverend Simon Barrington-Ward of Coventry, England, representing the Archbishop of Canterbury, to meet with both President Arafat and Mayor Freij of Bethlehem to discuss the needs of this historic community in the days ahead.

Both the President and the Mayor along with Church leaders of the Province of the Episcopal Church in Jerusalem and the Middle East, have a vision they want to share with us. I count it as a great privilege to present to you the need for a united Christian witness in Bethlehem for the millennium celebrations.

Manger Square in Bethlehem, the main pilgrimage area, needs total reconstruction and replanning. The current situation in Bethlehem finds a lack of qualified people to take on this particular kind of endeavour. To miss the goal of a renewal by the year 2000 would be a tragedy. The infrastructure as it now stands will not provide the necessary expertise to move forward. What this means is seconding people to do the primary and necessary task of city planning. Of course, one of the greatest joys of this will be to work alongside our brother and sister Christians in the Holy Land. It is amazing how many tourists and pilgrims come to Jerusalem, Bethlehem, Nazareth and all the other places that are so important in the life of Christianity and never meet the indigenous Christian population. This is a sad reality and it is time to change this dramatically. Therefore in co-operation with all the peoples I have mentioned above, I am asking members of the Anglican Communion throughout the world to become part of this special 'Bethlehem Millennium' celebration.

First, it is absolutely imperative that a 'Bethlehem Millennium Planning Committee' be established with members from around the Communion. This Committee would need to consist of people proficient in city planning, construction and commercial enterprises. It is my hope that organisations like Volunteers for Mission in the Episcopal Church USA and other Provinces would ask people to come on board to be part of this exciting venture. I see brother and sister Anglicans joining hands in doing the actual work that needs to be done to help the city of Bethlehem come alive for the great celebration of our Saviour's birth.

Second and foremost for us as Anglicans, we have been asked by the President and Mayor to take on a particular project. The Anglican project, and I believe we are indeed honoured to be able to do this, is the renovation of Manger Square. This is a monumental task, but it is something which will enable us to have a unique Christian presence as Anglicans in Bethlehem. I praise God for this opportunity and I hope we can target designated donors and other Anglican Communion resources to make this a reality by the year 2000.

What this means is, not only the co-operation of the Anglican Communion Secretariat in London, but in each of the Provincial Secretaries and Communicators in the various Provinces to make this project known. It is my hope that out of this meeting of the Anglican Consultative Council, we can send a strong message to our brothers and sisters around the world asking for their support in these two areas. Area 1—the establishing of the Committee and the finding of workers. This is as important as the fund-raising which is going to be necessary in Area 2. One will not work without the other and therefore, I am asking ACC-10 to endorse full heartedly, the pledge for the Anglican Communion to renovate Manger Square to make it a more holy, lively, and accessible place which will enrich the lives of every person who will come to pray at the site of Christ's birth. At the same time this project will help support the people, especially our fellow Christians, in the land that we call Holy and the city that we revere above all cities. The Archbishop of Canterbury has given his support to this project, and I hope we can all join him in moving ahead rapidly in the days to come.

Presentation by the Most Revd Samir Kafity on Jerusalem

Wednesday, 16 October 1996

In a comment in Hebrew in the Talmud, a writer wrote about Jerusalem the following: "Ten measures of beauty God gave to the world, nine to Jerusalem and one to the rest of the world." But wait, he also gave 10 measures of suffering and agony to the world, nine to Jerusalem and one to the rest of the world.

As I was coming up to the podium, Bishop Dinis said to me, "You are going to take us on a journey to Jerusalem. What are we to expect in Jerusalem?" I told him Golgotha is in Jerusalem but also the Empty Tomb is in Jerusalem.

Jerusalem is a subject which is now being discussed in the peace process between the Israelis, the Palestinians and the Jordanians. They have kept the issue of Jerusalem to the very end because of its difficulty and complexity. Jerusalem is the sacred city for Christians, Muslims and Jews. Its sancity to us as Christians, is very obvious. Everything in our faith happened in the Holy Land. It was not by accident that God has chosen the Holy Land for enacting his drama of salvation and, therefore, as Christians the sanctity of Jerusalem and the Holy Land are essential for our liturgical life, for our faith and commitment to the Gospel.

The Christians, in 1947, in the small municipal boundaries of the city drawn by the British Mandate, numbered 28,000 Christians in the city of Jerusalem. At the moment in 1996, after almost 50 years, the number of the Christians, all the Christians, of all the denominations, ancient and new, Eastern and Western, lay and ordained, are less than 9,000 Christians in the city of Jerusalem. Massive emigration.

There are more Christian stones and buildings and bells than Christian people and what makes Jerusalem holy is also the holy community of Christ that is living there. If the Christians had not emigrated during the past 50 years and were only increased by birth, the natural way of increase, there would now be more than over 100,000 Christians in the city of Jerusalem. There are less than 9,000. One congregation in your Province makes more than the total number of Christians in the Mother City of our faith.

I remember very well on his visit to us to mark 150 years of the presence of Anglicanism in the city, the Archbishop of Canterbury wishing that the city not be considered as Disneyland. That's why in my sermon I proposed the eighth sacrament for us Christians. Pilgrimage and journey and joining the living community, the random community in its life and witness in the Mother City of our faith, is an essential demand of the Gospel. Thanks to other Churches, that makes it imperative for the faithful to do their pilgrimage. Perhaps the Roman Catholic Church is the most active Church in developing pilgrimage to the Holy Land.

It is also sacred to the Jews and this is the place of their Second Temple, although Moses did not reach the land but there is a lot of sanctity in Judaism connected with Jerusalem and "the Promised Land." I am not going to politicize the Bible or use the Bible for partisan politics, but one cannot deny that there is a connection, a strong connection, of Judaism and the Jews with the Holy Land.

It is also sacred to Islam. For the ascension of the prophet Mohammed took place from Jerusalem according to the text of the Koran. It was their first object of prayer, now they turn to Mecca which is the second. But the first focus of prayer for the Muslim world is still Jerusalem. When the Caliph, the immediate successor of the Prophet Mohammed, visited Jerusalem with the Islamic armies, Arab armies, he was welcomed, he was welcomed and that was in the year 738AD by the Patriarch of Jerusalem, the Orthodox Patriarch of Jerusalem who was an Arab by nationality. Safronias met the Caliph, and the Caliph and his company stayed in the monasteries and the homes of the Christians of the city. The Caliph did not pray in the Church of the Holy Sepulchre or else it would have become a mosque. He prayed outside the Church of the Resurrection where a mosque is erected, which gives the characteristic of Jerusalem being sacred to Jews, Christians and Muslims. He also delivered the key of the Church of the Resurrection to the family called Musehbah and Abu Judhi and since the 7th and 8th centuries the Muslim community serves as the janitors and caretakers of the Church of the Resurrection. A new form of inter-faith, not only dialogue but co-operation and co-existence.

When the United Nations met in 1947, it was two years old. It was born as the League of Nations in 1945, in our Cathedral, Grace Cathedral in San Francisco. Two years later, they decided under Decision 181 to partition Palestine into two states; a state of Palestine, so the United Nations did not erase or wipe out the name of Palestine, and a Jewish state for Israelis. But they put Jerusalem as a special international zone between the two states and since then there are over 400 decisions taken by the United Nations recognising the specificity and peculiarity of the city of Jerusalem, that it can't be owned or monopolised by one party over/against the other two.

So, in all the decisions of the United Nations, Jerusalem is not recognised as the eternal capital of Israel. Jerusalem was divided between the Jordanian administration of the Palestinian land and the state of Israel for 19 years, from the year 1947 to the year 1967 when Israel military occupied Jerusalem together with the other occupied Palestinian Territories. They were unilaterally annexed so the inhabitants of Jerusalem did not invite Israel to unify the city. The word "unification" of Jerusalem is wrong. It was annexed unilaterally by the state of Israel and not a single country in the world, even the United States of America, recognised this annexation. For all Embassies of these countries are still in Tel Aviv, and the Embassy of Holland, the Netherlands, was in Jerusalem when the United Nations refused to recognise that Jerusalem is the capital of Israel alone. It was forced to move its Embassy from Jerusalem to Tel Aviv. This gave rise to the nervousness of evangelical Christians in Europe and the United States of America, and they themselves got together and established what is called the Christian Embassy in Jerusalem, as if the senate is somewhere outside Jerusalem and European Christians and American Christians are behaving as ambassadors of Christianity to Jerusalem. It turns out to be an Embassy which is there to support the state of Israel.

The history of Jerusalem, and I don't have the time to go through it, will show you the following facts. There was pagan rule of Jerusalem for 41% of the period, Hebraic rule, Jewish rule, only 13.4% Christian rule, and they were the crusaders who came by force as knights and priests to guard the holy places. To guard them from whom? They were not taken by either the Jews nor by the Muslims. They were still in the hands of Eastern Christendom, yet, Western Christianity came in two waves. One wave was military presence occupying the area during the crusades and ruled the country about 12% of its time. 32% of the country and Jerusalem were ruled by the Arabs of the Middle East.

If we look at the population of the world, we find a discrepancy of having Jerusalem owned only now by the Jews. They say it's an open city, yet it is open and closed at the same time. It is open for the friends of Israel, but it is closed for my own sisters and brothers who live in Ramallah, nine miles to the north of Jerusalem, and who could not come on Easter Sunday to celebrate Easter with their bishop. You have got to have a military permit to come to Church. This is why they claim that the city is open and they thank God it is open once and for all and united. 0.2% is the size of the population of world Jewry from the world family. 0.2% control Jerusalem. While we have 30% of the family of human beings are Christians and 30% or so Muslims, 60% of the population of the world has no right except at the courtesy or permission of the 0.2% who monopolise Jerusalem. So the situation is walking on a field of mines, unless Jerusalem regains its status and peace for all three children of Abraham, then you cannot hope for peace in the Middle East and peace in the world. It is very important for us Christians to remember that our roots are there and we cannot just give up for political reasons or circumstantial politics the place and sanctity of Jerusalem connected with us and our faith.

I want to read to you what the Orthodox Patriarch of Antioch, the late Elias (Arabah?), has said in a conference of total Muslim countries on Jerusalem, and then I am going to give you the position of the Vatican regarding Jerusalem, which they want to see as an international zone. The Patriarchate has at present only two explicities that state its Christian positions on Jerusalem. One is a mixture of biotitic and archaeological spirits that connects the Holy Land back to its Christian origins and attempts to justify the Zionist movement in crusading terms, turning the spiritual homecoming into a colonial venture. The other finds the hands of justice at work throughout Christian history and the presence of Jesus among the oppressed and the wretched of the earth. The Vatican, in a message from the Pope quoted by Father Mubarak from Paris, says, "is not Jerusalem the goal of this long journey on the path to liberty, liberty of humanity, in which we all are engaged together. Are we not, Muslims and Christians alike, dedicated to hope, determination and sacrifice. How can we forget Thee O Jerusalem when Thou art… humanities… to God and the symbol of the spiritual values that descended upon us from his whole inspiration. To ask the preservation of stones, even if they be sacred shrines, cannot be more important than the living presence of people, for the presence of God is where people live in constant devotion."

Such is our understanding of the Palestinian character of Jerusalem that, in his Good Friday message of 1974, Pope Paul VI called upon Catholics to tell their minds not to the Holy places, but tell us the Churches of the Holy Land which prevent the Holy places from becoming mere museums.

I can go on and on speaking about the importance and significance of Jerusalem and the Churches there for us, but I would like us, as an Anglican Communion, not to be silent while Jerusalem is being discussed in the international agenda of all three religions and all parts of the world.

Thank you to the Peace and Justice Network of our Communion which gave some special attention to Jerusalem in their last statement. A special mention has to be made of Jerusalem, the city equally sacred to Christians, Muslims and Jews. Any exclusive sovereign claim of the city has to be rejected. We cannot accept it or tolerate it. For justice to be made and peace to endure, Jerusalem should remain physically undivided but serve as two capitals for the two states, with East Jerusalem as the capital of Palestine. This is what the Anglican Peace and Justice Network have said in their statement.

Thanks also to the predecessor of Bishop Jim Ottley, Sir Paul Reeves. When he assumed the office of the Anglican Communion Observer to the UN, he collected all Anglican statements since ACC-7 to the Primates Meeting of 1993 in Cape Town, and there were 70 statements by the Anglican Communion, and various instruments of the Anglican Communion, speaking on the questions of justice, human rights, equality among the races, and against apartheid, including Jerusalem as a sacred city for all three faiths.

I want to tell you that for the first time in the history of Christian presence in Jerusalem, all the Churches without exception, from the successor of St. James, the brother of our Lord, who was the first Bishop of Jerusalem in the Orthodox community, to the Baptists and the Assemblies of God, we all join hands and hearts in prayer to issue the first Christian statement on the question of Jerusalem. We called the statement "The Sanctity of Jerusalem to Christians." It was published in the issue about the presence of the Episcopal Church in Jerusalem and the Middle East. It is republished in the West Asia Preparatory Meeting of the Bishops for Lambeth, and I plead with you that you read this statement and that perhaps the ACC and later the Primates in Jerusalem and Lambeth in 1998, would endorse the voice, the relevant indigenous voice of all the Patriarchs, Archbishops, Bishops and Moderators of the Christian Churches of Jerusalem and say, "Yes, there is a Christian voice." If we want to listen to the question of Jerusalem, we better listen to the relevant voice and the voice of the Christians who spoke about Jerusalem being important to all three religions and who tried to show the special stature of the city of Jerusalem. We as heads of Churches in Jerusalem did not advocate internationalising the city because we didn't know which nations were going to come to run it. We think that the inhabitants, Palestinians and Israelis together, could have special statutes for two capitals in one city and run the city as children of Abraham.

I want to end this brief presentation by saying that we all are conscious in the Middle East of our roots to Abraham and this might be the key for peace in the Middle East. The outgoing Minister of Religious Affairs in the State of Israel, Mr. Shimon Shitreet, a great lawyer and theologian at the same time, has started a movement which we all have joined: Muslims, Arab Muslims, Christian Arabs, and Israelis. He had the motto for the Ministry of Religious Affairs as, "Religion is the basis for peace," and before long his Prime Minister got shot at the hands of Mr. Amir, a member of the extreme Orthodox party in Israel. The hero of peace, Mr Rabin, became the victim of peace at the hands of those who want only to give exclusive answers to their own political theory and thinking and presence.

This evening I received a message from Jerusalem, and it's a terrible message. It has come through the *Jerusalem Post*, which is an Israeli paper. It seems that the option of war is going to be taking the lion's share rather than the option of peace in these last days in that region. So please, pray that the option of peace will win. Pray that Jerusalem will become a shared city at every level, not at special levels. The Palestinians are equally the children of God. They carry the same image and likeness of God like the Israelis. We don't want to show God as giving preferences. We don't want people to question the justice of God. I plead with you as a Communion to support the statement and position of your extended sisters and brothers, the Christians of Jerusalem who have now become vocal, very vocal about this issue.

Presentation by the Rt Revd Richard Harries on Human Sexuality

Thursday, 17 October 1996

There are, of course, a range of concerns under the general heading of 'Human Sexuality': the rejection by many of the traditional family unit, polygamy, pre-marital sex and so on. Homosexuality is only one amongst a range of issues. Furthermore, I recognise that in a number of Churches, for example, the Sudan, Rwanda, Melanesia and Brazil, it is simply not an issue, and indeed a number of Churches do not have a word for homosexuality in their language; the concept is unknown. By contrast, for Churches in the United States and Canada, this is the most persistent and deeply divisive issue facing their Provinces.

So, on behalf of such Churches, I ask for the understanding of others, as well as their insights. Also, although the issue of homosexuality is a pressing one for only a minority of Anglican Churches, it raises general questions of concern to all: for example, the relationship of Christian truth to the customs and way of life of the surrounding culture. This is a question whether the subject is polygamy or homosexuality. And the question of Anglican unity comes into focus again. Like the ordination of women, we could be faced in the future by one Province allowing what other Provinces fundamentally disagree with.

The 1988 Lambeth Conference recognised that there is much confusion on the subject of sexuality and unresolved issues within the Church. Further study was recommended. (Full text at end of paper.)

I want to begin by indicating briefly where some of the Churches in the Anglican Communion now are on this issue. Time forbids looking at other denominations or considering the whole history leading up to where Churches now are. I then want to deal more fully with different aspects of the issue under separate headings.

Church of the Province of Southern Africa

First, however, I will examine some of the other Churches, beginning with the Church of the Province of Southern Africa. The Theological Commission produced a report, *The Church and Human Sexuality,* which was presented to the Synod in September 1995. It was emphasised that this is a study document and the issue remains under consideration by the Church. The document examines the subject in an African context and discussed *Lobola,* customary union and polygamy as well as homosexuality. Although Archbishop Desmond Tutu in February of this year called for the ordination of practising homosexuals and referred to the issue as one of justice, that particular perspective is not reflected in the Theological Commission's document. The document comes to no conclusion but after indicating the disputed cause of the homosexual condition it urges the Church "to listen to the experiences of homosexuals," an experience which has been one of "almost overwhelming prejudice and hostility." It further suggests that the issue needs to be explored afresh in the light of new understandings of homosexuality on the one hand and the actual loving and caring practice of Jesus towards those whom the world has condemned (paragraph 7).

Episcopal Church in the United States of America

In the Episcopal Church in the United States, the subject has long been passionately debated. The latest contribution to the debate is a pastoral study document of the House of Bishops to the Church as a whole entitled *Continuing the Dialogue.* This was published in 1995 and its purpose is to prepare the Church for the next Convention in 1997. The document is a substantial one which recognises the deep division within the Church. The poet Rilke is quoted in the forward, to the effect that we must "learn to live the question, and perhaps one day we will live into the answer." But, guidelines are set out for living together as the issues are discussed, so that in answer to the question, "Where does the Episcopal Church stand?" Episcopalians can reply, "We stand together seeking God's guidance."

Church of England

In 1987, the Church of England had a contentious debate on the subject at its General Synod and since then the House of Bishops has tried to manage discussion on the issue. It produced *Issues in Human Sexuality,* which has on the whole been well received, though often misinterpreted. It argues that the divine intention in creation is for faithful, lifelong marriage and this is what the Church seeks to encourage. Sexually active gay and lesbian relationships cannot therefore be regarded as an equally valid option. However, there are of course gay and lesbian people in the majority of congregations. Some live celibate, chaste lives, others choose to share their life in a loving relationship with someone of the same sex. The conscience of such people is to be respected and their presence, and voice, in the Church affirmed. Clergy, whether heterosexual or homosexual have, like everyone else, a need for close and loving relationships, for intimacy. But they have a particular responsibility to witness to the Church's discipline which, whether people are homosexual or heterosexual, allows two ways of life, celibacy and marriage. I chair a small working party of bishops, set up by the House of Bishops, to continue to reflect on the issue, meet groups and individuals who have a point of view they wish to put across, and to encourage further debate.

Anglican Church of Canada

The House of Bishops of the Anglican Church of Canada produced a statement and guidelines in 1979, which were reaffirmed in 1991. However, more recently a major study programme, complete with study kit and video entitled "Hearing Diverse Voices, Seeking Common Ground" was produced. This was discussed by 170 Church groups in 1994, and the reports from these groups went to Synod in 1995. In England, bishops have also tried to encourage serious discussion at the parish level but they have not had the success of the Anglican Church of Canada. That Church is as divided as any other,but at their General Synod in June 1995, they affirmed "the presence and contributions of gay men and lesbians in the life of the Church and condemned bigotry, violence and hatred directed towards any due to their sexual orientation." And it encouraged continuing discussion and dialogue throughout the Church.

Anglican Church in Australia

I am not aware of any authoritive statement by the General Synod of the Anglican Church in Australia, but a recent article in *St. Mark's Review* traces the history of this question in two dioceses, Adelaide and Sydney, with their very different practical approaches to this subject. One conclusion in the report is:

> "In its official responses to homosexuality the Anglican Church in Australia has been more influenced by the cautious and ambivalent policy of the Church of England than by the more liberal position espoused by some sections of the Episcopal Church in the United States. Reports, resolutions and episcopal pronouncements have all been at the conservative end of the spectrum. On this issue no one can accuse the Australian Church of being 'trendy.'" ("The Limewashed Church.")

I wish now to discuss this issue under a number of different headings: the origin of the homosexual condition, organisations that claim to heal gay people, hermeneutics, the social context, tradition, reason, and the role of clergy.

The origin of the homosexual condition

From time to time claims are made that the gay gene has been identified. Equally often this has been disputed. The assumption behind those who look for and would welcome a genetic basis to homosexuality is that because it is thereby proved to be unchangeable, it would have to be fully accepted. But this conclusion does not necessarily follow. For example, when one claim to have identified the gay gene was publicised, the former Chief Rabbi of Great Britain, Lord Jacobovits said that if the techniques of genetic engineering continued to advance, the gay gene could be eliminated from the human gene pool. In fact, I suggest, that an underlying genetic factor, if there is one, is likely to be polygenic, due to a number of genes, rather than one.

Others look for a psychological causation. One of the most influential in Christian circles derives from the work of Dr. Elizabeth Moberley. She argues that people become homosexual or lesbian primarily because of a failure to make a close relationship with the parent of the same sex. She believes that this condition can be overcome by making a close, but non-erotic relationship, with someone of the same sex in therapy. This enables the person to move through a state of arrested development, to make mature relationships with people of the opposite sex. This psychological explanation has in its turn been rejected by members of the gay community. Recognising that many homosexuals, for example, do indeed have distant or bad relationships with their fathers and are close to their mothers, they suggest this is because a homosexual person is likely to have qualities of gentleness and sensitivity which are unacceptable in males in a macho society. It is the father, who, sensing these qualities in his son, distances himself from him, whilst the son draws closer to the mother, both by way of reaction and because she will exhibit more of these qualities.

It is clear, therefore, that the nature of the genetic causation of the condition is disputed, as is the psychological explanation and the relationship between the genetic and psychological factors. As Christians, I think our task is to strive for as much objectivity as possible in this area. It is clear that some people have a clear agenda, either to prove or disprove a genetic origin, or to prove or disprove a particular psychological explanation. We all have our biases and these should be recognised, but that said, scientific objectivity is that which we should be seeking. Another crucial point which comes out of this discussion is the simple fact that, for whatever reason, there are people of homosexual or lesbian orientation, who have not chosen to be that way and for whom the condition is in most instances irreversible. Through no choice or fault of their own, that's the way they are, that's the way they were made. They also are God's children.

The complication does not end there, however. Other people emphasise that the homosexual condition is not essentially anything, whether genetic or psychological, but is a social structure. This view derives in part from the well-known fact that there is not any one thing called homosexuality, there are homosexualities. In ancient Greece, for example, it was customary and accepted for an older male to have a close, erotic relationship with a younger male. This went in parallel with heterosexual marriage. Anthropologists and social scientists point to unusual customs in some tribes, which they label transgenerational homosexuality, involving initiation rites and transgenderal homosexuality, involving the exchange of male and female roles.

On this view then, sexual orientation is not anything fixed or final. It depends upon the culture in which we live, on how it is interpreted and expressed. Clearly there is an important truth here, one which is not inimical to a Christian perspective. For it means that our understanding of sexuality and its appropriate expression can be influenced, for good as well as ill, by the prevailing attitude of society. Nevertheless, at least some members of the gay community would resist the idea that a social explanation can account for everything. They would argue that there simply are people who are more attracted to people of their sex than to the opposite one. What forms society allows for this attraction and its expression may vary but the attraction is there from society to society, whether or not it is always linguistically recognised. The insights of those people from societies where there is no word for homosexuality would be particularly valuable at this point. Is there, despite this lack of linguistic recognition, the phenomenon of same sex erotic attraction?

Organizations that claim to 'heal' gay people

The question of causality leads naturally to the claim by some Christian organisations to be able to cure people's homosexuality or lesbianism. These organisations are particularly disliked by the gay community because they do not think of homosexuality as anything to be cured. They regard it as something to be accepted and celebrated as part of the rich variety of life. There have been demonstrations against some of these organisations. It is also true that there is some evidence of abuse in at least one and questions about the professional competence of the counselling given in some. But the heart of the dispute is the claim that homosexuality can be 'cured,' a claim which, of course, depends upon the assumption that the condition is primarily psychological rather than genetic.

My own view is that we should not reject these organisations out of hand because they often offer a first port of call to troubled evangelical homosexuals. In some evangelical circles where there is a very negative, hostile attitude towards homosexuality, young homosexuals sometimes find that these organisations are the first place where they can openly acknowledge and talk about their homosexuality in a context where they are loved and cherished. This is acknowledged even by thoughtful people who are opposed to their fundamental stance. But it is quite wrong, I believe, to suggest that every homosexual person, or even the majority of homosexual people, can be changed or cured. A better approach would be that of modern marriage guidance organisations. Their prime purpose is to help people face honestly where their marriage is at. Although, of course, they would like the couple to stick together, that is their underlying assumption. They may also have to help the couple face the fact that their relationship is destructive and they would be better apart. In a similar way ex-gay organisations might have to help people face the fact that they really are homosexual and are not likely to change.

There is also a fundamental contradiction at the heart of the philosophy of these organisations, one which is also present in other Christian groups. An attitude of love and cherishing is indeed shown but it goes along with a fundamental disapproval of homosexuality. So the young evangelical homosexual does indeed feel cared for but this care also conveys the message that his homosexual condition is unacceptable. His self-rejection, his self-hatred, are therefore subtly reinforced all the time. Of course we have to remember that a person's sexuality is fundamental to them, and it is therefore a rejection of their very being that is reinforced. If God's acceptance of us as we are is meant to convey an acceptance of ourselves as we are, does this not carry with it the implication that we should befriend our sexuality rather than reject it? There is, as I say, a fundamental contradiction here for Christians who wish to convey the love and acceptance of God whilst at the same time being hostile to homosexuality.

Hermeneutics

As Christians we seek to be guided by the Bible and this raises the whole question of hermeneutics, how the Bible is to be interpreted in our own context. It is easy enough to bring forward a number of texts from both the Old Testament and the New Testament which condemn sexual relations with the same sex. I am not going to discuss those texts again. They are clearly there. But is the activity which is condemned the same as that supported by committed Christian homosexuals today? Christian homosexuals argue for stable, faithful, permanent relationships. This is very far from the kind of casual and promiscuous same sex relationships which the Biblical writers might have had in mind. Furthermore, we now know that, whatever its origin, people do not simply choose to be homosexual. They find themselves that way. It is doubtful whether ancient writers thought of homosexuality in that way. It is more likely, though not certain, that they thought it was all a matter of choice. If it is all simply a matter of choice and we are free to choose one form of sexual expression rather than another, then moral approval or condemnation is possible. But if choice, at least as to the condition, does not enter into it, we have a very changed situation.

There are some Christian writers who argue that the Biblical writers knew quite well what they were doing. Homosexuality was widely accepted in the ancient world, particularly the Greco-Roman world, and the Biblical writers quite decisively rejected this in favour of God's purpose in creation of lifelong heterosexual unions for all people. Others would stress that our circumstances today really have changed, both in our understanding of the condition and the kind of homosexual relationships which we would regard as desirable, and they cannot therefore simply receive a blanket condemnation, whatever some texts might suggest. There are also other parts of the Bible which need to be brought into the picture, not least the attitude of Jesus himself to the marginalised, rejected people of his time. His approach would suggest a profound compassion to a group of people who have so often been victimised in history and who still today are subject to abuse and vilification. There are also other texts which bear on this issue, including, for example, the dispute in the early Christian community about different kinds of food, reflected in Romans, Chapter 14. The principal point which emerges there, is that on issues which divide us, we must respect one another's conscience and be sensitive in all our dealings with our fellow Christians. The implication of that for our own time is that heterosexual Christians and homosexual Christians should hold together in the Body of Christ, respecting one another's views and acknowledging our common loyalty to Christ, for the Bible is not interpreted in a timeless, trans-historical world. We are seeking to interpret and apply the Bible in our own times, just as those who wrote it, did so out of a particular social and political context.

The Context

The fundamental fact about our time, as far as this issue is concerned, is that the subject is discussed openly and many gay and lesbian people are willing to identify themselves as such. The Gay Pride Movement of the last two decades has resulted in a great many gay and lesbian people being entirely open about their sexuality and this is reflected in the way they and their concerns are talked about in the media. The Gay Pride Movement was further reinforced by the AIDS epidemic. Although AIDS considered world-wide is primarily a heterosexual disease, in the United States and Britain it has been associated with homosexuals. So people who are diagnosed as HIV positive have, as often as not, been therefore identified as gay or bi-sexual. Because of the changed situation, it has been argued that what was once the predominant attitude of society as a whole and is still the predominant attitude of the Church, namely public silence or disapproval of homosexuality, together with private tolerance, can no longer be maintained. The characteristic attitude in the United States, for example, amongst certain kinds of people, was a public reticence about the issue, whilst at the same time knowing and being entirely tolerant of particular homosexual people. This is certainly the stance of many Church people in the Anglican Communion. But can it hold for much longer? For people in the Churches are now willing to identify themselves as gay or lesbian in exactly the same way as people are in society as a whole. The public/private distinction may therefore become the same as it is for heterosexuals. If we know that a person is heterosexual in public, that leaves open the question about how they express their heterosexuality, whether they are chaste, promiscuous or engaged in a long-term relationship. Similarly, if we live in a society now where people are openly gay or lesbian, then the question of how they express their sexuality will belong to the private sphere.

So within the Church we could have more and more people who are content to declare themselves gay or lesbian, who are known and accepted as such, whose sexual relationships, if any, belong to the private sphere. This is the context of the society in which we live and could very well be the context of the Church in which we seek to interpret the Bible. This is a context in which gay and lesbian people will be allowed to speak for themselves, as Christian brothers and sisters. One of the main criticisms of a number of Church documents and Church statements, is that they treat homosexual people as 'them,' someone else as it were. The fact is that there are gay and lesbian people in almost every congregation in societies where the condition is recognised. More recent Church writings urge that the voices and the feelings of such people must be heard. Their stories must be told and listened to.

As I have listened to at least some of those stories, what I think moves me more than anything else is the pain of people growing up to discover that they are gay or lesbian in a culture that denigrates homosexuality. A heterosexual teenager can look forward to the time when they can have a true and lasting relationship of sexual love with someone of the opposite sex. Their first tentative relationships can move in that direction, have that goal in mind. But in our society at the moment there is no publicly acceptable and valid model for the teenager who finds themselves gay or lesbian. They have nothing to aim for which has public validation and approval. They grow up in a context where they have to hide their deepest feelings and develop strategies of discretion and secrecy in order to survive at all. Estimates of the percentage of people in society who are gay or lesbian very between 5% and 15%. Even if it is as low as 5%, there is a great deal of human pain around with which no Christian can be content.

Tradition

An Anglican approach to disputed questions involves the Bible, tradition and reason. Tradition is important to this subject, because tradition is being re-evaluated. Until comparatively recently it was assumed that the history of the Church was one of long, unremitting condemnation of homosexuality. The work of scholars suggests that this is not so. The name here is that of the late John Boswell, a Professor of History at Yale and a Christian. In an earlier book he argued that the revulsion against homosexuality as an especially perfidious sin really dates from the 14th century. Before that there was a much more relaxed attitude. His last book, *The Marriage of Likeness: Same-sex Unions in Pre-modern Europe,* as its title indicates, suggests that there was a ceremony for same-sex unions. Boswell has discovered and translated eight versions of this from before the 12th century and refers to the existence of other versions, in a variety of languages, right through to the 16th century.

It seems clear that some such ceremony did exist and that it has many parallels with a marriage service. The rubric at the beginning of the service for example, begins with the words:

> "The priest shall place the Holy Gospel on the Gospel stand and they that are to be joined together place their right hands on it, holding lighted candles in their left hands. Then shall the priest cense them and say the following…"

A key question is how certain words are translated. The service is called a prayer for or office of Adelphopoiesin. Literally this would be translated "Prayer for Making Brothers or Office for Making Brothers." Boswell translates it "Prayer for a Same Sex Union". My own reading of his book and the texts which he produces in full, is that this service was for a very special blessing of two people, but that it was above all a blessing of their union to the service of God and the assumption was that it should be non-erotic. Clearly, Boswell's work puts the tradition of the early and early

Medieval Church in a different perspective. We could also mention the passionate same-sex friendships which were part of that world, even when they were not associated with a particular service of blessing.

Another period which has been identified as formative is the end of the 17th century in Britain. Until that time male friendship could be celebrated as something natural and beautiful. There is evidence that men wrote love letters to other men. People argue that Shakespeare's *Sonnets* were primarily written to other men. By the end of the 17th century male friendship in this sense died and this coincides with the emergence of gay sub-cultures, as an inevitable reaction in a society which no longer overtly valued male friendship. Historical insights like this help us to get away from the idea of tradition as something which is fixed and unchanging, and it can lead us to question the assumptions and pre-suppositions of our own time.

Reason

Interpreting the Bible, in the context of our own time, in the light of tradition, involves the use of our reason. Reason has always been the third leg of the Anglican trilogy involving the Bible, tradition and reason. This reason has reflected not simply on what God has revealed through the Bible but on what he disclosed of himself in the created order. This gave rise to the whole tradition of natural law thinking, which has been very important for some forms of Anglican moral theology and remains so in my opinion. Reflection on nature leads to the conclusion that the divine purpose in creation is for lasting heterosexual relationships, with children as their natural outcome. It also suggests a male-female complementarity within the divine purpose. All that I believe remains true. We now know that there are a good number of people, certainly 5% of the population and perhaps 10%, whose sexual orientation is predominantly towards their own sex. Their human longing, their fulfilment, their very identity as human beings, is bound up with this orientation. It is not something which we can likely pass over. Part of the difficulty here is to find the appropriate language. Gay people strongly resist any implication that they are abnormal, or that their condition is a medical one which could be cured. The Roman Catholic Church and some Anglican Churches, whilst avoiding stigmatising particular individuals, will talk about a disordered condition, a disorder of nature. Again, the gay community resents this. They would like to see homosexuality as adding to the variety and richness of God's creation. So, for example, whereas most people have rather mousy brown hair, some people are red-heads. Red-heads are in a minority but their difference enhances humanity. Thoughtful members of the gay community argue that heterosexual relationships can still be regarded as primary, but this need not involve any kind of denigration of those who do not fall into that category. So, for example, in a family where two siblings are happily married but a third is homosexual or lesbian, if the gay person finds a partner with whom they want to share their life, this can be accepted as right for them, without in any way detracting from the primacy of the married relationships which the other two siblings enjoy. The upshot of this is that although reflection on creation can lead us to talk about the divine purpose in creation for the majority of human beings, there is a minority of people whom we have to take into account and about whom we have to talk in a sensitive and affirmative way. Finding the right language is not easy.

The role of the clergy

Then, finally, there is the role of the clergy.

In their report, the House of Bishops of the Church of England argued for the recognition of gay and lesbian people in Christian congregations. It said that their consciences should be respected and their voices heard. It also argued that clergy have a particular responsibility to witness to the tradition, and therefore the liberty which might be open to a lay person, is not open to them. The strength of this view is that it is where many Churches are today. Christians recognise that there are gay and lesbian people in their congregation, fellow believers, fellow members of the Body of Christ. No doubt many of these live celibate lives but some will probably choose to share their life with another person of the same sex. However, most Christians today do not feel comfortable with the idea of their parish priest sharing his or her life with someone of the same sex, certainly in the Vicarage. In a Church which is very strongly divided on this issue, where there is no consensus, the clergy have a particular responsibility to maintain the tradition until, under God, the Church as a whole comes to a different conclusion, if that indeed is what it does.

A contrary view however, is that the gay community desperately needs role models of faithful, stable, permanent, same-sex relationships, and clergy in such are an enormous support and help for those who would otherwise be swept up into a promiscuous gay lifestyle. Such clergy who are openly gay have an invaluable pastoral role in relation to the gay community. They are able to have this ministry because they are open about their sexuality, and they are sustained in it because they themselves are in a supportive and loving relationship.

These are, as I understand it, the main aspects of the issue as it confronts the Anglican Communion today. I recognise, as I said right at the beginning, that this is not an issue for the majority of our Churches. In others it is the most contentious and potentially divisive subject that now concerns us. Personally, I very much welcome this opportunity for a discussion from such a variety of cultural perspectives.

LAMBETH CONFERENCE 1988 RESOLUTION

SEXUAL ORIENTATION

153   Despite its basic assertions about marriage and family, there is much confusion in the area of the Church's doctrine and teaching about sexuality. *Transforming Families and Communities* witnesses to this on the basis of extensive Communion-wide consultations. Thus, on the vexed question of sexuality, it reports:

> The question of sexual orientation is a complex one which the Church is still grappling with many Provinces have traditionally maintained that homosexuality is a sin whilst others are responding differently to the issue. As sexuality is an aspect of life which goes to the very heart of human identity and society it is a pastorally sensitive issue which requires further study and reflection by Church leadership.

154   We recognise that this issue remains unresolved and we welcome the fact that study is continuing. We believe that the Church should therefore give active encouragement to biological, genetic and psychological research and consider these scientific studies as they contribute to our understanding of the subject in the light of Scripture.

155   Further study is also needed of the socio-cultural factors which contribute to the differing attitudes towards homosexuality, mentioned above, in the various Provinces of our Church. We continue to encourage dialogue with and pastoral concern for, persons of homosexual orientation within the Family of Christ. (Resolution 64).

Presentation by the
Rt Revd Dr Alexander Malik on Islam

Friday, 18 October 1996

I count it my rare privilege, pleasure and honour to have been asked to make a presentation on Islam before this august gathering. Looking at you as gathered from all over the Anglican World, I, at the same time, feel quite nervous and inadequate, particularly for two reasons:—

(a)   one that it is a difficult assignment to speak about a religion other than your own, and

(b)   secondly, that no specific topic or subject of Islam has been assigned to me. Just to be asked to make a presentation on Islam makes it very wide and general. However, I have divided my presentation into two parts:—

A. Islam in the present-day world
B. Christian response

A.   Islam in the present-day world

1.   The spread of Islam

When one looks at the world map, one cannot help but be impressed by the extent of spread of Islam all over the world. It originated in Saudi Arabia, but soon it spread to neighbouring countries and within a century it touched other continents like Europe, the Indo-Pakistan sub-continent and China. Right from its inception it kept its pace of expansion, influence and vitality. It had great empires like the Ummayids, the Ottoman and the Moghals. No one can deny its contribution in the fields of science, art, literature and architecture. Even in today's world its spread is most noticeable. Right from West Africa to the whole of North Africa and parts of Central and Eastern Africa, it has spread through the whole of the Middle East to South East Asia and parts of China. A number of newly independent states of the former Soviet Union like Uzbekistan, Turkmenistan, Azerbijan, Kazakstan are all Muslim. There are sizable contingents of Muslims in Europe, North America, South Africa and Australia. Black Muslims and immigrants from Islamic countries form a sizable group of Muslims in Western countries. According to one estimation there are about 1000 million Muslims all over the world and out of this, one-third live in Indo-Pak sub-continent countries like India, Pakistan and Bangladesh. In this way Islam is the second largest religion in the world both in numbers and in expansion.

2.   Islam as a political and economic force

After the Second World War, Islamic resurgence was most noticeable. A number of countries with a majority Muslim population got their independence both in Africa and Asia. Other Muslim countries like Iran, Iraq, Libya, Syria etc. have been very aggressive in their presentation of an Islamic standpoint in world politics and economics. The oil-rich countries are mostly Muslim and they use their petro-dollars for preaching and propagating Islam. Most of the mosques and Islamic centres built in Western countries are erected with petro-dollars. Recent Islamic fundamentalist uprisings in Iran, Afghanistan, Pakistan, Egypt, Nigeria, Sudan, Algeria etc. are most noticeable with a cry to enforce *Shariah* laws. Islam has made its impact on world politics and economics. Arabic has now become an international language. Special shops have been opened for *Halal* meat and special Islamic meals are provided on flights etc. All this is enough to show that Islam is a force to be reckoned with in today's world.

3.   Islam as a religious and spiritual force

Leaving aside the political and economic dimensions of Islam, even as a religious and spiritual force it ought to be studied and looked at carefully. Millions of people bowing before Allah at the time of annual pilgrimage depicts a moving scene, highlighting their commitment to the Islamic way of life. Not only at the time of pilgrimage but even in their daily lives their commitment to five times daily prayer, fasting during the month of *Ramadhan* and their effort to mould their lives according to the laws of Allah is remarkable. There are millions of people who quench their spiritual thirst by following the Islamic way of life and take Prophet Mohammed (Peace be unto Him) as their model of life. As such, Islam is both a religious and spiritual force and deserves our attention and study.

4.   Expression of Islam in the present-day world

In the present-day world, especially in the Western countries, Islam is usually associated with fundamentalism and terrorism. The happenings in the Islamic countries do not help remove this impression. As a matter of fact many Muslims do take pride in calling themselves "fundamentalists," as what they mean by this term is quite different from what it conveys to Western people. Moreover, the Islamic concept of *Jihad* (Holy War) further encourages them to kill and to get killed in the name of Allah and for the sake of Allah. The *Qur´an* says:

> "And fight in the way of Allah with those who fight with you ... and kill them wherever you find them and drive them out from whence they drove you out and persecution is severer than slaughter... and fight with them until there is no persecution and religion is only for Allah..." (Sura 2:190-193). "Fight those who believe not in Allah, nor in the latter day... until they pay the tax in acknowledgement of superiority and they are in a state of subjection" (Sura 9-29).

There are other verses as well which speak about *Jihad* (2:216-218; 4-89 and 91). All that is happening in Algeria, Afghanistan, Sudan, Egypt, and the Middle East is a logical corollary of *Jihad* enunciated in the Holy Qur´an as a duty for all Muslims. Therefore, what the Westerners call "terrorism" is perhaps a "religious duty" for Muslims.

In the present-day world, most of the Islamic countries are torn apart between the modern, open, liberal, democratic form of government and the "Islamic State" run on Islamic laws and principles on the pattern of the first four (Khulfa-e-Rashdin) Chaliphs of Islamic history. This cry is heard from West to East Africa, from North Africa to Afghanistan and even in smaller contingents of Muslims like Mindanao, an island of the Philippines. Even Turkey has in the recent elections given verdict in favour of the fundamentalists. Islam as such becomes an all encompassing philosophy of life including religious, social, economic and political. There is no division of state and religion, canon or civil law. It is proudly claimed that Islam is a perfect code of life and is a way of life which needs to be lived rather than discussed in a comfortable drawing room or taught in an academic institution. It was this compelling force which forced the Muslims of undivided India to demand a separate homeland for Muslims. This demand had its fruition in the creation of Pakistan in 1947. More recently, Mindanao got its autonomy from the Philippines on the same principle that the *Momins* (believers) cannot live with the *non-momins*. The same struggle is going on in Chechnya, a state of the former Soviet Union. It looks like the Russians will not be able to contain the armed *mujahideen* (people doing *Jihad*) and will soon bow her knees before the demand of the Chechnyians for a separate sovereign Chechnya.

There is a passionate struggle to enforce *Shariah* law in countries like Sudan, Egypt, Algeria, Afghanistan, Pakistan, Bangladesh and Indonesia, besides the others which already have _Shariah_ imposed like Saudi Arabia, Malaysia, Libya and some other Middle East Sheikdoms. Most of the present-day countries grant equal rights to their citizens irrespective of their creed, caste, colour or sex. But such an equality before law may not be available once the _Shariah_ is enforced.

Coupled with the desire to make Muslim countries Islamic States, another expression of Islam in the present-day world is the desire to convert the whole world to Islam. It is believed by the Muslims that Islam is the final and only true religion. Others like Judaism and Christianity, even though revealed through their respective prophets, i.e. Moses and Jesus, have been corrupted by the followers, with the result that only the _Qur'an_ and Islam have to be trusted and accepted. Pakistan is commonly called the "fort of Islam" against which no forces would be able to stand. There are a number of Islamic evangelistic associations engaged in the propagation of Islam commonly known as _Dawah_ both within and outside Pakistan. As state and religion are the same and Islam has been declared the state religion, it is incumbent on the state to make provisions for the spread of Islam. Islam is truly a "missionary" religion and the duty of evangelism is not only left to the individuals but the state is normally active and supportive of the Islamic evangelistic activities. Countries like Saudi Arabia, Libya, Malaysia, Pakistan and Indonesia are particularly active in this field.

In order to regain and re-capture the vision of the Islamic _Ummah_ (the whole community of faith), a number of Pan-Islamic movements are organised, i.e. The Organisation of Islamic Countries, The World Islamic Council, etc. There is a growing feeling that attack on one Islamic country is an attack on the whole Islamic _Ummah_. This trend is capturing the hearts and minds of many Muslims in spite of many differences among themselves. I personally will not be surprised that soon Islamic countries might create a United Nations of Islamic countries.

The most noticeable expression of Islam in the present-day world is the rejection of Western civilisation and culture. This rejection partly may be that the West is considered to be Christian and partly because of its modernist liberal and secular tendencies. On this, the educated Muslim is really torn. The West or the universal civilisation it leads, is emotionally rejected. It undermines, it threatens, but at the same time it is needed, for its machines, goods, medicines, war planes, the remittances from emigrants, the hospitals which might have a cure for calcium deficiency or the universities which will provide higher degrees. In this torn situation and failure to respond meaningfully to the modern world, Muslims commonly rely on Islamic fundamentalism. Therefore, slogans like _"Nizam-i-Mustapha"_ or "Enforcement of _Shariah_" or "Islamisation of Banking and Education" or "Enforcement of _Hadoods,_" etc are commonly heard and are used for popular election campaigns. Within this majority, there are some, though a small number, who feel that there could not be a truly "Islamic State" and one could not reverse the process of history. Such people are normally rejected by a taunt that they are corrupted by the liberal Western philosophies and are even termed *Kafirs* (non-believers). People freely use religion to legalise their doings. Any attempt to criticise Islam or Prophet Mohammed (Peace be upon Him) is not only discouraged but also prohibited. Violation of this law would land one in jail and later be hanged. Islam is being imposed from outside and with force of the legal system. Freedom of speech is guaranteed in the Constitution but not applicable to religion. Thus, disciplines like form criticism or the application of scientific methods of study are resisted and rejected. People normally fear making any attempt of modern interpretation of Islam or the *Qur'an* unless it suits the already accepted one. Therefore, Islam is in a state of flux, torn by a desire to have an ideal Islamic state over and against the modern state, between law and grace. The sum total of Islamisation is some Islamic countries so far have seen the introduction of certain Islamic laws and not so much of renewing of "inner persons," where all legal systems are conquered and triumphed over by an experience of "new birth."

B.   Christian response

Christians and their corporate body, i.e Church/Churches, are quite confused and puzzled as to how to respond to the growing challenge of Islam. Some even call it a "threat" to Christian Church and society. They become quite nervous when they see mosques and Islamic centres being built in great numbers in Western countries. According to *Radio's Voice of America's* survey, every alternate month a big Islamic centre or a mosque is being built in America. Westerners who are not used to this phenomena find it very difficult to accept the situation. Their worry is amplified when they hear Islamic organisations' involvement in terrorism, hijackings and bomb blasts, etc. The growing apathy of the Church further aggravates the situation. To them, it looks like Christianity is on the decline and Islam is on the rise. Faced with this situation, they develop quite an antagonistic attitude towards Islam and Islamic people. Thus their first response is usually negative towards Islam.

Not all the people subscribe to such a negative response. So they respond in a little more positive way, basing their rationale on the premise that all people have a right to subscribe to whatever faith or belief they want to. So they go out of the way to help, to be kind and considerate towards the people of Islam. This diaconal response to the challenge of Islam is advocated both in the Western Churches where Muslims are in a minority and in the Churches in Islamic countries where Christians are in a minority.

Like her Master and Lord, the Church has to engage herself in serving others: *"The Son of Man has come not to be served but to serve"* (Matt. 20.28). Service (diakonia) is a practical form of proclamation. Actions usually speak louder than words. Even in the life of Jesus, we see that practically every miracle of his aroused a response from his audience. The Church's different ministries of education, health care, adult literacy, emergency help, drug prevention, etc., are different forms of diakonia and are significant forms of mission. ACC-6, while discussing "Mission and Ministry," rightly says:

> "Just as Jesus was able to hold together proclamation and ser-
> vice, the Church must also hold the two together in the right
> balance. It is no longer necessary to put a wedge between evan-
> gelism and social responsibility and Christians should not be
> divided between those who see mission primarily as evangelism
> and those who identify mission with activities designed to
> relieve human suffering. Evangelism and social responsibility
> are partners. It is this vision of man as a social being as well as
> a psychosomatic being which obliges us to add a political
> dimension to our social concern (John Stott, *Christian Mission
> in the Modern World*, p.29). Jesus did not only heal the sick, He
> also challenged scribes and Pharisees on issues of Sabbath law
> and fasting (Matt. 2.23-28), dietary laws and divorce (Mark
> 10.2-12). The healing of a man who was sick for 38 years and
> his commanding him to break the Sabbath, was a challenge to
> the selfish structures of the society which put more emphasis
> on observing (unnecessary) Sabbath laws rather than seeing a
> man who had suffered for 38 years healed. We are therefore,
> called upon not only to do acts of mercy but to go to the root
> causes of human suffering and struggle for justice with hope of
> transforming the unjust structures which are by and large
> responsible for human suffering. Christ's followers are called,
> in one way or another, not to conform to the values of this
> world but to be a transformed and transforming people
> (Romans 12. 1-2; Eph. 5. 8-14)."

The third response is dialogue. Though dialogue is viewed by both the Christians and the Muslims with some apprehensions, e.g., His Excellency Sheik Zaki Yamani, the famed Saudi OPEC diplomat, in his foreword to Professor Montgomery Watt's *"Islam and Christianity Today—A Contribution to Dialogue,"* extols his approach, his attitude in challenging Christians and Muslims for a dialogue, and his "tireless persistence" which has "enhanced the chances of its ultimate success." But he bluntly warned:

"In the great debate between Christians and Muslims however, there are areas of fundamental principles where no amount of logical discourse can bring the two sides nearer to each other and therefore the existence of an impasse must be recognised. Issues like the Trinity, Divinity of Christ and the Crucifixion so central to Christian beliefs, have no place in the Islamic faith, having been categorically refuted by the *Qur'an,* on the authenticity of which there is no discord among Muslims. The discussion in this book of the Crucifixion and the "Salvation" it represents therefore will not be very convincing to the Muslim scholar and the attempt to find real parallels to it in Islam will have dubious prospects of success (Watt 1982 p. 9)"

In an ecumenical context, inter-religious dialogue is one of the significant ways to engaging in mission. As the Church's mission is basically addressed to those who do not know Christ and his Gospel and how God in Christ calls all peoples to himself, inter-religious dialogue becomes a means to proclaim and present Christ. In the light of the economy of salvation, the Church sees no conflict between proclaiming Christ and engaging in inter-religious dialogue. Pope John Paul II, in his *Encyclical Letter,* says that dialogue should not in any way detract from the fact, "that salvation comes from Christ and that dialogue does not dispense with evangelisation." He goes on further to say:

"Although the Church gladly acknowledges whatever is true and holy in the religious traditions of Buddhism, Hinduism and Islam as a reflection of that truth which enlightens all men, this does not lessen her duty and resolve to proclaim without fail, Jesus Christ who is the Way, the Truth and the Life. The fact that the followers of other religions can receive God's grace and be saved by Christ apart from the ordinary means which he has established does not thereby cancel the call to faith and baptism which God wills for all people."

In the same Encyclical Letter he writes

"Dialogue should be conducted and implemented with the conviction that the Church is the ordinary means of salvation and that She alone possesses the fullness of the means of salvation... Through dialogue, the Church seeks to uncover the "Seeds of the Word" a ray of that truth which enlightens all men"; these are found in individuals and in religious traditions of mankind. Dialogue is based on hope and love and will bear fruit in the Spirit. Other religions constitute a positive challenge for the Church; they stimulate Her both to discover and acknowledge the signs of God's presence and of the working

of the Spirit, as well as to examine more deeply Her own identity and to hear witness to the fullness of Relevation which She
has received for the good of all. This gives rise to the Spirit
which must enliven dialogue in the context of mission. Those
engaged in this dialogue must be consistent with their own
religious traditions and convictions and be open to understand those of the other party without pretence or close-mind-
edness, but with truth, humility and frankness, knowing that
dialogue can enrich each side. There must be no abandon-
ment of principles nor false irenicism but instead a witness
given and received for mutual advancement on the road to
religious inquiry and experience and at the same time for the
elimination of prejudice, intolerance and misunderstandings.
Dialogue leads to inner purification with docility to the Holy
Spirit, will be spiritually fruitful... dialogue can assume many
forms and expressions from exchanges between experts in religious traditions or official representatives of those traditions to
co-operation for integral development and the safeguarding of
religious values; and from a sharing of their respective spiritual experiences to the so-called "dialogue of life," through
which believers of different religions bear witness before each
other in daily life to their own human and spiritual values and
help each other to live according to those values in order to
build a more just and fraternal society" *(L'Osservatore Romano,
N. 4 28 January 1991. p.13).*

In the present day multi-religious, multi-lingual, multi-racial, multi-cultural
situation prevalent in most of the advanced countries, there could be no
fixed or stereotyped Christian response to the challenge of Islam. There
would be many and varied responses depending on the situation. The
main point in this response is that it has to be open, liberal and flexible.
This openness and flexibility does not mean that we should accept the
ideology of Islam without its critical evaluation (1-John 4:1) or reject it
without reason or compromise with it at the expense of Christian principles and "kingdom values." The presence of other religions or ideologies
should not deter us from sharing our religion or faith with others, but it
needs to be done with love and humility on the pattern of our Lord and
Saviour Jesus Christ.

THE REPORTS

Every group, every organisation, every entity like the Anglican Consultative Council must discuss and hear from the staff and various leaders as to the status of on-going programmes of the Church and its work. Indeed, Panama 1996 was no exception with thorough, sometimes amusing, and definitely informative presentations being made by various staff members. Of particular significance was the move forward on the organisation and care for the Networks of the Anglican Communion.

Address by the Most Revd Robin Eames on The Virginia Report

Monday, 14 October 1996

The report of the Inter-Anglican Theological and Doctrinal Commission

At the outset it is important to understand two points: (1) how this report came into being and (2) what ACC-10 is asked to do about it.

1.   How the report came into being

In the introduction on pages 4-5, there is a summary of several develop-ments which illustrate something important about our understanding of Anglicanism—we are in a process of continually refining our ideas, con-stantly reacting to developments in the Communion and the world, and continually learning how the perceptions of such a wide cultural, eco-nomic, political and religious family help us to face up to what it means to be a Communion. The truth is that what is contained in this *Virginia Report* is a further step along that road of self-discovery in faith. It seeks to take from all the Commissions and Reports mentioned in the Introduction and to move our thinking forward. In that process we have tried to dis-cover more about what it means to be an Anglican, and how we perceive the machinery, the 'instruments of unity,' should inter-relate. We are say-ing to the Lambeth Conference—this is where we believe we have come from—and these are some of the ways in which we think we can move for-ward. We start from a theological basis and move to practicalities. We have tried to root our suggestions in what is our view of God's revelation to the Anglican tradition.

2.   Considerations to be addressed by ACC-10

The Commission suggests there are three considerations which should be addressed by ACC-10:

   i)   Reflect on the concept of *Koinonia* and how ACC-10 sees that concept impacting the *Virginia Report.*

   ii)   Note and reflect on the principles set out in Chapter 5 (p35-40). Chapter 5 is in a sense the water-shed of our report. Before Chapter 5 we try to relate our theological reflections to the structures of Anglicanism as they have developed. Chapter 5 outlines the purpose and principles for developing our structures. Chapter 6 "bites the bullets" and suggests what ought to be the consequences of what has gone before.

iii)   So Chapter 6 will probably command most of our attention. ACC-10 is a fact and an important part of the route to the Lambeth Conference 1998. The *Virginia Report* is geared for Lambeth. What the Commission seeks are the comments of ACC at this stage before we complete our final draft for the Lambeth Conference. We do not anticipate widescale re-drafting, but I assure ACC that any comments made here will be taken on board as we prepare for Lambeth.

Before turning to the contents, let me pay a warm tribute to the Virginia Theological Seminary where we have conducted most of our work. But for the generosity of Virginia Diocese and the Seminary in Alexandria, I doubt if we could have achieved as much as we hope we have. They have together met a vast amount of our costs and I think ACC-10 needs to realise why we have designated our work as the *"Virginia Report."*

So much for the background and the task before us today. Let me now try to take a bird's eye view of the *Virginia Report*.

The Lambeth Conference of 1988, in Resolution 18, resolved that there should be further exploration of the meaning of communion, with particular reference to the doctrine of the Trinity, the unity and order of the Church and the unity and community of humanity. We have responded to that call in several ways: through the Archbishop of Canterbury's Commission on Communion and Women in the Episcopate, through the Consultation which produced *Belonging Together*—now the *Virginia Report* takes us a step further.

The *Virginia Report* centres its theological reflection on the understanding of Trinitarian faith. It suggests that the unity of the Anglican Communion stems from the unity given by the triune God: the same God whose inner personal and relational nature is itself Communion. We are called to incarnate communion in visible form by the mystery of God's life. We claim that that is the reason why the Church is called upon to review and reform its structures, those structures which link its various limbs together and provide the bones of unity—but we suggest we need to review them so that they nurture and enable the life of communion in God and serve God's mission in the world. The mission of Christ and the Church is celebrated and proclaimed in our liturgy, which shapes the Trinitarian faith of the people of God and empowers them for a life of ministry and mission. In particular we think of holy Baptism and holy Eucharist. Yet the one ministry of the Church, the Body of Christ, we argue, must find its motivation, its credibility and its integrity in the one ministry of the Lord of the Church. Without that certainty we believe the difference and variety among Christian ministries would soon become incoherent. God invites his people to accept and, more important, to enjoy diversity. As Anglicans we accept the concept of unity in diversity. It lies at the centre of the *raison d'être* of Anglicanism. The *Virginia Report* attempts to relate our understanding of that principle in the light of theological and practical experience to the 'instruments of unity.'

Interdependence is the final piece of the jig-saw. Those pillars of unity are themselves the consequence as well as the justification for interdependence.

By tradition the 'instruments of unity' are the Archbishop of Canterbury, the Lambeth Conference, the meeting of Primates and the Anglican Consultative Council. In Chapter 3 we try to analyse the Anglican principles of scripture, tradition and reason, but again we emphasise the relationship of theory to practice. What has our tradition to say about the way these instruments have developed? That discussion comes together in Chapter 4 as we recognise the levels of communion and analyse subsidiarity and interdependence. It is here that some of the real tensions of living together with difference comes to the surface. We quote in particular the issues surrounding the ordination of women to the priesthood question. Here we have to recognise how binding decisions can only be made at the level of a Province or in some cases at the level of a diocese. How do we discover the mind of Anglicanism? How do we protect and enhance international consultation? It is from the junction of such questions with our theological reflections that the concept of reception becomes prominent. Behind all we say is another attempt to respond to the proverbial question "What is an Anglican?"

In each part of this more detailed study of the 'instruments of unity,' we have posed certain questions. Those questions seem to us to arise from our theological analysis—they arise from the on-going search of Anglicanism for a clearer picture of itself and of its mission to the world—they arise above all else as the Anglican Communion seeks ways to respond to the prompting of God. We believe that theology is not just a source of re-assurance and comfort and justification. We believe theology compels us to ask questions so that we can see more clearly the way ahead. We believe these are highly significant issues and they are issues to which answers must be found—but answers which in themselves will be incomplete. I believe this report comes before the Church at a most exciting time—a time of possibility. I hope and pray that you in the ACC-10 will help us to answer these questions. The Commission would welcome the reflection of ACC-10 on the questions, as we seek to prepare our final wording for the Lambeth Conference.

Mission and Evangelism Report 1: MISSIO Report by the Revd Canon Roger Chung Po Chuen

The mandate to MISSIO

The Mission Commission of the Anglican Communion, MISSIO, was set up by the Joint Meeting of the ACC and Primates (Resolution 43, p164, ACC-9 Report) in Capetown, January 1993, with the following responsibilities in mind:

1.   To provide a forum for Provinces in which the mission of the Church can be reviewed in this decade (e.g., justice, peace and the integrity of creation, interfaith and other concerns).

2.   To encourage new mission structures to emerge in the Communion.

3.   To develop a partnership of Churches and their agencies acting together to exchange and share God-given resources for the benefit of the whole.

4.   To maintain an overview of the Partners in Mission process within the Anglican Communion.

5.   To develop the Decade of Evangelism e.g., the meaning and development of evangelism in different cultures.

6.   To develop the database for mission begun by Mission Agencies Working Group, MAWG, with a view to its usefulness for the whole Communion.

7.   To follow up the Anglican Encounter in the South Conference. (See Page 34, section 1: A-D of the *Mission Issues Strategy and Advisory Group II, MISAG II Report.*)

8.   To follow up the Movement for Mission Conference.

9.   To report to the ACC and receive relevant items responsibility from the ACC.

10.   To provide encouragement, input and support for the Director for Mission and Evangelism of the ACC.

Also in this first Report is a brief account of some of MISSIO's other discussions, its work in progress, and possible future work. It ends with four resolutions arising out of issues discussed at our meeting in Ely, England, in January 1996.

We praise God for the many signs in our Communion that we are moving into 'mission mode.' And we pray that the work of MISSIO, even in these earlier stages, will help Anglicans world-wide to *"sing to the Lord a new song!"*

Full details about the mission and strategy of MISSIO are contained in the MISAG II Report, *Towards Dynamic Mission* (London, ACC, 1992, pp 40-51).

Sing a New Song: A first report from Missio

Two of the responsibilities given to MISSIO have received particular attention since the inauguration of the Commission and therefore comprise two important components of this our first report, *Sing a New Song: A Vision of Transformation and Celebration.*

A: G-Code Conference: Mid-point Review of the Decade of Evangelism

The first of these is MISSIO's task to develop the Decade of Evangelism. The Decade has been a remarkable feature of Anglican life since 1991, capturing the imagination of member Churches in a way that few other initiatives have done. ACC-9 asked for a mid-term review of the Decade (Resolution 44 [d]).

Under the dynamic leadership and vision of Canon Dr Cyril Okorocha, ACC's Director for Mission and Evangelism, MISSIO oversaw the holding of a significant gathering Global Conference on Dynamic Evangelism Beyond the Year 2000 (G-CODE 2000) at Kanuga, North Carolina in September 1995 for that purpose. It was probably the most representative meeting of Anglican lay people, clergy and bishops since the 1963 Anglican Congress in Toronto, and it was widely acclaimed to have been wonderfully successful. The conference was self-funding (i.e. outside of the Inter-Anglican Budget) and ended up with a generous surplus which the Planning Group committed to follow-up and distribution of the Conference Report.

We commend the comprehensive report of the Decade of Evangelism Midpoint Review *The Cutting Edge of Mission* for study and application. (See also the separate brief report on G-CODE Mission and Evangelism II.)

B: Theological reflection

The other main item in *Sing a New Song* is MISSIO's first response to its mandate "to explore ways of developing theological perspectives for mission and evangelism for the Communion" (ACC-9, Resolution 43[b]).

MISSIO has been aware, of course, of the theological diversity found around the Communion, and therefore within its own membership. While we have been greatly enriched by that, we have come to believe that the Communion needs to move beyond the mere acceptance of diversity, towards a more creative engagement with it which can be a unifying factor amidst plurality.

The section of theological reflection in *Sing a New Song* is MISSIO's initial contribution to such creative engagement. We commend it to the Communion for the greater enrichment of our common commitment to the *Missio Dei.*

With the foregoing in mind, we offer to the Communion, as we launch into the 21st century, the following vision for transformation and celebratio, a vision of a Church in mission mode.

a.   A Transforming Church

God is moving in history right now. The breaking down of walls, the ending of divisions, the dawning of peace, provide humanity with possibilities for new life, new freedom, and the mutual enrichment that can result from a creative celebration of our diversity. Such moments are fragile, as the continuing litany of conflicts around the world bears all too ready testimony.

If the Church is to be a sign of God's presence and activity among the nations, *"the kingdom come on earth as it is in heaven,"* then She must give increasing attention to the task of mission, which has at its heart the recognition that the earth is the Lord's, and that it is about the transformation of the life, not only of individuals, but also of society, nations and the created order (cf John 10:10).

Such transformation does not come without cost. For many within the Communion, following the example of Jesus has meant laying down life, marginalization, racial discrimination, deprivation of property and other forms of persecution. God's love for the world, revealed in the self giving, sacrificial death of Christ, continues to be enacted today, and for the sake of the world we are invited to walk the way of the Christ of the Cross. The Scriptures provide us with abundant evidence that God's purpose is the redemption of the world through our Lord Jesus Christ. Scripture, therefore, challenges us to live and work so that the just and gentle reign of God shall be the common experience of all humanity. To fulfil her mission in the 21st century, the Church must change under the Holy Spirit's power so as to become:

i.   A Church rooted in community

The Church we long to see is, therefore, a network of worshipping communities, both great and small, which are:
- rooted in context by way of being relevant;
- living out the vocation of God to live in love (John 15:33-35);
- seeking the welfare of all God's people irrespective of racial or cultural differences;
- living in the spirit of Jubilee (Leviticus 25, Luke 4:18-19), in forgiveness and generosity.

We look for episcopal and diocesan structures that will be:
- servant in nature;
- focused on local communities of faith;
- broad in vision
- facilitate a worldwide Communion where every member is given a full sense of belonging.

ii.   A Church of Jubilee

Jesus came not only to announce *"good news to the poor, liberty to the captives, freedom for the oppressed, sight to the blind,"* but *"to proclaim a year of favour from the Lord"* (Luke 4:18-19, NJB; cf Isaiah 61:2). We long for a Church that will live in the spirit of Jubilee—the *"now"* of *"the acceptable year of the Lord."* We long for a Church which brings healing to a wounded humanity, a Church which speaks, acts for and is in solidarity with the vulnerable. We look to the bishops at Lambeth 1998 to act cooperatively and ecumenically in promoting a year of Jubilee in the year 2000:

- for the remission of debt to the poorest nations;
- for freeing of all prisoners of conscience;

- for the return of lands to those made landless;
- for restraining the greed and oppression of the World Bank, the IMF and other multinationals.

iii.   Committed to the *Missio Dei*

Furthermore, we suggest that the Churches of the Communion be strongly encouraged to tithe their income for mission, as a witness to the importance of sharing resources for the sake of the Kingdom of God. Evidence from history shows that the power for mission is more than economic power yet our giving can be a measure of our commitment to God's mission.

iv.   A revitalised Church living in the simplicity of God's love

Our prayer and vision is for a revitalised Church which, in witness and communion, is a true sign of God's Kingdom in context:

- celebrating God's faithfulness;
- rooted in biblical faith;
- dynamic in mission and evangelism;
- creative and joyful in worship;
- caring in fellowship;
- generous in giving for mission;
- committed to social transformation through transformed people.

b.   The way to the future

We call upon the ACC and the Lambeth Conference to help us move from where we are now towards the vision that God is giving us. We are grateful for all the signs of hope throughout the Communion of a Church ready to *Sing a New Song*. We celebrate God's faithfulness in our story up to now, rejoice in the present and anticipate the future in hope. In the light of our history and present experience, we suggest the following line of action as we look to the future

i.   Evangelism: beyond stereotypes

The Kanuga mid-term review of the Decade of Evangelism (September 1995) showed that Anglicans around the world are gaining confidence in sharing their faith in Jesus Christ with others. We should like to encourage this trend. We should also stop to ask what the Spirit is saying to the Churches through the current vitality and growth of the Two-Thirds World Church. We urge the Communion to move beyond the stereotypes and crippling dichotomies between 'evangelism' and 'social action' into holistic evangelism. We urge a recovery of the Biblical and historic centrality to the life of the Church by making known the good news of God's Kingdom revealed in Jesus through all we are, all we do, and all we say. Evangelism beyond stereotypes is holistic.

ii.   Mission: beyond the boundaries

The goal of all mission is to glorify God. We urge a more open but firmly Christ-centred recognition, and celebration of the diversity of Anglican mission theologies which underlie the Five Marks recommended by ACC-8 (*Mission in a Broken World* p101).

iii.   Theological education: beyond distinctions

The Church 'in mission mode' (Lambeth 1988 Resolution 43) is one in which everyone is called to be a disciple and a witness, as the community of the baptised is mobilised for worship, ministry and mission. We urge a thorough-going re-assessment of the curricula of our seminaries and other training institutions (including extension, in-service and continuing education), so as to make mission the basis and goal of ministerial and theological formation.

iv.   Spirituality: beyond expectations

If there has been one clear lesson to learn from the stories of Churches in mission, it is the centrality of prayer to mission. Time and again, the unexpected has happened as a result of the local Church's commitment to prayer, often with fasting. The reality of spiritual conflict challenges the rationalism of much of our Communion; but it should come as no surprise to us (cf Eph 6:10-13). So we urge a new willingness to wrestle in prayer for a fresh encounter with God's love, forgiveness, justice and holiness in personal and communal life. We also seek a rediscovery of Christian spirituality, in which the whole being of each disciple and of every faith community is open and available to God for continuous renewal and revitalisation for redemptive service in the world.

v.   Church: beyond uniformity

Are our inherited modes of being the Church locally and nationally becoming obstacles and irrelevant? We urge a willingness to allow new structures to emerge, and a commitment to develop new networks so that in all our diversity we can still hold together in serving God's mission as a Communion.

vi.   Episkope: beyond hierarchy

We endorse without reserve the comments and recommendations of MISAG II about episcopacy (*Towards Dynamic Mission* [1992], pp29-30), and encourage our bishops to review their ministries in the light of that document. We wish only to add that leadership by example is vital to the bishop's role in mission, and that the pattern of bishop-in-synod is an important and distinctive feature of Anglicanism. (We have written a letter of encouragement on this subject to our bishops worldwide which is being circulated with the G-CODE 2000 Report: *The Cutting Edge of Mission.*)

vii.   Bible: beyond ideologies

The growing Churches of the Two-Thirds World remind us that there is an exciting rediscovery of the Scriptures, as the wellspring of our worship, witness and action. It is a fresh reading of the Bible, in which the ideological baggage of past interpretations is put aside, that allows the whole people of God to relate the whole Word of God to the context in which they live. We urge, in particular, the development and use of small community resources for encountering the Bible, so allowing the Word of God to shape the emerging Church. In the words of one of the leaders of the Two-Thirds World Church at the Decade Review Conference: "We have no high Theology, we simply follow the Bible." Such hermeneutic naivety may sound revolting to the Western mind; but what could the Spirit be saying to the Churches through those among whom there is apparent power and phenomenal growth at the moment.

viii.   Ecumenism: beyond division

We rejoice at so much of what has emerged in the first years of the Decade of Evangelism. We urge that mission initiatives in each diocese and parish be seen as local experiments in unity, and that moves to bring Christians together be seen as local adventures in mission; and furthermore that we should explore ways of making mission the basis and goal of our ecumenical initiatives.

ix.   Other faiths: beyond suspicion

Many people with no previous Christian commitment are coming to Christ through the witness of Anglican people and communities around the world. This is a cause for rejoicing. But we are also aware that in some contexts, Christians feel threatened by people of other faiths—often with very good reason. We look for a willingness to find a common ground for dialogue and peaceful co-existence with people of other faiths.

c.   Conclusion: Beyond the Decade

As we conclude this reflection, a question comes to mind: is God calling the Communion to new life in the power of Christ's resurrection? But resurrection is necessarily presaged by death. Death to cherished traditions, death to ingrained prejudices; but it is also death to stale and outmoded self esteem and therefore a call to a new and revitalised life in service and hope.

So we have a vision of a transformed Church. This vision takes us beyond Lambeth 1998, beyond the Decade of Evangelism, and even beyond the proposed Anglican Congress in the year 2001. It is our hope that the Communion will sing a new song through a transformed life, a life in the spirit of jubilee, rooted in Biblical faith and lived in the simplicity of God's love. In that hope we commend these reflections to the Communion for implementation and for continued support and prayers for MISSIO as it seeks to fulfil its mandate.

C: Structures for Mission

Mission structures in the Anglican Communion are in a state of change and development. In some places, much of the work previously done by established synodical agencies is being decentralised as local expression of the Church seek more active participation in the shaping and carrying out of mission. Indigenous mission movements are emerging and growing in the global 'South.' In the report of the recent Anglican Encounter in the South and in the preparatory materials for the next Encounter in 1997, firm convictions are expressed about the nature of mission that opens the possibility of new and exciting ways of participation in the *missio dei*. The call is for a 'grass roots Church' which is unequivocally committed to mission.

New Reality in World Mission

A fresh focus before us is the emergence of a new reality in world mission which challenges our previous concepts of partnership. The mission field today is no longer unidirectional with one region as a sending base and the other as a receiving base. What we see rather is a web of movements around the globe: 'from everywhere to everywhere.' How should we as a Communion respond to this new reality? MISSIO hopes to develop some guidelines for this changed reality. To help it do this, MISSIO invites synodical mission agencies, voluntary societies and interested groups and individuals from around the Communion to submit concrete suggestions toMISSIO, Anglican Communion Office, Partnership House, 157 Waterloo Road, London SE1 8UT, England.

D.   Emerging frontiers for mission

MISSIO has begun to examine and explore a number of important challenges to existing patterns of Anglican mission, including urbanisation, world poverty, the AIDS pandemic, refugees, and so on.

A continuing concern is that of self-reliance and leadership development. MISSIO is exploring the adequacy of the traditional 'three-selfs' formula of Henry Venn and Rufus Anderson in the light of at least two things: on-going dependency between Two-Thirds World and First World, and (more positively) the nature of our Communion as a *koinonia* engaged in mission 'from everywhere to everywhere' and continuous recognition and exchange of resources this calls for.

The issue of 'unreached peoples' is another MISSIO concern. But how do we define 'unreached peoples'? Would that include the unreached in our modern mega cities, and neo pagan societies? And what about the super rich who are prisoners of their own wealth and haunted by an inner spiritual poverty?

The need for a spirituality of mission is also on MISSIO's agenda. The question of 'spiritual conflict/warfare,' in particular, is one MISSIO plans to address. Reports and papers on this subject, from those with first hand experience in this field, are requested and should be sent to MISSIO at the ACC Office.

E.   Work in progress

Among the issues on our agenda are the following:

- The Anglican Encounter in the South scheduled for February 10-15 in West Malaysia; its significance for Lambeth 1998 and leadership development in the South;
- Revamping the MAWG Database with the assistance of Church House Statistics Department;
- Setting up an electronic 'mission convene' for more effective coordination of and information on mission personnel and resource movements;
- Updating and strengthening the Companion Diocese Links as a vital aspect of the PIM process;
- Continuing to service the PIM process;
- Continuing reflection on mission as the basis for ministerial, theological and spiritual formation;
- Exploring ways of following up the findings of the Decade Mid-point Review Conference;
- Reflection on the place of prayer, spirituality and spiritual warfare in mission;
- Exploring ways of revitalizing the Communion's Development network;
- Reflection on practical and missiological questions in relation to human well-being, social and economic justice and mission;
- Care of the environment as an aspect of mission and its practical implications;
- Reaching the 'unreached peoples' and how this relates to available resources; Relating self-reliance to the call to interdependence and mutuality;
- Understanding the new paradigm shift in mission and how this relates to established western agencies and the new mission initiatives from the South.

In preparation for the next meeting MISSIO has assigned various tasks to its members individually and in small groups, based on these issues.

F.   Future work

MISSIO plans to meet in Brazil, in September 1997, in preparation for Lambeth 1998. MISSIO's final meeting is scheduled for 1999 in Israel/Palestine to reflect on mission so far and to set concrete goals for the next millennium. Apart from relationships with other religions and the thrust of expansionist Islam, one major missiological issue that emerged from the G-CODE Report is the whole question of 'The Gospel and Apologetics.' MISSIO is challenged to reflect on this. The 1999 meeting will also reflect on the agenda of the proposed Anglican Congress of 2001.

G. Resolutions

In the light of our findings so far we appeal to the ACC to give careful consideration to the following resolutions:

1. Decade of Evangelism

This meeting of MISSIO, giving thanks to God for the success of the Mid-point Review of the Decade of Evangelism (G-CODE 2000), held in Kanuga in September 1995, asks the ACC:

a) to receive the report on that Review, *The Cutting Edge of Mission;*

b) to circulate that decade report throughout the Communion, in translation where necessary; and

c) to look for ways to take forward the 10 'Emerging Issues and Future Directions' which were identified as priorities for the Communion as a result of the Decade Review as outlined in the G-CODE Report to ACC-10 and in *Sing a New Song.*

2. Proposed Anglican Congress

Welcoming Resolution 1 of the Joint Standing Committee of ACC and Primates (March 1995) to hold an Anglican Congress, possibly in the year 2001, MISSIO:

a) re-affirms Resolution 44 of ACC-9 on the Decade of Evangelism, and in particular section (g) which called for a "significant Communion-wide celebration of the renewal of our commitment to mission and evangelism;"

b) notes that an earlier proposal to hold a 'Movement for Mission' gathering (possibly in 1999) as a response to ACC-9's call, has been superseded by the gathering envisioned for 2001;

c)   urges that the "celebration of the renewal of our commitment to mission and evangelism" be integral to the proposed 'congress,' and that the gathering be seen as promoting the hopes of Lambeth 1988 (Resolution 44) for the Communion to become more of a "movement for mission," "going beyond care and nurture, to proclamation and service;" and

d)   requests that some members of MISSIO, as the Communion's Commission on mission and evangelism, be appointed to the planning group for the proposed 'congress' from the earliest stages.

3.   **Jubilee 2000**

In view of the Biblical pattern of the jubilee, *"the year of the Lord's favour"* (cf Luke 4:18-19) which expected the remission of debts and restoration of the land to the dispossessed every 50 years, MISSIO urges the Anglican Communion and its member Churches to promote the spirit of the jubilee for the year 2000, by:

a)   co-operating with other Churches, agencies and governments in support of international movements for the remission of Two-Thirds World debt by the year 2000; and

b)   seeking, under the leadership of their bishops, concrete actions in the local Church and in their local context that reflect the spirit of forgiveness and reconciliation implicit in the Biblical jubilee motif.

4.   **Giving for Mission**

We challenge the Churches of the Communion to move beyond maintenance thinking by giving mission the top priority place it deserves in their budgets.

The Revd Canon Dr Cyril C Okorocha
Director for Mission & Evangelism

The Revd Roger Chung Po Chuen
For The Rt Revd Yong Ping Chung
Bishop of Sabah, Chairman, MISSIO

THE MISSION COMMISSION OF THE ANGLICAN COMMUNION (MISSIO)

The Rt Revd Brian Kyme	Australia
Dr Eleanor Johnson	Canada
Mr John Clark	Europe
The Revd Canon Ron Taylor	New Zealand
The Revd Canon Patrick Mauney	USA
Mrs Margaret Larom	USA
The Rt Revd Datuk Yong Ping Chung	Southern Asia
The Revd Paul Kwong	Northern Asia
The Revd Sam Sahu	South Pacific
The Rt Revd Riah Abu El-Assal	North Africa Middle East
The Rt Revd Benjamin Kwashi	Western Africa
The Revd Stephen Mung´oma	Eastern Africa
The Revd Canon Dr Sabastian Bakare (from August 1996)	Southern & Central Africa (StoS)
The Revd Roger Chung Po Chuen	Francophone (ACC Standing Committee member)
Dr Hugo Vergara	South America Spanish Speaking
The Rt Revd Jubal Neves	South America Portuguese Speaking
The Revd Canon Harold Daniel	West Indies & Central America
The Rt Revd Jason Dharmaraj	India (Ecumenical)
The Revd Michael McCoy	Southern Africa & South to South (up to the end of 1994; Consultant at Ely January 1996)
The Revd Canon Peter Price	Consultant at Singapore 1994

Mission and Evangelism Report II: Report on the Mid-Point Review of the Decade of Evangelism by the Revd Canon Dr Cyril Okorocha

A: Background

At the 1988 Lambeth Conference the Bishops passed the following resolution:

"This Conference, recognising that evangelism is the primary task given to the Church, asks each Province and diocese of the Anglican Communion, in co-operation with other Christians, to make the closing years of this millennium a 'Decade of Evangelism' with a renewed and united emphasis on making Christ known to the people of his world." [Resolution 43]

The Communion formally launched the Decade of Evangelism in 1991 and the Revd Canon Dr Cyril Okorocha was invited from Nigeria as a 'gift' from the Church in Nigeria, to co-ordinate the Decade throughout the world and take on, in addition, the portfolio of Director for Mission (defunct since the unfortunate death of The Revd Canon Martin Mbwana) of ACC. Cyril brought with him a holistic view of mission, which blended the two responsibilities excellently along the lines of the ACC's definition of mission (ACC-8 pp101f). The Communion-wide response to the Decade vision was varied, but there appears to have been a positive universal attitude to the idea. In the words of Canon Colin Craston, "In my 40 years of ministry, I have never known any concept that captures the imagination of all Anglicans, irrespective of tradition or nationality, the way the Decade vision has done."

But so as to take nothing for granted, the meeting of the ACC and Primates in Cape Town 1993 asked for a mid-point review of the Decade of Evangelism to assess the progress made in the first half and to reflect on the future.

In September 1995, 120 representatives of the Provinces of the Communion met at the Kanuga Conference Centre, N. Carolina, USA to report to each other on the progress of the Decade in their Churches, to identify issues and priorities for the future in a context which did not fail to celebrate the diversity of our world-wide Anglican family. The full report of this Conference, which some people have described as an 'Anglican Pentecost,' *The Cutting Edge of Mission* needs to be studied for a greater appreciation of its message. (Available at the Anglican Communion Office, 157 Waterloo Road, London SE1 8UT, and in provincial offices as well as major bookshops.) A copy of this book has been sent to every ACC member and every bishop of the Communion in preparation for Lambeth 1998.

Funding

There was no provision for the Decade Review in the inter-Anglican budget so it was entirely self-funded. We praise God for the generosity of his people which we experienced and which made the conference possible and for lessons of faith, risk-taking and God's faithfulness learned as a result. I am happy to report to the glory of God, that the conference was fully funded and there is a generous surplus for follow-up.

B: Evangelism—The central task of the Church

Reports at Kanuga revealed that evangelism, in its various forms, is moving to a more central place on the agenda of the Provinces of the Communion, as a result of the call for a Decade in 1988. They also revealed a diversity of understandings of evangelism and a wide variety of approaches as Anglicans sought to relate the Gospel to their local situations. For example, the Church in Nigeria responded to the Decade by consecrating and sending nine missionary bishops, in one day, to largely Islamic Northern Nigeria, to make disciples and share the love of Christ. In this way, bishops, they argued, are first and foremost missionaries and vision-bearers. Pakistan combined its usual outreach programmes with intensified ecumenical anti-drug programmes and Church building projects to provide a Christian presence for witness and rehabilitation. Korea, on the other hand, started a programme of shelter for all through a house sharing scheme, as their own expression of mission in context.

Nevertheless, there were some underlying common themes.

For example, all the reports viewed mission and evangelism as an integrally connected 'seamless robe.' Whereas evangelism was generally understood to deal with the sharing of the Gospel in order to awaken or re-awaken personal faith in Jesus Christ, this could not be done without relating to the personal and social contexts of those concerned. All the reports agreed that evangelism, in spite of these local understandings, was central and essential to the life and witness of the Church. It was the cutting edge, the sharpest point, of the broader task of mission. Any Church not seriously engaging in mission was a disobedient Church and stood the risk of extinction and of becoming a mission field for other religions.

Evangelism impacts on the wider aspects of mission. For example, it challenges the quality of life and welcome of the Church communities into which new believers come. It raises questions of Christian nurturing. It raises issues about the role of Christians in society and their service to the world at large. As was clear from the reports, evangelism provides challenges to the economic and social injustices of our world, to age old issues like racism and neo-colonialism and the role of the Church, especially in the West and individual Christians in those situations. This last question focused on Rwanda and Burundi, which was the cradle of the East Africa Revival and yet where in recent years, there have been most horrifying cases of genocide and inter-ethnic intolerance. That tragedy remains a pain in the neck of the Church in that region and in some way an anguish for the whole of the Communion. But we heard reports from Rwanda at the conference.

C: Emerging issues and future directions (The 10 Points of Decade so far)

The reports from around the Communion identified the following issues as priorities to be addressed in the second half of the Decade and beyond.

1.   Issues of training and nurturing from chaplaincy to prophetism

To shift the Church from maintenance to mission, we need to shift emphasis in ministerial formation from chaplaincy to prophetism. We seem to train our clergy to become community chaplains committed to gentle nurturing and maintenance. They wait for people to come to 'Church.' But a missionary congregation, takes 'the Church,' the ministry of the Church to the people in the larger community. No wonder the issue identified as top priority was the need to revise the training, nurturing and formation of clergy, so as to prepare them to participate and give leadership in evangelism in the holistic sense of mission. Equipping and empowering the laity was also emphasized. Both clergy and laity need opportunities to gain confidence in telling their faith stories. Clergy in particular need encouragement and help to engage in ongoing theological formation.

2.   Issues of spirituality and worship

There was a strong call for freer worship and contextualised liturgy. Our common pattern of Anglican liturgy has helped to bind us together, but needs to be revised to reflect local cultures. Evangelistic endeavours need to be undertaken under the guidance of the Holy Spirit, and should be strongly supported and surrounded by personal and corporate prayer. Personal devotion and communal worship lie at the heart of renewal in evangelism—which often includes 'spiritual war-fare.' Clergy and lay leaders need training in this direction. The whole Decade Review Conference, G-CODE 2000, was borne on the wings of lively imaginative worship and sustained by intercessory prayer.

3.   Repentance and humility

There was an acknowledgement that humble repentance is a necessary precondition to bold evangelism. In each part of the Communion there is a need for the Church to repent of its past and present sins, and this is an on-going process which may in some cases involve restitution. Examples from Japan and New Zealand were received positively and formed a challenge to other nations and Churches.

4.   The role of lay people

The central role of the laity in evangelism was strongly affirmed. There is a need not merely to give tasks to lay people, but rather, to empower them by truly delegating authority and encouraging and enabling them to get on with the job in their homes, places of work and daily lives. The important role of women in witness was particularly highlighted. In many parts of Africa, especially West Africa, women, largely through the ministry of the Mothers' Union, lead the Church's mission and form the well spring of its social and spiritual life.

5.   A Church open to all people

The emphasis on evangelism is vital, But so as not to lose gained ground, local congregations/Christian communities need to become more welcoming, nurturing and open to enquirers. They also need to provide neighbourhood, house-oriented or 'cell' groups which newcomers can join. The hierarchical structures of our Anglican Church need to be modified to allow a more equitable sharing of responsibilities.

6.   Leadership and visioning

Delegates called for strong and prophetic leadership from the bishops of the Communion. There is a need for bishops to practically and financially demonstrate their commitment to evangelism, and to articulate a clear evangelistic vision. They carry a responsibility as vision-bearers for the Communion.

There was therefore a call to free both bishops and clergy, as vision-bearers, from administrative burdens so as to exercise their prophetic ministry and visionise for the people as they spend time with God in prayer and study.

7.   Youth

There was a strong call to explore and harness ways of ministering with the youth, by implementing whatever changes are needed in order to attract youth, as well as the need for affirming and encouraging youth in the work of evangelism and in their spiritual and moral formation. "Youth," we learnt, from the young workers, "do not believe in theories, they follow sketches, the life of the leadership."

8.   Cooperation with other Christians

In the second half of the Decade, Provinces need to reassess their ecumenical co-operation in evangelism as urged by Lambeth 1988.

9.   Other faiths, ideologies, unreached people

There was special concern about strengthening our witness among people of other faiths. Mention was also made of the challenge of materialism and secularism. We should support efforts to reach the unreached both in the modern and mega cities of the wealthier parts of the world and in the less developed places.

10.   Issues of social and environmental justice

a)   Evangelism is the central task given to the Church, and it was felt that this means a call to live like Christ in concern for the poor, the weak, the oppressed and to uphold the integrity of creation. Churches were urged to pray and work to overcome structures and systems that perpetuate poverty, oppression and environmental degradation.

b)   Within the Church it was felt that Provinces and dioceses should reflect their commitment to the vision of becoming a movement for mission by giving mission a priority place in their budgeting. Churches should do more teaching on tithing and mission-oriented giving by the members.

D.   Some practical suggestions for mobilizing the Church

Working groups at the Conference suggested some practical ways to help the Church address the emerging issues and future directions identified above. These suggestions need to be adapted to fit local situations.

1.   Seminary training

There needs to be a Communion-wide review and revision of seminary curricula and staffing to prioritise mission and evangelism. To shift the Church from maintenance to mission, we need to put mission at the heart of ministerial formation.

2.   Exchanges of personnel

These exchanges should increase, and can happen in a variety of ways and in all directions.

3.   Team and group visits

These are short-term, focused visits, to meet specific requests. We can learn from each other's experiences.

4.   Translation and adaptation of resources

There is a need for more resources in languages other than English, and of culturally- sensitive adaptations.

5.   Sharing stories

We would be helped by hearing one another's stories, including faith stories and accounts of successful and unsuccessful efforts in evangelism. We need to affirm one another by recognising that everyone has an important and useful story to share for the common good.

6.   Regional gatherings

Gatherings are one of the important ways we meet each other, encourage and support each other, exchange our stories, and celebrate our oneness and rich diversity.

7.   Electronic networking

We need to make the best possible use of the technology that is available. But we also need to help the less privileged Churches with modern technological know-how and tools.

8.   Evangelism assessment/evaluation

We found that those Churches with the clearest and least complicated goals made the most progress. For example, Nigeria's missionary bishops emphasise that bishops are vision-bearers. In Sabah Diocese's mission 1-1-3 program, each member works and prays to bring another worshipper in three years. The aim is to double the Church membership in three years. Texas Diocese's Mission 1-1-10, is similar to Sabah's but has a different context and the time scale is 10 years. The point is to have clear views and measurable goals.

9.   Budgets

The Church at all levels should budget sufficient funds to enable the work of evangelism. Examining our budgets is one way of measuring our commitment to evangelism.

10.   Mission structures and programmes

The programmes and structures which have been established to assist the Church throughout the Communion to fulfil its broad mission goals should be modified as necessary to assist with current evangelism needs.

11.   Ecumenical endeavour

Local parishes and dioceses need to be encouraged to approach the evangelistic task ecumenically, in cooperation with other Christians in their own communities.

E.   Some questions to help us move forward

These questions are intended to stimulate thought, leading to positive action. They should be adapted as necessary for local situations.

For the Anglican Consultative Council

1.   Sharing of resources

What and where are the identifiable resources, human and

material, that can be used for evangelism, and how can these be effectively shared around the Communion?

2.   Language and translation

Are some language groups in the Communion being marginalized in the study of theology and at conferences, and what can be done to correct this anomaly?

3.   Funding

Does the evangelism budget adequately reflect the priority of this Decade of Evangelism?

4.   Mission from below

Are we willing to learn from the younger more vibrant Churches of the South or is their economic disadvantage yet another obstacle in the way of empowerment for them and enrichment for all?

For Bishops/Dioceses

1.   Vision and encouragement

Evangelism is the cutting edge of mission. What is your vision for the spread of the Gospel, recruitment, training and sending of labourers for the ongoing task of mission? (See MISSIO's letter to the Bishops of the Communion)

2.   Training

How central is the practical training in evangelism in the curriculum of your institutions of lay and clergy training?

3.   Relevant liturgy

How do you encourage your people to adapt liturgy to better reflect your culture and the local situation and to make worship a more lively and creative encounter with God?

For Parishes

1. Sensitivity to local needs

What do people find attractive in your congregation?

2. Welcoming community

In what ways can you improve your welcome to others?

3. Building confidence for evangelism

How does your parish help members to share their faith at home, at work, with neighbours and in the wider society?

4. How open and friendly are your members to

a)   people of other Christian denominations;
b)   new converts and enquirers;
c)   people of other faiths and cultures in your neighbourhood?

For all

Look at the list of emerging issues and practical suggestions. In each list which are the top three priorities for you in your situation? Do you have any other priorities? What will you do about them?

F: Five key observations

1. A demographic shift

We learnt about the phenomenal growth and vibrancy of the younger Churches, suggesting a dramatic shift in the 'centre of gravity' of the Church, in terms of numerical growth and liveliness, away from the traditional places in Europe and North America to Asia and Latin America and especially Africa. We learnt that in spite of material poverty, political and social marginalization and persecutions as well as pressures from other religions, Christianity in Africa seems to be growing faster than the population.

2. A reversal in missionary movement

It looks as though there is a new missionary movement following the demographic shift in the world Church. It is as yet unstructured and spontaneous. Christians from the South coming to the 'Global North' as students, migrant workers and economic refugees suddenly find themselves impelled by the power inherent in the faith they embody and from their experience in their home Church, into becoming unofficial missionaries in their host countries. We heard many stories which point to mission and evangelism as a movement, not due to money and technological know-how, important as these are, but of the power of God that brings salvation.

A great question we would not resolve was this: Should this new movement be allowed to remain haphazard from everywhere to everywhere? or should the older mission agencies lend their experience to make it more creative? Or will structuring and bureaucracy stifle the move of the Spirit? What is the Spirit saying?

3.   Leadership for the younger Churches

We saw the need to train relevant and qualitative leadership for the Churches of the South:

a)   to help secure the future of the Church;
b)   to make partnership meaningful, as it will then be more on the basis of equality, mutual acceptance and respect.

4.   Confidence in the Gospel

It looks as though the Churches' honest engagement with evangelism and mission at any age is directly proportional to its degree of confidence in the validity of the Gospel and of the message of the Bible for that age. "We have no high theology, we simply follow the Bible," confessed the Bishop of Sabah. He claims this accounts for the current phenomenal growth of the Church in his diocese, in spite of the official negative legislation by an Islamic national government.

5.   Power of prayer

We learnt that prayer is more than saying one's prayers. It is engagement with God. Intercessors sustained the conference through prayer. Mission and prayer are inseparable.

6.   Power of forgiveness

We saw the healing power of forgiveness and its centrality to a fruitful Christian life and collective witness.

Report on Guidelines for Membership by New Provinces by the Revd John Rees

Monday, 14 October 1996

Introduction

Whilst I love the Anglican Communion dearly, I am under few illusions about the burning enthusiasm that this topic will engender amongst you all.

The Anglican Communion has an inherent scepticism about law, lawyers and all their ways. After all, the first Lambeth Conference was called precisely because the lawyers appeared to have made such a mess over the case of the Bishop of Natal. Owen Chadwick sums it up well by saying, "Just as Pope Pius IX needed a Council of Roman Catholic Bishops to tell Italian politicians that they had no business interfering with the Church, so Gray needed a Council of Bishops to tell the lawyers that they had no standing to determine whether Colenso was a Bishop or not" (in Coleman, *Resolutions,* Toronto 1992, p vii).

As if the law were not tedious enough, the topic itself does not excite the imagination. Herbert Hensley Henson described one day's business at the Lambeth Conference in 1920 that "the discussion in the afternoon bored me stark. It dealt with the multiplication of Provinces in the Anglican Communion. I deserted and went to the Athenaeum" (*Retrospect* ii, p 7).

Clearing the ground

I want to make it absolutely clear that the purpose of this exercise is not to alter in any way the delicate balance that presently exists between the various Anglican 'instruments of unity.' It may help if I briefly summarise what these are.

The Archbishop of Canterbury

The first of the four unifying instruments is the Archbishop of Canterbury himself. He is variously described as being "the primary focus of unity," "the *primus inter pares,*" or as having "primacy of honour."

It lies with him to call together the bishops at Lambeth every decade, to convene the Primates' Meeting, and in relation to the ACC, he is its President, its only *ex officio* member, he is not subject to retirement, and (joy of joys) is *ex officio* a member of all its committees (Article 6 [a]).

The Communion defines itself by reference to him: it is "a fellowship, within the one Holy Catholic and Apostolic Church, of those duly constituted dioceses, provinces or regional Churches in communion with the See of Canterbury" (*Lambeth Conference Report,* 1930, Resolution 49). He is, in himself, a "personal symbol of unity" (ACC-7 *Report,* p 130). The See and the person are in one sense separable, but in another, quite obviously inseparable. I came across a memorable quotation from Richard Chartres the other day, in which he describes travelling around the Anglican Communion with Robert Runcie, and how "they kept bumping into the ghost of Geoffrey Fisher." He was, I hasten to add, describing a time before Michael Ramsey's death, or I imagine they would have encountered his massive shade as well!

The Archbishop of Canterbury's role, then, is pivotal in the Communion.

The Lambeth Conference

The Archbishop of Canterbury, as we have seen, invites or "gathers" the bishops of the Communion for the Lambeth Conference. The Conferences themselves have no legal authority. That is by design. The first Conference would not have been held at all had not everyone been agreed that this did not constitute a formal Synod or Council of the Church. The Archbishop of York, for one, would not attend the first conference, partly for fear that it might be thought to be a body that had legal powers.

We are adamant about this as a Communion, and this concern is rehearsed at almost every gathering of any of the instruments of unity, almost as if it were an article of faith. In a sense, it is. One comprehensive recent statement may suffice, combining dogma, aspiration and realism: the bishops at Lambeth in 1988 reminded the Communion that "we do not see any inter-Anglican jurisdiction as possible or desirable; an inter-Anglican Synodical structure would be virtually unworkable and highly expensive" (*Lambeth Conference Report* 1988, p 217).

Nevertheless, "meetings start to gather authority if they exist and are seen not to be a cloud of hot air and rhetoric. It was impossible that the leaders of the Anglican Communion should meet every 10 years and not start to gather respect; and to gather respect is to slowly gather influence, and influence is on the road to authority. It continued to have that absence of legal authority which some of its founders wanted and which of necessity was denied to them. But in most Churches some of the most important parts of authority are not based upon the law" (Chadwick, *op cit*, p x).

The Primates' Meeting

The Primates' Meetings have become a regular feature of the Communion's life over the last 20 years, arising out of a suggestion of Donald Coggan, discussed and resolved upon at Lambeth in 1978.

They have only the authority of the Primates who take part, but that is not an inconsiderable weight of authority. For example, when it was decided to prepare a list of Churches forming part of the Anglican Communion in the late 1970s, the list initially prepared by the ACC was circulated to the Primates so each could confirm that his own Church was in communion with the others. It is published in the ACC Handbook with the following note: "Since the Anglican Communion does not have a central body with canonical authority, the list is authorised by the Archbishop of Canterbury and the Anglican Primates" *(Handbook,* 1994, p 19). For it must be remembered that we are dealing with a network of autonomous bodies, each of which must be clear that it is in communion with the others. Without that mutual recognition there can be no communion.

A question was raised this morning about the United Churches in the Indian sub-continent. They provide a good example; each constituent part of the Anglican Communion has had to come to its own conclusion as to whether they are bodies with which it can be in communion. In the case of the Church of England, for a considerable time the difficulty turned upon the continuing existence of ministers of the Church of South India who had not been episcopally ordained.

This illustrates the interaction of our instruments of unity; each Province has had to decide for itself, but each will have taken into account the decision of the ACC at Singapore in 1987 to normalise the relationship between the United Churches and the ACC, and its recommendation to the Lambeth Conference and the Primates' Meeting to receive them as full participants (ACC-7, Resolution 17).

Anglican Consultative Council

There is a case for saying that in one shape or another, the Anglican Consultative Council has existed since 1897. Clearly that is not an accurate statement of fact, but it is a fact that there have now been committees or individuals for the best part of the last 100 years entrusted with the task of consulting with and communicating between members of the Anglican family of Churches and beyond (see, for example, *Lambeth Conference Report* 1897, Resolution 5).

The ACC as we now have it is, of course, the creation of Resolution 69 of the Lambeth Conference 1968. It alone of all the four instruments of unity has a legal structure and clearly defined functions. It is a charity incorporated under the English Charities Act 1993, and its Constitution is set out in the Handbook (pp. 7-10, 14, and 15).

It should be noted in particular that it is the only one of the instruments which provide a place for lay representation.

The delicate balance of authority

You may by now be becoming puzzled by the multiplicity of unifying bodies we have to deal with. Do not be confused by it—you need not be. The fact is that as Anglicans, we believe in dispersed authority, not top-down management. Theologically, we look to scripture and tradition and reason/conscience in our process of reception and discernment of the mind of God. Some unkindly characterise this as woolly-mindedness, or indecisiveness; we say it is part of God's calling to us to be a people who are responsive to the world he has called us to live in, and at the same time faithful to all that He has given us from the past. We are "a learning Church" as well as a teaching Church, and it is one of the glories of our tradition.

What holds good for our theology holds equally good for our structures. The Lambeth Conference in 1988 noted with approval that "in the Communion as a whole, the instruments of Communion or the organs of consultation provide appropriate checks and balances for each other... [we] seem to have a view of dispersed authority which relates not only to the sources of authority but also to its exercise" (*Lambeth Conference Report* 1988, p 298).

So this balanced mix of authority should not puzzle us. Rather, we might be asking ourselves how it could be otherwise in a Communion which is characterised by a voluntary, not enforced or enforceable submission to "mutual attentiveness, interdependence and accountability" (*Inter-Anglican Theological and Doctrinal Commission, Draft Report*, para 3.44, 1996). It is characteristic of Anglicanism that our structural as well as our theological authority is dispersed.

All of which, though lengthy to set out, is important in this context. Let there be no misunderstanding: the purpose of this exercise is not in any way to tamper with the delicate balance that exists between the authority of the Archbishop of Canterbury, the Lambeth Conference of Bishops, the Primates' Meeting, and the Anglican Consultative Council. Streamlining the role of the latter does not imply any diminution in the importance of the others.

The purpose of these proposals

Provincial Constitutions

Essentially then, our concern is to ensure that what the Lambeth bishops were looking for when they set up ACC as a unifying instrument in 1968 is being given effective expression in the conditions included in our Communion nearly 30 years later.

From the outset one of the central concerns has been "to advise on inter-Anglican, provincial, and diocesan relationships, including the division of Provinces, the formation of new Provinces and of Regional Councils, and the problems of extra-Provincial Dioceses" (Article 2 [c]).

Early on, the ACC produced broad guidelines for new Provincial Constitutions, and their recommendations have been noted and observed quite extensively over the years. You have them amongst your papers, not as documents for comment and amendment, but by way of reminder. Almost by definition (by virtue of the time-limits on membership in the ACC constitution), none of you can have been members at the time when these guidelines were passed; in the nature of things, the "institutional memory" may have failed, and for some of you, this may be (and some of you have told me that it is) the first time you have found that such a resource exists.

However, in recent years, it has become apparent that there need to be clearer lines of communication between those involved locally in preparation of new Provincial structures and the ACC. It may well be that in the past informal means of communication were perfectly adequate, and certainly that may have been the case at the time when most of the new Provinces were developing out of relinquishment by the Archbishop of Canterbury himself of his metropolitical authority. But times are changing, and changing rapidly. The pressures for change are as often political as ecclesiastical.

I do not think it is good enough, as the Communion gets ever larger and faces ever more complex problems, for us to rely on casual conversations and informal contacts. "Mutual attentiveness, interdependence and accountability" in current conditions demands more than that. As with the existing guidelines for the content of provincial constitutions, if they do nothing else, guidelines on the procedure for consultation will serve as a checklist or *aide-memoire* to ensure that valuable steps in the consultation process have not been overlooked. I fear at the moment that valuable resources available for the Communion through the Consultative Council are not being used—just because people do not know they exist, or because it does not occur to them to ask.

There is a need to be proactive. For that reason I want to urge you to adopt the following guidelines, setting out a procedure for consultation. This can then be incorporated into a separate document, along with the existing guidelines on content of constitutions, for publication and circulation within the Communion.

The suggested draft is as follows:

> *1.   For the Primate or any other Council or body having metropolitical authority for the relevant dioceses to make contact with the ACC as soon as a proposal for formation of a new province is under serious consideration.*

> *2.   This referral might (and ideally would normally) be accompanied by an invitation to the ACC for a visit by the Secretary General, or by someone nominated by the Secretary-General, to the dioceses or region, if possible to co-incide with some other activity of the Anglican Communion requiring the Secretary General's presence in the area. The purpose of the visit would be to discuss the application of the ACC's guidelines to the specific situation in the local area.*

> *3.   Once initial consultation had taken place, and it was agreed in principle that it would be expedient to form a new Province in the region, the promoters would appoint a drafting committee, to consider the outline draft constitution set out by the ACC. They would address any issues arising from it that had not yet been considered by the promoters, and set up clear lines of communication and a timetable for consultation with the dioceses concerned, with their metropolitical authority, and with the ACC.*

> *4.   The drafting process in itself is likely to take some considerable time, but the ACC can provide significant assistance in advising both on the content of constitutions (by comparison with those used elsewhere in the Communion), and on the arrangements that may need to be made for that stage of the discussion.*

5.   *On receipt of the first (and any subsequent) draft constitution by the ACC, the Secretary General may appoint a committee, or call upon individual consultants, to make observations on its behalf for further consideration by the promoters and their advisors.*

6.   *Having agreed on the form of the new constitution, the proposers are asked to submit their application for revision of the scheduled list to the ACC not less than 15 months ahead of the next meeting of the full Council.*

7.   *The Secretary General in accordance with Article 3(a) will then consult with the Primates, either at their next scheduled meeting or individually, to seek the two-thirds majority approval required by its constitution.*

8.   *The proposal for revision of the schedule (to add the new Province to the scheduled list) will be put on the agenda for approval at the next full meeting, subject to any outstanding consents of Primates.*

9.   *The Secretary General will be charged with informing the Archbishop of Canterbury at every stage as to the ACC's view on the eligibility of the applicant body for recognition as an autonomous Province of the Anglican Communion.*

I hope these are straightforward and commonsensical. Their purpose, as I have tried to explain, is not to alter the delicate balance between the unifying instruments of the Communion, but merely to clarify, and to enable the ACC to fulfil its part of the process of development in the Communion more effectively and in line with the vision of the bishops at Lambeth in 1968.

Some Constitutional housekeeping

There is an internal amendment I would also like to suggest, to correct what I think was probably a mistake in drafting when the Constitution was changed to take account of the creation of the Primates Meeting in the early 1980s.

Members will observe that the ACC Constitution provides a definition of "Primates," which introduces a degree of circularity into the process of amending the scheduled list, and which the Council may wish to address.

The definition provided in the Constitution refers to them as being the heads of "each autonomous Province of the Anglican Communion." In consequence, a Primate or presiding bishop of a newly formed Province, which had not had any consultation with the ACC, should himself be counted amongst the Primates to be consulted by the ACC in relation to a revision of the scheduled list.

This emphasises the difference between membership of the Anglican Communion (which as we noted earlier is essentially a doctrinal and ecclesiological question) and inclusion in the scheduled list for membership of the Anglican Consultative Council (which is essentially a legal matter defined in the ACC's own constitution).

If it were thought prudent by the Council to address this issue, one way of doing so would be by restricting the requirement for assent to those Primates only who are Primates of autonomous Provinces already listed in the schedule to the ACC Constitution. That would bring the provision in line with the amendment provision in Article 10, where only those already listed are to participate in such decisions.

Conclusion

People say that lawyers are unnecessary because they take for ever to state the blindingly obvious. That is only in part a fair criticism. Often things fall into place in our minds only when they have been unpacked in the (admittedly) tedious way I have tried to do this afternoon.

I hope that the points I have tried to make are blindingly obvious, but what I hope has also become clear is that there is more to the life of our Communion than legal structures. Our structures merely provide a skeleton. The skeleton needs to fit together in the right way, but what we are offering here will not be any more than dry bones unless the Spirit of life breathes into all our efforts a fresh willingness and commitment to work together in fulfilling a shared vision for the Communion, which means so much to us and which, we trust, in the purposes of God has so much to offer our troubled world.

Report on Liturgy by the Revd Paul Gibson

Thursday, 17 October 1996

Work

I work as Co-ordinator for Liturgy for the Anglican Consultative Council for one-quarter to one-third of my time, on secondment from the Anglican Church of Canada. My goal is to facilitate communication in the Communion, not only among those responsible for liturgical renewal but also among those who are concerned for the defining and unifying function of worship in our Communion. In fact, I suggest that worship operates as a fifth 'instrument of unity,' unofficial and unlegislated, but real. ACC-7, in its proposal of a Liturgical Commission, quoted the following sentence from the document, *For the Sake of the Kingdom:* "The Church's liturgy carries the common mind of the community, and it is this 'mind' with its characteristic questions, interests and assumptions, that receives, and in receiving interprets, the Bible and the creeds"(Paragraph 60).

It is my belief that although local liturgies are becoming increasingly varied in form and cultural expression, we will continue to be able to maintain and discern the common ground of historic Anglicanism even in this period of accelerated change. But this requires communication and mutuality of resources, a process envisioned by ACC-7 in its suggestions that a commission would keep liturgical revision under review, offer encouragement and support, study and reflect on inculturation, study and evaluate ecumenical liturgical developments, and finally, "attempt to discern liturgical features and principles in which, as the future unfolds, the Anglican Communion could recognise its continuing identity and encourage fellowship with other Christian Communions." (I note in passing the recognition this meeting of the ACC has given to communication on worship in the life of the Communion by assigning a section to work on this subject.)

At a modest level, this is what I try to enable. I have developed a collection of Anglican liturgies produced in the last 30 years which is housed in Partnership House and is available to students and scholars. It continues to be expanded. I maintain a connection with provincial offices as needed. I am available (and frequently approached) by e-mail, post, and telephone to members of the Communion all over the world for consultation on liturgical details of all kinds. But more and more of my time once available for this task is now devoted to providing staff support to the International Anglican Liturgical Consultations, their steering committee, and the conferences and meetings they promote and foster.

International Anglican Liturgical Consultations

The Consultations perform in fact the tasks which were envisioned for a commission which was never established. They began as a caucus of Anglicans at the biennial congress of *Societas Liturgica,* the ecumenical academy. They have now expanded into major meetings with broad representation every four years, and small conferences during the intervening two-year points. They have the disadvantage of a self-selecting system of representation which favours affluent regions of the Communion. On the other hand, they have the advantage of a much broader range of expertise than a small commission could hope to assemble, and they create a large network of informed participants who can carry their message more deeply into the Church's life. More than 70 people attended the 1995 Consultation in Dublin. Several Provinces have made significant efforts to bring greater north-south equality to the membership of the consultations.

Dublin 1995

The Findings of the 5th International Anglican Liturgical Consultation in Dublin, Republic of Ireland, in 1995 were included in the documentation supplied to members of this meeting of the ACC. (See *Renewing the Anglican Eucharist.*) A synopsis of this document appears in my written report. The Dublin Consultation and a conference which preceded it two years earlier were both designed to provide principles and guidelines for consideration in the Communion, as the development of Eucharistic prayers continues and members of the Communion pursue a style of praying which is better inculturated, more inclusive, more aware of the social dimensions of the Gospel, and richer in both form and content. In particular, I draw the attention of members of the ACC to the three paragraphs on the second page of my written report, in which I have attempted to provide a digest of the principles and recommendations of the Consultation, grouped under headings which I have chosen to identify as what I perceived to be their areas of concern.

First, under the heading of **Order** (1, 6, and 8), the Consultation identified the assembly, from which no baptised person may be excluded on such grounds as age, race, gender, economic circumstance, or mental capacity, as the celebrant of the Eucharist. The assembly itself is an ordered community with a variety of roles, and the liturgical functions of the ordained arise from and are related directly to their pastoral responsibility. All the Churches, leaders, laity and clergy must be open to renewal and continuing formation.

Second, under the heading of **Faith and Practice** (2, 4, 7 and 5), the Consultation suggested that we may expect to find Anglican unity in the future expressed in a structure which balances word, prayer and sacrament, and in a common approach to Eucharistic celebration more than in uniformity of texts. Eucharistic theology should articulate the sacrificial character of all Christian life and worship without blurring the unique atoning work of Christ. The place of expressive, even vivid, language, symbol, and metaphor should be recognised. The centrality of thanksgiving to the Eucharistic prayer (which includes memorial and invocation) must be emphasised. Local tradition should contribute to the embodiment of proclamation, music, symbol, and ritual.

Third, under the heading of **Vocation and Ministry,** the Consultation acknowledged the Eucharistic celebration not only as the model of God's transformation of the world in the Word made flesh, but as the way in which broken individuals respond by offering themselves to be made one in that transformation, "reaffirming the baptismal commitment to die to self and be raised to newness of life, and embodying that vision of the kingdom in searching for justice, reconciliation and peace in the community." Liturgy is a key to personal spirituality and social justice.

I urge study throughout the Communion not only of **Renewing the Anglican Eucharist** (the findings of the Dublin Consultation), but also of the preparatory documents produced by the conference two years earlier which have been published as *Revising the Eucharist: Groundwork for the Anglican Communion.* Both have been published by Grove Books. Those who wish to follow more closely the Dublin Consultation's suggestion that Anglican liturgical unity may in future be expressed in structure rather than in uniformity of texts should give particular attention to Thomas Talley's seminal essay in *Revising the Eucharist: Eucharistic Prayers, Past, Present and Future.*

Future Consultations

The steering committee of the Consultations will meet in South Africa next month to plan a conference for next year, which we hope will lay the groundwork for a full Consultation two years later. The Consultations are moving towards the study of ordination and ordination rites. This will involve not only an opportunity to review our ritual practice but will also require an evaluation of our ecclesiology, our sense of the meaning of *laos* and the place of ministry (whether charismatic and/or ordered) within the life of God's people, our understanding of the relationship of ministry and mission, as well as the appropriate forms of prayer and gesture through which ordered ministries are recognised, confirmed, and conferred.

Inculturation

As noted in my written report, the Consultation in Toronto in 1992 led to a regional conference in Africa on African Culture and Anglican Liturgy. The findings of this meeting have been published as *Anglican Liturgical Inculturation in Africa: The Kanamai Statement* (also published by Grove Books). I believe the *Kanamai Statement* is important not only for Anglicans in Africa and not only for Anglicans whose culture is neither Mediterranean nor North Atlantic, but for all who are concerned with the incarnation of Christianity in the identity of a people (whether aboriginal, modern industrial, or whatever). I recently commended the *Kanamai Statement* to those in Canada who are concerned with the liturgical expression of First Nations Canadians

If I may be forgiven a somewhat simplistic metaphor, I will suggest that Anglican worship is like some delicate and interesting wines which are said not to travel well. The export of English cathedral worship to the former colonies has only occasionally been successful. However, it is possible to take cuttings of those vines whose wine it is difficult to transport and plant them in other soil, where they will produce not the same wine as in their source but a product with its own distinctive and interesting qualities. I suggest that the time has come for many Provinces to recognise that there are some ancient liturgical qualities preserved in Anglican tradition which they wish to maintain—reverence, a balance of contemplation and doxology, predictability, respect for individuals, a coherent liturgical use of scripture, to name but a few—but maintain within forms of expression, verbal and symbolic, which are entirely local. This process is not easy, but it is brilliantly challenging, not only for some Provinces but for all, because we have all become conscious of continuous social and cultural change. I gather that the export of the English cathedral tradition to Wapping and Lewisham may not have been easier than to the former colonies. We must remember that all liturgy, without exception, is inculturated; the question is, which culture?

In addition to studying statements like the report of the Kanamai Conference, I urge Provinces to support initiatives towards regional consultations on liturgical challenges like inculturation. This support should take the form not only of money but also the selection of the most appropriate and creative leaders. The goals originally envisioned by ACC-7 can best be realised by the widest possible conversation and communication. Provinces without strong and vigorous liturgy committees should seriously consider their creation, so they can participate more effectively in the international and ecumenical conversation and also provide a network through which the spread and study of information may be encouraged at home.

In closing I want to pay tribute to Archbishop Brian Davis's contribution to the Consultations as liaison between them and the Primates' Meeting. He has been an active and valued member of the steering committee and has worked with us as a visibly committed insider. Most of all I want to thank him for the support he has given me and for the candour and friendship which has marked our working relationship.

Report on Ecumenical Affairs
by the Revd Dr Donald Anderson

17 October 1996

Bishop Mark Dyer has spoken of the meeting of the Ecumenical Advisory Group and some of the major subjects that have become paramount concerns in the last 10 years: our understanding of the goal of unity and the importance of reception as we move toward that goal. He has also spoken of the "categorical imperative" of the ecumenical calling; God calls us into a communion *(koinonia)* of common faith, common life and common witness. That includes a concern for the unity of this Anglican ecclesial family, but constrains us to reach out to all baptised Christians in a journey together toward full visible unity.

Ecumenical engagement and praxis is important at every level of the Church's life, but there is also a unique and essential international task which must be done for our case through the Anglican international instruments of consultation and unity. Ecumenical relationships with other Christian world communions encourage, undergird and resource local, national and regional engagement. I would like to draw your attention to some of the international nuts and bolts, the processes and structures through which we work with ecumenical colleagues, and for which ACC has special responsibility.

First, the bilateral dialogues. We are presently engaged in bilateral relationships with six world communions. A description of their work is outlined for you in the *Agros Report*, pages 38-54, but I will make a brief comment about each.

1.   Anglican-Lutheran Relations

Our attention has been captured by the major advances that have taken place in northern Europe and the USA, but you should also know that there is vibrant Lutheran-Anglican engagement in many other places, among them especially Brazil, Canada, Namibia, Southern Africa and Tanzania. ALIC is unique in that it is not primarily a theological dialogue but a commission that monitors regional dialogue, attempts to help regional dialogues to be in touch and consistent with each other, and provides consultation and study when there is a need. For example, it has sponsored a series of consultations in eastern and southern Africa, and its most recent study on the diaconate is on your tables. The diaconate is not a Church-dividing issue, but one of interest to Christians of every tradition; ALIC offers its study not only to the Lutheran and Anglican Communions but to the whole ecumenical community, in the hope that it will be useful in our common study of the nature and task of ministry.

With the completion of these tasks, and the progress of both the Porvöo agreement and the Concordat, ALIC has asked that thought be given to a new shape for the future. The EAG, in response, offers the recommendation on the bottom of page 42 of the *Agros Report.*

2.   Anglican-Methodist Relations

The report *Sharing in the Apostolic Communion* was given to you as you arrived. An internationally agreed statement is only a first step, however important. It clears the ground of some of the historical debris and underbrush that has separated and hidden us from each other. But, given the variety of Methodist and Anglican Churches, it does not relieve national and local Churches of the responsibility of face to face engagement, dialogue and co-operation. For that reason, the report recommends (at the back, page 39) that there be a working group to encourage those actions in each place, which will lead to full, visible unity.

3.   Anglican-Oriental Orthodox Relations

This forum continues a long-time relationship of the Communion with five ancient, non-Chalcedonian oriental Churches. There is increasing contact with them, particularly in diaspora because of immigration from ancient homelands to Australia, Canada, England, and the USA, where we face many common issues, both missional and pastoral. The forum undergirds that regional activity, and we expect it to lead to more focused theological dialogue on the international level with at least some of the five Churches.

4.   Anglican-Orthodox Relations

The dialogue continues work on an agreed statement on the trinitarian basis of communion. A full account is in the *Agros Report* and needs no further comment.

5. Anglican-Reformed Relations

Anglican-WARC relations take the form of a Joint Working Group because on both sides it was felt that we have not adequately responded to the 1984 Anglican Reformed International Commission Theological Report *God's Reign and our Unity*. The mandate of the JWG is summarised on page 49 of the *Agros Report,* together with some recommendations of the EAG.

6. Anglican-Roman Catholic Relations

ARCIC hopes to complete a third study of authority, discussing scripture, tradition and the Magisterium, including a section on primacy, next year in time to publish a document in time for the 1998 Lambeth Conference. With this publication, ARCIC will have completed its current mandate and, as the EAG recognises, thought will need to be given to the shape and content of the next stage of this Anglican-Roman Catholic International relationship. It is worth noting that ARCIC, as well as the EAG, is convinced that reception is an area which needs greater attention, both because the reception of ARCIC I was not entirely satisfactory (we were both doing it for the first time), and because a number of ARCIC II documents have not yet received careful scrutiny.

All six of these dialogues are the responsibility of the ACC, and the ecumenical staff is responsible for their care and feeding: preparation of documentation and the meetings themselves, logistical support and travel, and all the details that accompany successful communication, conversation and co-operation with ecumenical colleagues.

The ACO ecumenical staff is two in number. Besides me, there is a very important person, Mrs. Christine Codner, whom many of you will have met as the person in charge of the Secretariat at this meeting. When she is not at ACC meetings, we work together, and on this last opportunity I would like to make known to you my deep appreciation for her dedication, friendship and the superb quality of her work.

In addition, I am theological secretary of four of the bilaterals, including the Anglican-Lutheran International Commission, the Anglican-Methodist International Commission, the Anglican-Roman Catholic International Commission, and Anglican-Reformed. I share the secretaryship of two, the Anglican-Oriental Orthodox Forum and the International Commission of Anglican-Orthdox Theological Dialogue, with Canon Richard Marsh the Archbishop of Canterbury's ecumenical secretary. Here I would like to pay another tribute to Richard for the easy co-operation and friendship that has contributed so much to the quality of the working relationships between Lambeth Palace and the ACO.

The World Council of Churches

You will also find a brief comment (*Agros* pages 55-57) on the WCC, to which I will not add, except to note that the ACO collated an expanded Communion response to the WCC's request for comment on the *Common Understanding and Vision of the WCC*. This was shared with the Communion two years ago.

In addition to bilaterals and multilateral relations with the WCC, the ecumenical staff are responsible for informal talks with the Roman Catholic Church and the Ecumenical Patriarchate year by year, and are called to organise and sponsor a variety of annual and occasional ad hoc meetings: for example, last autumn on Porvöo/Concordat; this November on COCU.

Finally, the ecumenical staff of the ACO have been responsible for the meeting and work of the Ecumenical Advisory Group. I have outlined its activities in a short foreword on page 5 of the *Agros Report* and will not repeat the details here. However, I draw your attention to the recommendation of the EAG emerging from its reflection on the work of the bilateral dialogues (page 53), which recommends that the EAG be replaced by an Inter-Anglican Standing Commission on Ecumenical Relations, with, I expect, a budget comparable to the present EAG.

Communications Report
by Canon James Rosenthal

Thursday, 17 October 1996

Symbols of our time

My vision for communications comes from the Empty Tomb and the story in the Scriptures. The first communicators, as I see it, were the women confronted by the angel in the now empty tomb in Jerusalem. The angel asks the question, *"Whom to you seek?"*

They said, *"Jesus."* The angel replies, *"He is risen as he said,"* and what follows is my inspiration. The angel says, *"Go and tell the disciples,"* (the equivalent of saying go tell the Primates, ACC, Lambeth Conference, the Archbishop of Canterbury). The greatest of all news is ours, yours and mine to tell and to tell everyone.

At the Anglican Communion Office we tell the stories that you tell us, that you share with us and that we discover on our various visits around the globe.

Now to illustrate the complexity of the commission we have, I want to share a recent survey with you. This poster (poster of the Compasrose) displays a symbol—what does it mean?

Do you know what a recent survey showed to be the most recognisable symbol in the world? Yes, it is McDonalds. Does anyone not know what McDonalds is? It is of course the multi-billion dollar food operation from the USA found all over the world.

The second most recognisable symbol—the shell—is not the shell of baptism of the great Shrine of Santiago de Compostela, but can you guess? Yes, Shell Oil—around the globe known and seen by all.

This card shows the third, not first, most recognisable symbol, the cross of Jesus Christ. As we say on Good Friday, behold the wood of the cross on which was hung the world's salvation.

The cross is number three and the hamburger is number one.

How do we communicate? How do we convey who we are and what we are about?

Many parts of the Communion simply do not have the means to address any communications operations—no magazines, no newspaper, no video and no telecommunications. It has already been pointed out what the cost of a magazine subscription might mean in Zaire—one month's salary! In visiting the various provinces I am almost embarrassed at the degree of importance that people place on the magazine; it is incredible.

I must preface my remarks by saying that my words to you as the ACC will only be heard by those who accept and believe that Anglicanism has a vocation and ministry in this day and age and into the next millennium. I can not argue for communications with anyone who does not hold this as a starting point.

The communications work we do, small staff and all, is totally based on our ability to convince others that we need help from those who share a vision for Anglican Christianity. We have been and continue to be fortunate.

I have to say publicly that I am a bit bewildered by the fact that this presentation comes after you have set your priorities. I can only hope that you have heard the word communications mentioned in almost every presentation from UN to Rwanda.

Videos

The video work has been faithfully carried out over the years by St. Martins Video Ministry and the Diocese of Texas in the person of the Revd. Dr. Robert Browne. We will witness his latest project created in cooperation with our office this Thursday and remember there is a free drink for all who stay up to watch this excellent video! If this will ever be a budget item, time will tell.

Telecommunications

Our telecommunications work has been supported by Trinity Church Grants Programme for many years, and I personally am so grateful to Dr. Dan Matthews and Fr. James Callaway for this support. Praise God it continues to this very day. I must also say hearty thanks to the ECUSA for the time and expense they have put into our telecommunications on the Internet and World Wide Web. The work is co-ordinated by the Revd. Kris Lee, as co-ordinator of the Quest Managers. This work must now increase and, as introduced, the Revd. Dr. Joan Ford will be responsible for such programmes in the future. I am fully aware that telecommunications is fashionable and manageable for some and a distant dream for others. We are attempting to bridge that gap. It will cost money on the local level and the international level, and indeed if you have an e-mail address please give it to the secretariat as soon as possible.

Anglican World

That, of course, leads me to the printed page and *Anglican World,* our chief means of communication, of mission and outreach and how we best tell our story as a global family. How grateful I am for the numerous expressions of support and the increased awareness of this magazine in such a short period of time. The potential is great but can only be accomplished by your telling others about the magazine. We recently took an ad in a major Anglican newspaper, and the cost was enormous! In a way *Anglican World* can be viewed as competitive, but support from other magazines and newspapers will not happen unless we pay; I must say with the exception of *Anglican Digest.* As for links with our ecumenical friends, I need not tell anyone the enormous number of international magazines produced by our Roman Catholic friends. Can we not have one?

One letter from a chaplain in the Sudan said it all to me. He said to me that I was one of the only people who kept a promise about getting information back to the Sudan after a visit. I indeed sent many copies of the magazine to him for distribution. The response, he states, was *"fantastico,"* as we say in Spanish; some people had never seen a camera or photos of themselves. A sense of pride and dignity was shown to a people that have been stripped of almost everything. The Sudanese Episcopalians have much to teach us!

The magazine tells our story and what a story it is. If we expect people to support work around the communion, they must know what the situation is and I believe *Anglican World* is the best way and most valuable way to do this. The incorporation of an attractive format speaks of the need for photos, as they help transcend language barriers, yet I am seeking from the meeting names of people able to help create summaries of *Anglican World* in French, Portuguese, and Spanish.

Again the response is overwhelming. Read the letter to the editor in this issue. It says it all to me. It shows a healthy pride, the same pride I have in what I do as your director of communications.

Remember three years ago *Anglican World* produced no income at all, but with more exposure through ACC members the number of paid sub-scribers can rise dramatically. Our advertising is on the increase as well, which speaks of the acceptance of the quality of the magazine to the wider community. Help me identify more advertisers, please.

At this time in our history as a Communion, *Anglican World* is how we com-municate the best. Can we really live with ourselves if we do not tell the story of the Rwandas and Sudans of our Communion. Even other journal-ists recognised the value of our Rwanda coverage, since we received sever-al awards for it and the dissemination of the photos from the Archbishop of Canterbury's visit were used in hundreds of diocesan papers!

The need for clear communication

But what about communication in general? What about the section here at ACC about communicating our beliefs? Does it make a difference?

One book I would like to mention is the one created by the Primus of Scotland through the Affirming Catholicism group. *This is Our Faith* is available from the *Anglican World* off page sales scheme.

Yet, might I offer some practical reflections without being controversial. This summer I visited a part of Europe, for holiday and part of my lay canon work for the Diocese in Europe. I visited three Anglican Churches.

None of them had signs that bid me welcome, none had the times of ser-vices listed and none said that they were "Anglican." One did say "English."

What about our terminology? Back to McDonalds—and you imagine McDonalds saying, well because of this or that, in Spain we better call McDonalds Restaurants—McCarlos? or in England will we call it McSmiths? What people know is McDonalds. So we have Church of this or that, Anglican, Episcopal and more. I remember once receiving a mes-sage at the ACO that St. Johns Church phoned me. Well, no number was given, no city, no denomination, no way of saying who was who.

In other words, when communication is broken, it's broken! Our symbols say things about who we are; they are important.

The Compasrose is an attractive symbol, and I urge its use widely as a sym-bol of the Anglican Communion, the Churches in Communion with the See of Canterbury. One flare I would like to raise is the use of the term Anglican being adopted by non-Anglican dissident Churches, especially in the USA. It is very sad. Just yesterday I spent some time with bishops from Province IX of ECUSA, the Latin American dioceses. One diocese in particular is under fierce attack from self-appointed "Anglican" bishops who are claiming the rights to the name. How sad.

Another interesting symbol we have is that of the primates. Well, if you have ever heard Archbishop Emeritus Desmond Tutu on this, you know what I mean. These primates call themselves Primus, Presiding, President and Archbishop, here and there. Yes, it is autonomous but does it communicate well? The person on the street does not have the time or energy to sort out our subtle ways. One of the most often asked question at Westminster Abbey is "Is this a Roman Catholic Church?" Here, where more people are exposed to Anglicanism than in any other place, the average person has no idea that this is a living witness to our faith as received and expressed by Anglicans.

The symbol of the Anglican family is important. Our encounter with the wider family on visits or at meetings like this is true communication. This is why the visits of the Archbishop of Canterbury are so important. He does not go alone, he is not a pope, but a symbol of 70 million people.

Communication is a two-way street. I beg you to be diligent in getting information to us. Each time Nicola Currie and I sit down to put together *Anglican World*, we realise we have enough good news to span double the pages. The good news is there. I am sick and tired of the perpetual telling of bad news even by our own Church press. I say, "shame on them." Of course we must be honest and clear and transparent, but for the sake of the kingdom we must enable and inspire with the good news that is taking place in every Province. Good news whether preached or printed is to inspire. Look at England. Many people think the *Church Times* is an official paper of the Church of England; well, it is not. Yet for many it is the only voice of English Church news, at least the most prominent. We must not rely on others to tell our story.

Frankly, if we do not communicate we are lost.

The Lambeth Conference is a place for a major emphasis on communication, and we have a 50 member volunteer team coming to Canterbury for that event. The years coming up to the Primates' Meeting in 1997 in Jerusalem, the Lambeth Conference, the next ACC meeting and indeed the proposed Anglican congress are our times to shine, to be known, to share the faith as we have received it with others. Now is specially God-given time to be on the move. Let us not be foolish and let it pass by.

The angel told the women to go and tell. Now I admire and have great affection for all of you, and though I will not call you "angels," I do want to hear from you the command and commission for my ministry. I pray God that ACC will commission me to "go tell" and I ask for the strength and ability to do the same. For Christ's sake. Amen.

Celebrating the Gifts of God among the People of God: The Ministry of the Anglican Communion Office at the United Nations

by the Rt Revd James Hamilton Ottley
Anglican Observer at the United Nations

Sunday, 13 October 1996

I am grateful for the opportunity to be with you here this evening. I am especially thankful to be able to share the exciting news about the ministry of the Anglican Communion Office at the United Nations.

Whenever I speak I like to let people know a little bit about the person who is speaking. My father was born in St Vincent, a small island off Trinidad, and I am sure that my great grandfather came from Africa. My mother was born in Costa Rica and her parents came from the island of Jamaica. My wife is from Puerto Rico and I was born in the Republic of Panama. Therefore, I speak some English and some Spanish. In this little country of Panama, there is an Anglican Church. The Anglican Church has been in Panama for about 144 years.

There are very few places in the world where you and I might visit and not find an Anglican Church. We are the second international, global Church in the world. And, as a Church, we have been in the forefront defending the issues of peace and justice in the world. Examples are the work of Archbishop Desmond Tutu in South Africa and Archbishop Robin Eames in Ireland.

On one occasion a General scheduled a visit to a particular military base. On that particular base there was a particular soldier who always seemed to say the wrong thing, or was in the wrong place at the wrong time. So the Commanding Officer of that post thought that on the day of the General's visit he would definitely place that particular soldier in the kitchen, far from the eyes of the General.

Lo and behold, the day came and the General came, and you know where he went? To the kitchen. And you know who he saw? The soldier.

"Soldier," said the General, "what are you doing?"
"Washing pots, Sir," the soldier replied.
"Washing pots?" inquired the General.

"Yes, Sir!" the soldier exclaimed.

"Soldier, if this was a national emergency and we needed every soldier, what do you think that you would be doing?" asked the General.

The soldier stopped, he scratched his head, he thought for a moment.

"Washing pots more rapidly, Sir!" he exclaimed.

We do what we can. We do the best that we can, with what we have.

I begin then with the premise that we are who we are, and that all people, all people, are inherently good. We are all made by God, in the image of God. We exist because of God's grace, created to love and to be loved.

If this premise is true, then it means that in order for this world to be a better world, then all the people of God need peace, security, health, education, shelter, food and equal opportunity. People must be at the centre, the focus of all that we do.

In Psalm 137:4, we read, "How could we sing the Lord's song in a foreign land?" This was said in the context of a time when people looked back on their past, wept about their past, and looked with despair and some trembling, but with some hope to the future. We live in a world which is still filled with many similar concerns and fears. As Christians, as people of faith, we are called to witness our faith in a world whose values and value systems may be in conflict with our own, and so we too feel like foreigners in an unfamiliar, foreign land. How then can we sing, what shall our song be?

The Anglican Communion is in this world and we believe that it must respond to the basic needs of human beings, as it responds to their spiritual need for nurturing. The Anglican Communion offers its ministry with the following as part of its ethos:

a.   We are a Church rooted in Holy Scripture.

We believe that the Holy Scriptures of the Old and New Testaments contain all things necessary to salvation and being the rule and ultimate standard of faith (Lambeth Conference 1888, Resolution 11).

b.   We are also a Church who believes in the value and power of tradition and in reason, in experience.

As Anglicans, we believe in the Bible, in the power of tradition. The Bible, the Book of Books about God, grace, creation, the acts of God, compassion and hope, is definitely at the core of who we are. The past is important to us, but we also believe in the right to analysis, reflection and action. We are people of different cultures, languages, of different ethnic backgrounds—a richly diverse global family, held together by our common roots. As Anglicans, our faith is rooted in Holy Scriptures and the Holy Eucharist, and lived out in evangelism and service. We believe, we pray, we celebrate, we evangelise, we serve.

I said once, and I repeat here, the beauty and the mystery of Anglicanism lies in its ability to honour, respect and celebrate diversity. As the world becomes more interdependent, and interactions with other races and cultures are more frequent, respect for diversity is imperative. Mutual responsibility and respect becomes a must for all religions, for all who look to God for purpose and strength.

The Anglican United Nations Office has identified five main areas of concern: human rights, the international economy, the advancement of women, the environment, and disarmament.

1.   Human rights

In the area of human rights, as part of our work, this Office investigates and responds to violations of human rights, as we are able, whether it is in Pakistan, the Sudan, Guatemala, Argentina, Burundi, Rwanda, Liberia, USA or Mexico, to name a few countries who have been referred to us. Our report on human rights is available for your review.

2.   The international economy

With respect to the international economy, our ministry has focused on the international debt crisis. The Copenhagen Declaration on Social Development states: "We acknowledge that our societies must respond more effectively to the material and spiritual needs of individuals, their families and the communities in which they live throughout our diverse countries and regions. We must do so as a matter of urgency, but also as a matter of sustained and unshakable commitment through the years ahead."

The Declaration also states the global wealth of nations has multiplied seven-fold in the past 50 years, and international trade has grown even more dramatically. However, it is noted that the gap between developed and many developing countries, particularly the least developed countries, has widened. The gap between those who have and those who do not have basic economic resources has widened. Despite the economic growth that has been observed, about 1.5 billion people in the world today live in absolute poverty, most of whom go hungry every day. Seventy percent of those people are women and children.

Over 120 million people world-wide are officially unemployed and many more underemployed. Secondly, it should be noted that more women than men live in absolute poverty. And, finally, it must be recognised that some of the political and economic violence which we experience in our world is a spiral which is exacerbated by the debt crisis. This Office has been involved in this life or death' issue. In a Greek drama, a prominent character expresses this thought which came to mind as I developed this presentation, "Life begins on the other side of despair." While this is true for some, despair means death for others. The problems of hunger, and of despair, mean death to many. We hosted a conference on the International Debt Crisis. Copies of the report are available.

In preparation for the 'Social Summit,' the Anglican United Nations Office participated in a conference relating to ethics, spirituality, and social progress. Here is part of what I said then: "In the Church we speak often of the respect of the dignity of every human being, and in that we include children, women and men, with the understanding that all people need to be respected regardless of their poverty or wealth, their culture, their language, their social standing, their gender, their religion or the colour of their skin."

3. The advancement of women

Another area of concern of this Office is the advancement of women.

Speaking to the plenary, I also said: "It troubles me to see a world where human beings are victimised on the basis of their gender. It troubles me to hear that women are treated as second-class citizens. It troubles me to hear painful stories of young children who are denied food, clothing and shelter, the basic necessities of life, simply because they were born female. It troubles me to see pictures of bodies of women who were set on fire and burned to death because a dowry was too small. It worries me to see refugees and displaced persons who are wandering aimlessly and internally uprooted, with no place to go nor no one to turn to. It troubles me to think that a girl-child has been denied quality health care and access to education."

This Office was instrumental in taking the leadership role on a statement on gender, that we believe impacted the discussions on gender at the

Fourth World Conference on Women. Copies of that statement are here for your perusal.

We have been involved in discussions on the banning of anti-personnel landmines, micro credit, especially as they affect women and children.

At this point let me say a few words about landmines. In the last 50 years landmines have become famous as weapons. Approximately 64 countries are contaminated with over 110 million uncleared landmines, claiming a civilian victim every 15 minutes, or approximately 2,000 victims per month. Two to five million new landmines are placed in the soil each year; there are approximately 1,000 million stockpiled, waiting to be sowed, and the arms industry continues to produce five to ten million mines each year. Anti-personnel landmines are sold for $3.00 to $10.00. They can be home-made.

The Report of the United Nations General Secretary (September 6, 1994) states that it would take about 1,100 years and $33 billion to clear landmines that are already planted.

4.   The environment

The fourth area of our concern has to do with the environment. If this is to be a better world, then our air, water, flora, and fauna must be protected. When God created the world and looked at it, God said it was good. We must preserve the sanctity of creation. It was from the dust of the earth that human beings were formed and from whence all living things have sprung, according to Genesis 2:5-8. Thus the relationship was formed between human beings and all of creation. If we destroy the environment, we destroy ourselves.

This Office has taken a very active part in the whole issue of the environment. We were in Brazil. And, just recently, the Revd. Dr. Jeff Golliher represented us at the Conference on Habitat in Istanbul, Turkey. A copy of his presentation to the conference is also available.

5.   Disarmament

In the area of disarmament, we are currently conducting research into how Church structures at the local level can get involved in promoting the cause of peace. Part of this involves lobbying governments and international organisations to support measures which eliminate illegal landmines, the sale and transfer or arms and munitions, and other weapons of mass destruction.

6.   Other issues

Many of you have probably seen the headlines of the horrible massacre that took place in Rwanda in April of 1994. I was asked by the Archbishop of Canterbury to visit Rwanda last year to prepare the way for his visit. I was invited to Burundi, to evaluate the crisis and explore peace-making options. This Office has been invited to Geneva to speak on landmines and human rights, and to Colombia, Ecuador, to speak on gender and women, and on Anglicanism. We have been asked to share our findings in Honduras, London, and throughout the USA. Our report on violence against women, prepared by Ruby Norfolk, has been reproduced in the newspaper of the International Federation of Women Lawyers and has been circulated widely around the world.

In a nutshell, our ministry has a global reach. We have been consulted on the issue of Tibet, on indigenous people's rights in Argentina, on a UK prisoner in Pakistan, on chemical waste in Panama. We are also working as a liaison between UNICEF and Liberia.

We have been involved with educational seminars on the rights of the child, sponsored by UNICEF and carried out by the NGO Working Group on the Rights of the Child, of which we are active members.

The Anglican UN Office assumes a prophetic, educational, and pastoral ministry

We believe that this office has a prophetic ministry, an educational ministry and a pastoral ministry to perform. As a prophetic ministry, we confront injustices. We call upon nations to put people at the centre of policy making and enforcement. Our pastoral ministry needs to focus on members of the diplomatic community. Diplomats and their families are people with the same fears, anxieties, joys and hope. We need to find ways to let them know that this Office is here for them.

Just recently, at the conclusion of the celebration of a Eucharist here at the Episcopal Church Center Chapel, a young man from the United Nations, who had attended the service, came over to me and said that he wanted to talk to a clergy person. We went up to my office and did just that. Johncy Itty tells of similar stories.

We have been part of a partnership with UNICEF, concerning Liberia; what to do with the child soldier. We are exploring other partnerships with UNICEF and UNIFEM and will do so also with UNDP. Our pastoral ministry is local and, in a very peculiar sense, international.

Our educational ministry helps members of the Anglican Communion to understand how our global interdependence is affecting many of us differently. We write briefing papers to help us all understand these forces and processes. We weigh the effects and possible solutions that will alleviate suffering and promote dignity. We do research and share the information as needed. Even as we disseminate information to the Anglican Communion, we seek to educate the United Nations on the harm caused by some international policies, and, of course, we always seek to educate ourselves. I have requested that every report, briefing paper, or article ends with questions, ideas, which can lead into further educational possibilities.

This is a very exciting ministry at a very exciting time in our history. We have been blessed in our Office with an excellent staff: Ruby Norfolk, Associate for the Advancement of Women; Johncy Itty, Associate for Human Rights; Jeff Golliher (part-time), Associate for the Environment; and Barbara Hernandez, Administrative Assistant; and Nancy Cortner, as part-time Grants Coordinator. We have a wonderful Advisory Council and a host of friends.

Many people have shared their enthusiasm about the impact of our ministry. Theologically and incarnationally, we are all yoked together and there is no better example than these partners who shared the following comments with us.

The Fellowship of Reconciliation, Task Force on Latin America and the Caribbean, a non-governmental organisation, wrote to us and said: "Thank you for signing the August 30 (1995) letter to President Clinton on toxic contamination and clean-up of US military bases in Panama. "The letter was a strong signal to the Clinton administration that US religious and peace leaders want our country to be accountable for the mess the military generates. We've been notified by the National Security Council that President Clinton was briefed on the issue prior to the meeting with President Perez Balladares on September 6 (1995), and that a response will be forthcoming.

We are pleased to note that some of our material has been considered to be helpful to those in leadership positions. Ambassador John Weston, the British Ambassador to the United Nations, noted: "Thank you for your letter of August 23, with which you enclosed a report on your recent visit to Burundi. I have taken the liberty of copying it to relevant FCO Departments in London, as I am sure they will find it helpful."

We are especially pleased by the prayerful support and good wishes we receive from some of the prominent Church leaders within the Anglican Communion. In a recent letter to me from the Church of the Province of

Southern Africa, it was noted: "Archbishop Desmond (Tutu) wishes to congratulate you on the fine production of your publication Anglican Observer at the United Nations. It is very informative and occupies a special place in the Anglican Communion."

A number of Church leaders have expressed their support for this ministry in various ways. A few of these persons from various parts of the Communion have shared their views by phone. (At this point in the presentation there was an audio-visual presentation.)

Thanks to God, our ministry has touched and continues to touch the lives of a number of people.

As we talk about the UN, as we speak about the world-wide Anglican Communion, we need to also share the great capacity for sharing information through the World Wide Web. We can appreciate this in a presentation which Dr. Itty has prepared on the computer screen. (At this point in the presentation there was a display.)

As you can see, God has given us a number of opportunities to witness our faith in this world. This is but one small example. The Anglican Communion Office is earnestly committed to a ministry in serving the Communion at the United Nations.

To make this ministry possible, Trinity Parish has been very generous in the past and up to this year gave us a grant of $75,000.00. The Presiding Bishop of the Episcopal Church was very generous in his contribution to support this ministry. There have been a number of gifts from our friends, and many others have expressed their commitment to this ministry. There have also been many other people who have volunteered their talents, skills and gifts to support this ministry.

We have initiated a good thing here. We want to move forward. We believe in people. We believe that God intends for all people to give of the little or much of what they possess. It may be "washing pots;" it may be the sharing of ideas, or the sharing of resources. We cannot do it alone. We need help.

As I said before, we live in a world which is still filled with many similar concerns and fears. As people of God we are called to witness our faith in a world whose values and value systems may be in conflict with our own, and so we too feel like foreigners in an unfamiliar land. How then can we sing? What shall our song be?...

We believe that this Office can establish the kind of partnerships, the educational opportunities, the prophetic ministry and the pastoral care which is centred on people that could help us all make this world better for all of us.

The Anglican United Nations Office needs your support. It needs for you to stand with us, enabling this ministry to be an instrument for peace and justice.

So let us stand and sing to the Lord a new song, we who are part of the mosaic of the world. As a people of faith, let us stand together and celebrate the gifts of God among the people of God in all that we do in our ministry (as a Communion). Let us boldly share with others the richness of who we are and what we are as faithful stewards and servants in God's most glorious creation.

Thank you. May the Lord continue to bless us all.

Report on Rwanda
by the Rt Revd David Birney

Wednesday, 16 October 1996

A new school, beautiful school, a large school of over 70 rooms. No students, no teachers—only skeletons in room after room—the dry bones of some of the more than 50,000 human beings gathered by government troops with the promise, assurance, that they would be protected, only to be shot and hacked to death. Their bodies were thrown in great pits by the soldiers who were obeying the 10 commandments. These were not the commandments given through Moses to the Hebrew people, but the commandments developed by the ruling majority party of Rwanda, to justify the murder of approximately one million of their fellow countrymen. They were members of the minority ethnic group with whom they had intermarried, with whom they attended school, worked together, played together, and prayed to the one God together. They were brother and sister human beings who shared the same language, the same culture, the same history. There is no word in any language to describe the absolute horror of the genocide of 1994. In the midst of the total chaos which followed, refugees from the minority group and more moderate members of the majority, who had been living in neighbouring countries, returned home and overthrew the majority government, sending hundreds of thousands of them into Zaire, Tanzania, Burundi, Uganda, as refugees and establishing a new government committed to the pursuit of justice, reconciliation and peace.

In the aftermath of 1994, one could ask—why did this happen? What evil, demonic force was at work that led one group of people to shout a loud "no" in answer to the question, "Am I my brother's keeper?"

Many reasons, many explanations, many excuses, many rationalisations are offered. At their root, I believe is one overriding reality, and that is that too many people believed a lie, a gross falsehood, to be the truth. It was a lie, a falsehood having its foundation in the colonial era of Rwanda (and Burundi's) history, when the Europeans made the fateful decision that the minority group was in every way a superior race to the majority, more European in physical appearance, therefore brighter and more intelligent than the majority and more capable of being educated and trained.

When the winds of self-government, self-determination, and independence began blowing over the African continent, it became obvious to the European power that the majority group would come into power. Therefore, they shifted their allegiance and support from the minority group to the majority and continued this support in various forms up to the time of the genocide.

This lie, this falsehood of the superiority of one group over another rooted itself deeply in the consciousness of the people. It became truth, a horrible truth, and it gave birth to deeply held prejudice, suspicion, lack of trust, hatred, resentment, and a justification for persecution and murder within the two groups of the population. The government and military leaders of the majority referred to the minority as "cockroaches," and exhorted the common man to deal with the minority as they would with cockroaches in their home. Step on them and mash them to death.

The Roman Catholic Church claims the allegiance of the majority of Rwandan Christians. The Anglican and other non-Roman Churches are considerably smaller. Despite their differences, one must ask, "Do they not share a belief in the one God; do they not both proclaim that man's salvation is found in God's son, the Christ; do they not both seek God's will, God's guidance, God's strength in the Holy Spirit of God; do they not share the same story of redemption as found in Holy Scripture in which the God of justice, the God of love, the God of reconciliation, the God of peace, reveals himself?"

If the answer is "yes," which I passionately believe it to be, where was their common voice, their common witness when the genocide began? Where was your voice; where was mine? Who dared risk standing up and shouting "stop"? Who dared to proclaim in the name of God that murder is evil, wrong, and an insult, a slap in the face, to the God in whose image humankind is created?

The voice of much of the Church in Rwanda was silent; the voice of much of the world-wide body of Christ was not heard. The voice of the United Nations which had proclaimed after the Nazi atrocities in Germany, "never again," could barely be heard. Had the Church, had the human family sold its soul to the devil? The throne of Caesar seemed to have replaced the altar of God as the object of man's devotion.

In the aftermath of the genocide, much of the Christian Church in Rwanda is struggling to regain its soul. Some of the bishops and clergy of both the Anglican and Roman Churches are believed to be implicated in the planning and the execution of the genocide. Some have been killed; some are living in exile; others are in prison. The trust of Christians in their spiritual leaders is being sorely tested. After more than two years there are still some dioceses of the Anglican Church without episcopal leadership. One bishop has been denied legal recognition by the government because of allegations against him rooted in the genocide. The Church has yet to be able to agree on a constitution for the ordering of its life. A growing number of clergy and people are deserting the Anglican Church in protest against its apparent paralysis. A growing group has come together to press for reforms in the Church, in an attempt to free it from some of the abuses of the past to which the House of Bishops appears to be turning a deaf ear. The government is becoming increasingly impatient with the power and other struggles in the Church which are preventing it from taking its role as a force for justice, reconciliation, peace, and morality in society.

Yet, in the midst of the present confusion, there exists a reminder of God's people in both the majority and minority groups. Men and women on fire with the love of God, who in the terrible days of the genocide, proclaimed by word and deed that in Jesus all persons have been reconciled to God and each other, and who today by their witness are calling the Church to a revival in the spirit, to a new birth and to a new life that matches or excels in power the East African revival which had its birth in Rwanda over 50 years ago.

The Anglican Communion owes a great deal of gratitude to his Grace, the Archbishop of Canterbury, to Canon John Peterson, and to Canon Andrew Deuchar, for heeding St. Paul's words to the Christians in Corinthians that when one member of the body suffers, the whole body suffers. A short time following the genocide the Archbishop, accompanied by the others, visited Rwanda to express solidarity with the Church there, to encourage the new government in its quest for justice and peace, and to share with them a vision of a reborn Church and nation. Two years later appreciation is still being expressed for this act of love, encouragement, and solidarity. The visit has been followed up by other initiatives from Lambeth and the ACC.

I pray that this gathering will not only applaud these initiatives but offer its ongoing support and encouragement to the Archbishop, Canon Peterson and the staff of ACC in their ongoing relationships with the Anglican Church in Rwanda.

I commend to you for your prayer the people of Rwanda, the government and the Church, in its struggle to move from the bonds of the past into a present and future in bonding to the spirit of God, reflecting in its common life the Lord Jesus who came not to be served, but to serve.

In this vein, I would ask you also to urge the leadership of the Church in

Rwanda to press forward to discover an acceptable, legal, and locally approved way to elect and consecrate bishops for those dioceses without episcopal leadership and, soon afterwards, to call a Provincial Synod in which a constitution for the Province can be agreed upon.

Finally, in the quest for peace, may the Church never abandon its call to be God's instrument of justice and reconciliation, without which no peace can be a lasting peace.

Sisters and brothers, pray that the schools and valleys of dry bones in Rwanda and throughout the world may be brought to life, having been touched by the word and spirit of the Lord.

SECTION REPORTS

The apparent success of ACC-10 was, I believe, due to the careful planning in asking members to look to the future. Indeed, in the areas of worship, ministry, relating to society, communicating our belief in God, it was possible for people from various walks of life, various cultures, various expressions of Anglicanism, to focus together on these foundational aspects of our work. Importantly, it was at this level that friendships were formed and positive dialogue occurred.

Section 1 Report
Looking to the Future in Worship

CHAIR:	The Very Revd David J. L. Richardson, Australia
SECRETARY:	The Revd Barbara Clay, Canada
COMMUNICATOR:	Canon James Rosenthal, Staff
CO-ORDINATOR FOR LITURGY:	The Revd Paul Gibson, Canada
MEMBERS:	The Rt Revd Maxwell S. C. Anikwenwa, Nigeria
	Mr Samuel K. Arap Ng'eny, Kenya
	The Revd Austin R. Cooper, USA
	The Revd Canon Colin Craston, England
	The Most Revd Brian N. Davis, Aotearoa, New Zealand and Polynesia
	Prof. Adrian Deheer-Amissah, West Africa
	The Most Revd Robert Eames, Ireland
	The Rt Revd Samuel Si Htay, Myanmar
	The Very Revd Robert Jeffery, England
	The Rt Revd Bernard Malango, Central Africa
	The Most Revd Livingstone Mpaylanyi-Nkoyoyo, Uganda
	Mr Antonio Ortega, Mexico
	Mr Theodore Phailbus, Pakistan
	Ms Sylvia Scarf, Wales
	The Rt Revd Dinis S. Sengulane, Southern Africa
	The Rt Revd Sumio Takatsu, Brazil
	The Rt Revd Tevita Talanoa, Papua New Guinea
	The Revd Hector Zabala, Southern Cone

Preamble

The Church's self-offering happens as Christian people offer themselves to God and to their neighbours in actions which speak of love and goodness, of mercy and justice. Such self-offering is identified as Christian when the Church meets together as a visible body to worship the Lord, especially in Eucharistic worship. Worship is our response to God's call to us to be in relationship with him. The very visibility of worship means that concern for worship cannot be sundered from concern for evangelism.

Nevertheless, many who belong to the Church report that they find worship irrelevant to their lives. Among these are the young who view worship as the religious expression of the elderly. Yet the liturgy of the Church is not and cannot be allowed to be the private property of any particular group nor of any particular individual, for it is the common possession of the whole people of God.

And what is it for? We offer praise in worship not because God needs our worship but because we need to offer it. Worship is concerned with helping people to bring their lives to God, their whole lives, and having brought them, to find them transformed by grace. Worship is throughout about renewal: the renewal of persons, the renewal of the Church, the renewal of the world.

When Christ's sacrifice and its power are proclaimed and known in worship, the liturgy is the means by which the crucified and risen Lord draws the world to himself and so to the Father.

This Section is divided into five smaller groups to discuss different aspects of worship.

Group 1:   To provide a liberating and healing liturgy that is thoroughly based on the fullness of God.

1.1   We encounter God in the Bible as the friend and liberator of orphans, widows, strangers, pilgrims, slaves and outcasts. One of the pattern-setting stories in the Bible is the account of the Israelites' salvation from slavery in Egypt. Jesus, as Saviour, reveals God as the power of salvation for everyone. He ate and drank with notorious sinners, blessed children, and treated women as equals. He himself assumed the form of a servant (Philippians 2.7), emptying himself of all signs of dignity and power. He died as an outcast, literally outside the city walls (Hebrews 13.12). He insisted that those who wanted to be leaders in the community of his followers must be servants of all (Mark 9.35). His community is, in fact, a fellowship of servants who are becoming his friends (John 15.15) and acceptance of that role is one of the few conditions of membership.

1.2   A recurring theme in the Bible is that God is not infinitely far away but, *"in the midst,"* dwelling among the people who accept the gift of freedom (Psalm 46). *"Great in your midst is the holy one of Israel,"* wrote Isaiah (12.6). We need to recover this sense of the divine presence as the power of liberation and equality, working from within to break down the divisions of gender, race, status, power and even styles of religious devotion, because it is fundamental to the teaching and ministry of Jesus.

1.3   Our liturgy must again reflect this biblical vision. Our readings and prayers should reflect the stories of women and children and all those whose marginalization (for whatever reason) is contrary to our Christian commitment to freedom and equality. Our liturgy should begin on a note of praise to God through Christ for the new style of life we have been given. Only after we have been united in praise for our baptismal freedom should we turn to instruction. We must listen to the worship aspirations of young people, which may give the whole congregation new insights into styles of liturgy which celebrate and therefore appropriate God's gift of a reign of freedom and healing.

Group 2:   To provide a liberating and healing liturgy that enables a praxis for mission, i.e., "Go! Tell! Do!"

2.1   As a praxis for mission, our liturgy should incorporate all the joy which flows from the assurance of the forgiveness of sin. Worship, in word and action, will need to be accessible to both newcomer and the faithful alike. The educational aspect is essential, as is the element of joy. What is experienced and taught within the preaching of the Word and the celebration of the sacraments, both Baptism and Eucharist, must enable the people of God to "Go, tell, do" to fulfil their mission to a broken world. This is a challenge to those committed to proclamation of the Word to recover the ministry of preaching.

2.2   The prayers offered at the liturgy should model for lay and clergy leaders how to lead others in prayer, so that with confidence, in difficult situations, all may be helped to use their gifts in an appropriate manner: those charged with visitation of the sick and shut-in, extraordinary ministers of Holy Communion, house groups, leaders of prayer groups and healing services—all can minister effectively.

2.3   Education and preparation are key elements in all that we do. Lay people who are acknowledged as leaders of the larger community, whether in business, education, government, or wherever, should be encouraged to take responsibility in Church assemblies and encounters as well.

Group 3:   To provide a liberating and healing liturgy that is a celebration of the senses and all of God's gifts.

3.1   Our senses are God-given and they, with all God gifts to us, express the communication of God with all creation. Renewal comes as worshippers engage through sights, sounds, smells, with customs and culture, while maintaining a link with tradition, as set forth in our experience of being catholic and reformed.

3.2   A variety of styles and a balance in leadership enable participation on a broader base, making it possible for laity to move rightfully from the posture of spectator to that of leader, alongside bishops, priests and deacons, each with their respective roles. It is important that what is considered essential is honoured, while at the same time those planning worship need not be afraid of fresh ideas and new expressions.

3.3   The signs and symbols we use in our celebration (bread, wine, water, the cross, actions in the liturgy) are often learned at an early age, and it is good that they should be. There is a responsibility to the tradition to teach them. It is good that the faithful understand why passing the peace, using incense, raising our hands in praise, liturgical dance, to name but a few things, become part of our worship. Liturgy must compel and attract young and old, rich and poor, male and female. Moving from "habit" to "renewal" makes what we do and what we say true celebration.

3.4   Leading worship with confidence and a sense of purpose will move God's people into the future in a way that will make a difference in the lives of those who gather as a community. To such a community, others will naturally be attracted as worship moves us to encounter and action in the world.

Group 4:   To provide a liberating and healing liturgy that honours the mystery of life and death, ritualising life passages in various contexts.

4.1   All human life is expressed in terms of ritual acts which enable people to relate to each other in community and life to have order and balance. Many of these rituals go unacknowledged, like forms of greetings between people, the routines of daily life, communal meals and the patterns followed in business and industry to enable communication and cooperation.

4.2   Other forms of ritual surround key points in human life relating to birth, death, adolescence, and marriage. There are also rituals relating to the cycles of nature and the seasons. All these may be given a religious context and significance. The Church often provides the place and manner of these rituals.

4.3   In all parts of the world, inherited patterns of religious ritual have been questioned as outmoded and regarded as pagan or dismissed as meaningless. At the same time New Age movements and others are seeking new patterns of ritual which relate to life today. One of the problems which surfaces is that for many life has become dysfunctional and lacking in focus. This makes the use of rituals hard to assimilate.

4.4   The Church has the opportunity to acknowledge the important place of ritual as relates to the whole person and to affirm the psychosomatic and communal nature of the human personality. We should be aware of the danger that, by unquestioned acceptance of rituals, we may affirm things which are degrading human dignity.

4.5   In seeking to re-establish rituals in the Church, we need to respect the traditions of the past and learn how to use them in a way which affirms human dignity and justice. We see opportunities for new patterns of ritual in relation both to the fundamental rites of passage on the one hand and events such as finding employment, celebrating retirement, celebrating life, and reclaiming in Christ's name relationships which have been broken by evil. For instance, Church practice could (without compromising the centrality of Christ's saving grace) adapt such rituals as

- introducing a child to the sun (a ceremony performed by Kenyan women four days after the birth of a child, in which the infant is taken out of the house for the first time),

- calling the child (a Kenyan clan ceremony about a month after birth in which the child is given a name linked with the names of ancestors),

- rituals (recently developed in some Western Provinces) for use after a miscarriage or a stillbirth,

- rituals on the conclusion of a war, to celebrate a good harvest, or in relation to certain kinds of death.

4.6   In some places some of these rituals are already in the process of incorporation into Christian practice. For instance, members of the the Mothers' Union visit a newly-delivered mother to welcome the new baby with gifts and prayer.

Group 5:   To provide a liberating and healing liturgy that upholds and informs the priesthood of all believers in their Baptism and in their daily work and worship.

5.1   In recent years there has been a growing recovery of the notion of baptismal priesthood. This is not the priesthood of each believer individually, but the priesthood of the whole body and therefore of each member as they share in the life of the body. There has been recognition that the word "priest" as it refers to an ordered ministry is usually derived from the Greek word "presbyter", although in the ancient religions it has another meaning. If we are going to speak of "baptismal priesthood" we must decide what meaning we are giving to the word, and how it applies to Christians and their community.

5.2   In many ancient religions, and also in the Old Testament, priesthood is about the offering of sacrifice, often by killing an animal or destroying an object, to make a bridge (pontifex) between the worlds of sacred and profane. A priest acts for the people, performing actions which bind them together in themselves and with their gods or God.

5.3   The attribution of priesthood to Jesus Christ is a significant theme in the New Testament and in subsequent atonement theology. His death is described as a sacrificial action in which he is both priest and victim, a theme developed especially in the letter to the Hebrews. But we may miss the point of his priesthood if we think of his death only in terms of ancient religious rites, as another but more important event in the long history of the practice of sacrifice.

5.4   We believe it is important to set the sacrifice of Jesus Christ within the framework of his life his ministry of teaching and caring in which traditional and accepted assumptions about power, status, and religious privilege were reversed. His sacrifice consisted of a life devoted to healing the sick and eating and drinking with outcasts and sinners, and we must see his death within the framework of that whole. The death of Jesus displays the totality of self-giving to which all his life was devoted.

5.5   The New Testament describes the sacrificial priesthood of Christians also in terms of their style of living. Paul appeals to the Romans to present their bodies as a living sacrifice, which is their spiritual worship (12.1). Like Jesus, their sacrifice is to be seen in their living; their priesthood builds the bridge between the physical and spiritual dimensions of human nature. Justin, an early Christian writer, told his pagan neighbours who accused Christians of impiety because they did not offer the usual sacrifices of their culture that the sacrifice of Christians was thanksgiving. The authentic marks of Christian sacrifice remain loving commitment to others (i.e. justice and responsibility) and thanksgiving to God for creation and the gift of new life in freedom, and these are the marks of the priesthood of the baptised community.

5.6   We do not offer animals or food or libations of drink or flowers or even money. Because we have already been made to share in the life of Jesus whose whole life was sacrificial, we too offer our lives in thanksgiving to God. This is our baptismal priesthood.

5.7   We are aware that many lay people today are disenchanted with the roles that the Church offers to them. Leaders and their goals seem far away. Priesthood appears to have been taken over by presbyters. Worship seems unrelated to the rest of their lives. We must renew not only the texts of our liturgies (a task massively undertaken throughout the Communion), but also the style in which our liturgies are celebrated, so the baptised priesthood of the Church may recognise its true vocation. The liturgy must constantly remind us of the connection between the Eucharist and Jesus' table fellowship with those whom others disvalued. It must also remind us of the hunger of those who have no bread, and of the personal care he gave to his followers in washing their feet before dinner.

Conclusion

6.1　The purpose of common prayer is to enable people to recognise their togetherness, to participate actively in the actions which represent our faith, and to convey a sense that the actions of worship belong to them. The function of the ordained is not to lead from outside the assembly and from above the assembly, but from within the assembly (as fellow members) and from underneath the assembly (like the invisible foundations on which a building rests), enabling the whole community to recognise that the authentic sacrifice, the sacrifice of Jesus Christ, is to be realised in their lives as they are shaped by responsibility and thanksgiving.

6.2　The prophets remind us again and again that God does not need worship; God needs justice and kindness and the humble friendship of pilgrims. It is we who need worship because it is in turning our eyes away from ourselves to the holiness of God that we find our true destiny. A hymn-writer, gazing in wonder at the appearance of the stars at evening, saw in the night sky a likeness to the spiritual quest which all our worship mirrors.

> Now all the heavenly splendour
> breaks forth in starlight tender
> from myriad worlds unknown;
> and we, this marvel seeing,
> forget our selfish being
> for joy of beauty not our own.

Recommendations from Section 1

7.1　We need to recover this sense of the divine presence as the power of liberation and equality working from within to break down the divisions of gender, race, status, power and even styles of religious devotion, because it is fundamental to the teaching and ministry of Jesus.

7.2   We must listen to the worship aspirations of young people which may give the whole congregation new insights into styles of liturgy which celebrate and therefore appropriate God's gift of a reign of freedom and healing.

7.3   What is experienced and taught within the preaching of the word and the celebration of the sacraments, both Baptism and Eucharist, must enable the people of God to, "Go, tell, do," to fulfil their mission to a broken world. This is a challenge to those committed to proclamation of the word to recover the ministry of preaching.

7.4   Lay people who are acknowledged as leaders of the larger community, whether in business, education, government or wherever, should be encouraged to take responsibility in Church assemblies and encounters as well.

7.5   It is important that what is considered essential is honoured, while at the same time those planning worship need not be afraid of fresh ideas and new expressions.

7.6   In seeking to re-establish rituals in the Church, we need to respect the traditions of the past and learn how to use them in a way which affirms human dignity and justice.

We must renew not only the texts of our liturgies but also the style in which our liturgies are celebrated, so the baptised priesthood of the Church may recognise its true vocation.

Section 2 Report
Looking to the Future in Ministry

"Patterns of Ministry for the New Millennium"

CHAIR:	The Revd Samuel I. Koshiishi, Japan
SECRETARY:	The Rt Revd John Paterson, New Zealand
COMMUNICATOR:	Deaconess Margaret Rodgers, Australia
MEMBERS:	Dr Christina Baxter, England
	The Revd Basimaki Byabasaija, Zaire
	The Rt Rev Sylvestre Tibafa, Zaire
	The Rt Revd Simon Chiwanga, Tanzania
	Mr Mawaraidzo Kututwa, Central Africa
	The Rt Revd James P. Mason, Melanesia
	The Rt Revd Michael H. G. Mayes, Ireland
	Mr Edward S. Mungati, Uganda
	The Rt Revd Charles J. Mwaigoga, Tanzania
	The Rt Revd Phillip Newell, Australia
	The Revd Prudence Ngarambe, Rwanda
	The Rt Rev Vinod A. R. Peter, India
	The Revd J. Prabhakara Rao, India
	Lady Brenda Sheil, Ireland
	The Rt Revd Peter Sugandhar, India
	The Rt Revd Sylvestre Tibafa, Zaire
	Mr Robert Tong, Australia
	Mr Bernard Turner, West Indies
	The Revd Canon David G. P. Williams, Wales

Preamble

Surrounded by the beauty and busyness of this ancient city, and encouraged by the warm welcome, hospitality and fellowship of the people of the Anglican Diocese of Panama, the members of Section II of ACC-10 turned their consideration and discussions towards the future shape and context of the ministry of Anglicans into the Third Millennium.

The following is a summary statement of their deliberations. It should not be viewed as a final statement on any of the issues raised, but it is clearly informed by the situation from which each participant comes. Though provisional, it can be regarded as a developed consideration on the present and possible future shape of ministry, which is informed by the diversity of practice and context presently experienced throughout the Communion.

The report commences with an initial statement which provides a theological basis for the more concrete deliberations on particular ministry issues which follow. The areas pursued in small group discussions are indicated in the sub-headings. The report concludes with a number of recommendations.

Introductory theological statement

1.0   There is one ministry of Jesus Christ in which all Christians participate by virtue of their Baptism. By Baptism we mean the complete rite of initiation with water and laying on of hands, administered responsibly in accordance with the principles outlined in the World Council of Churches document *Baptism, Eucharist and Ministry*. In accordance with this understanding, we believe that baptismal liturgies need to be more explicit about what that baptismal ministry is. This suggests that in the initial catechumenate, and in our continuing formation and re-formation, we need processes which enable us to learn how to minister and to discover how God has gifted each member. This is a joyful task which we want to embrace wholeheartedly. We note that in a missionary Church, the predominance of adult or family initiation is to be expected.

1.1   This ministry of the baptised is the fundamental ministry of the Church, with the function of ordained ministry being to serve, equip and enable this ministry to take place. If the ministry of the baptised is to be Christian where they live, then it follows that this is chiefly not sanctuary or churchly ministry, but rather a matter of being a Christian parent, employee, employer, unemployed person, or a voter, etc., with integrity. We need to help people to find out how to exercise these world-focussed ministries. The pattern for us all remains Christ who had a world-focussed ministry.

1.2   Within the general ministry of the baptised, some people will have special charisms or gifts. They will exercise these gifts as they respond to the call of God and the call of the Church. Special gifts are to be welcomed, but also to be scrutinised as the New Testament encourages us to do. The variety and richness of God's gifts are to be encouraged, but it must be ordered lest disruption emerges in the Church. There is a great variety of ministries which develop, when flexibility, openness and freedom to experiment in this area are encouraged.

1.3   We discern a tendency today to start with the ordained ministry and to see lay ministry as in some way derived. Our assertion is that the opposite is the better approach, with the ministry of the whole body coming first. The current experience of the Church in some places suggests that when we think of ministry as being derived from those who are ordained, our theology and practice can be stifled and inhibited.

1.4   In every area of ministry, lay and ordained, we need to learn to be mutually accountable and to trust one another.

1.5   The threefold ordained ministry developed in a Church which was engaged in mission and in a context of hostility. However, since Constantine, it has been shaped in the West to serve a 'Christendom' model which assumes a friendly environment in which the culture helps to form Christians. If the threefold ordained ministry is to remain viable today it must recover its role and relevance in a new age of mission. The ministry of the whole people of God is integral to the mission of the Church, yet the traditional understanding of the bishop as the orthodox preacher of the faith of the Gospel must not be lost.

1.6   Although Anglicans say that they adhere to the threefold ordained ministry, this is both untrue and true in practice. It is untrue inasmuch as the diaconate is generally temporary and usually constitutes probation for intending priests. So, for the most part, the ordained ministry is little more than twofold. However, we also notice that in many parts of the world, there are other categories of ministry which really fill this vacuum; examples include Readers in the Church of England, or Evangelists and Catechists in parts of Africa. We think there ought to be a fresh look at the ordering of ministry so that it really serves the mission of God; much of our current ordering needs either to be reformed or transformed. For instance, we think that the nature and possibilities of the permanent diaconate should be considered. It is now time to undertake a mission audit of the ways in which Anglicanism expresses the episcopate, presbyterate and diaconate.

1.7   What is the purpose of ministry? We think that this is best expressed in the marks of the Church as one, holy, catholic and apostolic. Ordered Christian ministry is:

- to promote the unity of the whole Church, (one);
- to foster its sanctification (holy);
- to keep the Church focused on its universal mission (catholic);
- and to ensure that it remains apostolic, that is, sent with the same message as the apostles.

1.8   God the Holy Trinity is a community of undivided love, in which Father, Son and Holy Spirit are both differentiated and yet united. The Church reflects that pattern of unity-in-diversity, and it is bound together from many different cultures and with many different gifts into one Body. In such a Church, there needs to be those whose prime task is to ensure that these gifts are exercised in the community of love which is the life of God himself. If the ordained are to do this effectively, they must themselves model God's differentiated unity, in a collaborative, collegial ministry. As the Church and the world see different kinds of leaders working together for the good of all, they themselves gain insights into its possibilities and potential.

1.9   In the past, the strength of the Anglican ministry has been in the quality of its pastoral and teaching ministry, but we believe that in the current missionary situation we need to give attention to the calling out of apostles, prophets, and evangelists, whom, along with pastors and teachers, Ephesians assures us, God desires to give to the Church (Ephesians 3.11).

1.10 The enabling power of all ministry is the Holy Spirit, given in Christian initiation to all Christians, who grow into maturity as they 'daily increase in God's Holy Spirit' which is the Church's prayer for all who are confirmed.

Patterns and expressions of ministry

The first area explored by this group concerns patterns and expressions of ministry, and the material below is a summation of discussion.

2.1   The theology of the ministry of the whole people of God as the foundation of all the particular ministries of the Church has developed rapidly in many parts of the Anglican Communion and elsewhere, but this development is by no means uniform nor have its profound implications been fully understood.

2.2   The wide variety of ministries depicted in the New Testament gradually became incorporated into offices held by a smaller number of people. This came about by force of historical circumstances and clearly enabled the Church to survive the crises it faced in early centuries. However, it also had the negative effect of producing almost a caste system within the Church, in which the ministry of all became the prerogative of some, and everyone else became little more than a 'baptised proletariat.' It also had the effect of divorcing ministry from community and is in a large measure responsible for the crisis in ministry today.

2.3   Even where the principle of the ministry of all the people of God has taken root, it is still too often seen in terms of back-up support for the 'real' (ordained) ministry, so that the Church remains in many places a community gathered round a minister instead of being the ministering community it is called to be.

2.4   Much clearer and more critical thought needs to be given to the variety of functions of ministry. This includes Church-related ministries, which include youth leadership, administration, liturgical, pastoral, educational, and also community-facing ministries, for example value-bearing, faith witnessing and defending, caring, reconciling and transforming. These ministries must be identified, called and equipped, and have people authorised to exercise those functions, with attention given to their co-ordination and oversight so that the whole body may be built up and strengthened.

2.5   Within the context of the ministry of the whole body, the ordained ministry has its particular place, but here there is particular need to distinguish between vocation and career. Over the centuries the two have become confused so that ordination and highly trained professionalism are almost identical. This has led to what has been called a 'sacramental captivity,' whereby gathered communities are deprived of sacramental worship unless a trained professional presbyter is available to them. Urgent consideration should be given to how the Eucharist may be provided in places where priests are absent for economic, deployment, political emergencies or other reasons. Since the laity are currently denied access to sacramental ministry in some places, member Churches of the Communion should give urgent consideration to resolving that problem, by studying the theological and practical issues raised by those who advocate lay presidency or 'extended communion.'

2.6   To further the growth of the ministry of the whole people of God, attention should be paid to how ministry has developed in some of the African Churches, where liturgical, pastoral, catechetical and other functions have been shared amongst much greater numbers of people. Futhermore, especially in those provinces which had many centuries of 'traditional' one-person professional ministry, there is much to be learned from the pioneering work of Roland Allen, Wesley Frensdorff and others in the development of ministry as a community product, as distinct from something imported from the outside.

2.7   In many provinces, the diaconate has been a subject of study and debate. Despite theories to the contrary, it is now for the most part a year long apprenticeship for the presbyterate. Instead, we find that the office of Lay Reader, especially where it has been combined with pastoral duties such as marriage/confirmation preparation, has almost become the equivalent of a permanent (distinctive) diaconate. We note the findings of *The Hanover Report* of the Anglican-Lutheran International Commission, published in 1996, entitled *The Diaconate as Ecumenical Opportunity*. This report is currently before the member Churches for study.

2.8   Episcopal ministry is integral to the Anglican understanding of the ministry of the Church. Thought needs to be given to the possible variety of ways in which it is to be exercised. Like all other ministries it is to be seen as both personal and collegial so that the Trinitarian principle of interdependence and mutuality may be seen. The development of contemporary collegial oversight within Anglicanism is noted here. In areas of close interdenominational co-operation, there is the welcome growth of ecumenical oversight exercised jointly by the bishop, moderator, and superintendent of all participating denominations. This is still comparatively rare but it is an important initial step of understanding épiscope in an ecumenical context, with the ultimate aim of coming together in formal unity *(Episcopal MinistryThe Report of the Archbishops' Group on the Episcopate, 1990. Church House Publishing, London, 1990, p. 283, para 659.).*

Training, resourcing, equipping for ministry

Another Section 2 sub-group focussed its deliberations on training and equipping for ministry.

3.0   It is clear that the purpose of the Church in the world is to carry out God's mission, and the primary model for Christian obedience to this mandate is Christ. The New Testament foundational concept of reconciliation is integral to understanding this mission mandate for the people of God. God reconciled us to himself through Christ and gave us this ministry of reconciliation [2 Corinthians 5:18-21]. This work of reconciliation entrusted to the people of God also requires them to engage with their fellow human beings, society and the creation to pursue human dignity, justice, peace and an equitable sharing of resources.

3.1   Furthermore the Gospel commission of Christ to his disciples develops our understanding of the nature of Christian mission and ministry. See, for example, Matthew 28:19-20, "go, make, baptise, teach," or John 21:15-19, *"feed my lambs, feed my sheep,"* or Luke 4:18-19, *"preach good news to the poor," "proclaim release to the captives," "set at liberty those who are oppressed."*

3.2   How are the people of God, the laos to be equipped? Christ has given gifts *"to equip the saints for the work of ministry for building up the body of Christ"* [Ephesians 4:11-16]. These Spirit-inspired gifts must be used and exercised diligently, with due care and discipline, otherwise they will wither and die. Love of God and for the people of God is the motivation and the context for the exercise of the gifts of ministry [I Corinthians 13]. Openness to the leading of the Holy Spirit will provide avenues for ministry [Acts 16:6-10].

3.3   The local congregation is often the initial circumstance where gifts of ministry are first recognised, identified and practised. The development and formation of Christian character should start with the young. Imaginative programmes using modern education tools (where appropriate) should supplement and support Christian nurture in families. The formation of the life and character of the Christian minister should be just a continuation of this process in the life and being of the individual, which commenced in the local congregation.

3.4   The local context will then consequently become the springboard for public ministry in a wider setting. Usually it will be desirable or necessary for formal education or training to be undertaken to develop ministry skills and 'sharpen' the particular, individual gift of ministry. This is an absolute necessity if the calling is to the ordained ministry. Yet it must not be forgotten that there is a similar necessity for the development, nurture and training for the ministry of the laity.

3.5   Formal training for stipendiary ministry, as indeed for all ministry, should have a solid Biblical basis. However, care should be taken so that the training is not just an academic degree in theology divorced from its application to the world. Theology must be grounded in a thorough understanding of context, so that it is relevant and speaks to the heart and the situation of every human person. If this situational grounding is absent, the theology is other-worldly and can be irrelevant to the contemporary context of ministry. It is also essential that ministry skills training and spiritual development be indivisible companions of the academic theological process, so that the Christian minister, whether lay or ordained, is fully equipped for mission in God's world.

3.6   Flexibility in the length and content of training may be desirable to fit particular needs. It should be recognised, for example, that training for youth work or itinerant Bible teaching may be found to be inadequate when an individual develops a sense of vocation for the ministry of leadership within the congregation.

Contexts for Ministry

Another sub-group explored some of the urgent questions facing ministry throughout the Communion. These included the areas of reconciliation, peace, justice, trauma counselling and other social problems which frequently impact upon Christian ministry. These issues can be experienced by Anglicans not only in urban settings but also in situations of extreme civil strife, oppression, poverty and persecution. They cannot be ignored if the ministry is to be received as relevant and appropriate to hearers and seekers after the truths of God.

Reconciliation

4.1   As set out in paragraph 3.0, Section 2 accepts that the ministry of reconciliation is a primary motif of ministry. God has reconciled those who are alienated to himself through Christ and given them the ministry of reconciliation (2 Cor 5:8-20). A further consequence of the reconciling work of the Cross of Christ is that divided humanity is reconciled (Ephesians 2:14-16). Not only is humanity reconciled but so also is the whole created order (Colossians 1:19-20). So Christian ministry must encompass this many-faceted Scriptural understanding of reconciliation through Christ. Those who have found forgiveness in Christ will be reconcilers, bringing together those who are hostile because of ethnic, political and religious differences. Care for the created order is also part of the ministry of reconciliation.

Peace

4.2   Those who are reconciled are at peace with God and with each other through Jesus the Prince of Peace. This is a basic premise of Christian proclamation, but it must also be lived and demonstrated in all relationships, individual and corporate, both within and outside the Church. If this is not the case, relationships and lives will powerfully deny to listeners and observers the proclamation in the name of the Prince of Peace. Christians must live, model and minister peacemaking (Matthew 5:9). This may involve individuals, Churches and even the Communion as a whole in taking a lead in providing forums for peace discussions, in initiating peace negotiations in appropriate contexts, and building bridges of personal relationships where they have broken down.

Justice

4.3   God is the God of justice. The prophetic call to the people of God continues to ring true and have profound meaning for our present age. *"He has shown you, O man, what is good, and what does the Lord require of you but to do justice and to love kindness and to walk humbly with your God"* (Micah

6:8). This remains a basic motivation for ministry. God's ministers, lay and ordained, cannot remain impervious to the insistent prophetic demand for active involvement in doing justice and mercy. God's ministers, acting on the prophetic model, will also be prepared, when necessary, to rebuke and call to account those who are agents of injustice and oppressors of God's people. They will also encourage those in government and the judicial systems to be impartial ministers of justice and mercy and to restrain evil and injustice.

Trauma

4.4   Many Christians today, through their own personal experiences and through observation of the traumatised state of many refugees, internally displaced and uprooted people in the world, understand the urgent need for the Christian ministry of trauma counselling. In countries where there are developed Christian programmes, they should be offered as centres of training and healing, and the spread of such work must be encouraged. Clergy and lay training should include appropriate segments which will prepare participants for this ministry. An understanding and exploration of the work of the Holy Spirit, the Counsellor and Comforter, in the life of the individual, will supply the foundation for this ministry (see John 14:25-27).

Social

4.5   There is a wider range of social problems experienced in every community throughout the world, which serve to dehumanise God's people and which must be challenged by the Church. Every Province must continue to initiate and develop activities and programmes which will serve the whole community, and which will encourage the whole people of God to view their life as one of servant ministry to their community in the name of the living God.

Conclusion

5.1   Section 2 offers its work to the Communion with the prayer that the ministry of the people of God will be exercised with due diligence and obedience to the commission of Christ, the Lord of the Church.

Recommendations from Section 2

6.1   That member Churches of the Communion be encouraged to continue to develop lay ministry within each community of faith, as well as to the wider community.

6.2   That the attention of the bishops attending the 1998 Lambeth Conference be drawn to the distress expressed by some lay people at the denial of their right to meet and minister.

6.3   That the Anglican Liturgical Consultation be asked to recommend ways of making baptismal liturgies state more explicitly the ministry of all the baptised.

6.4   That each member Church of the Communion be asked to study *The Hanover Report* of the Anglican-Lutheran International Commission relating particularly to the diaconate, in the continuing exploration of distinctive diaconal ministry.

6.5   That member Churches be asked to study and act on the implications of the statement in 1.3 that all ministry, including that of the ordained, is derived from the ministry of the whole people of God.

6.6   That the Anglican Communion Secretariat be requested to compile a list of ministry resource centres and ministry studies for circulation throughout the Communion.

6.7   That member Churches be asked to give urgent consideration to situations where access to sacramental ministry is limited or impossible, and in particular to study the theological and practical questions raised by those who advocate lay presidency or 'extended communion.'

Section 3 Report
Looking to the Future in Relating to Society

"I came that they may have life and have it abundantly." (John 10.10 RSV)

CHAIR:	Mr George Koshy, South India
SECRETARY:	Mr Ghazi Musharbash, Jerusalem & the Middle East
COMMUNICATOR:	Mrs Nicola Currie, Staff
MEMBERS:	The Revd Canon Dr John W. Baganizi, Uganda
	Ms Judith G. Conley, USA
	Ms Rachel B. Beleo, Philippines
	Mr Is-hag K. K. Kannedy, Sudan
	Dr Vidya S. Lall, North India
	The Ven. Bolly Lapok, South East Asia
	The Revd Dr John Jae-Joung Lee, Korea
	The Revd Canon Malusi Mpumlwana, Southern Africa
	The Revd Canon Mkunga H. P. Mtingele, Tanzania
	The Very Revd Vincent O. Muoghereh, Nigeria
	Mr John M. Rea, Scotland
	The Rt Revd Fernando Soares, Portugal
	The Rt Revd Joseph Wasonga, Kenya
	Prof. Whatarangi Winiata, Aotearoa, New Zealand and Polynesia

Preamble

The theme of the Conference was "Being Anglican in the Third Millennium." The Section worked to produce a statement of vision for the Church's role in the world in the future.

Jesus announced the coming of God's Kingdom. He taught his disciples to pray to the Father that his Kingdom might come on earth as in heaven. He called his followers to be in the world but not of the world, and to be salt and light to the world. The Gospel of Christ does not encourage escape from the world but rather engagement in the world as agents of the Kingdom. It is in the light of the coming Kingdom Jesus announced that Christians understand the relationship of the Church to the society and the wider world.

In society today there are signs all around that we live in a fallible, broken and fallen world. Although as Christians we work to make the world a better place to live in, we recognise that in purely human terms there can be no perfect or complete social, economic or political solutions to human needs. Only God can heal and redeem (John 16.33).

The Church is called, by the grace of God, to provide signs, both within its own life and within the cultural context in which it lives, of God's transforming love and justice. Whenever the Church is faithful to this vocation it provides hope that God's Kingdom will one day come in its fullness.

"The Church is the advent in history of God's final will being done *'on earth as it is in heaven.'* The Church is the icon of the future towards which God is directing the history of the world. A faithful Church signifies by its life that it is the living promise of God's purpose in the midst of today's history" (*Virginia Report* II 2.14).

The section identified four main areas of concern about the Church's role in the world and identified a number of suggestions for action which could be pursued within the Churches in the Communion.

1.   Sustainable Development

1.1   Following the collapse of the socialist economies, there has been an increasing globalisation of the world economy. A growth model based on a free market economy has gained prominence all over the world. But free enterprise and free market policies which are not guided by a commitment to social concern and justice will lead to greater injustice, conflict and social turmoil within society. Concern for people's welfare does not come automatically with increased wealth.

1.2   The Church has a dual ministry of caring for God's people and caring for God's creation. The Church therefore supports sustainable development which meets the needs of God's people. It also supports the removal of impediments to an equitable sharing of the fruits of economic development, including the burdensome servicing of international debt and other barriers to education, health, housing and the basic essentials of life.

1.3   Anglicans need to be wary of the false 'theology of success' where

God is described as the one who brings financial success and success viewed in secular terms.

1.4   Suggestions for action

•   In view of the Biblical pattern of the jubilee, *"the year of the Lord's favour,"* (Luke 4:18-19) which expected the remission of debts and restoration of the land to the dispossessed every 50 years, the Section urges the Communion to promote a spirit of the jubilee for the year 2000 by cooperating with the Anglican Observer at the UN, other Churches, agencies, and governments in support for the alleviation of the developing world's debt by the year 2000.

•   The Section suggests that the Anglican Communion works with other Churches and agencies in discussion and advocacy with the IMF, World Bank and other financial institutions to show how, together with the misuse and mismanagement of borrowing by some governments, their policies still adversely affect millions of people.

•   The Section recommends that the Church promotes education and awareness amongst its people about the issues involved in the question of international debt.

•   A call is needed for the Provinces of the Communion to utilise fully the offices of the Anglican UN Observer's Office.

•   A call should be made for the Church to re-proclaim the theology of stewardship.

2.   Tackling the root causes of human rights' violations and injustice

2.1   The Church helps realise God's Kingdom in its work in education, health care, social services and all its social outreach. In addition to this role of caregiver and provider, it is also called upon to challenge society when people are dehumanised or are unable to realise their full potential as children of God.

2.2   The Church has a prophetic mission to fight against injustice, human rights' violations, violence against women and children, militarisation, and oppressive social, economic, and political structures. The Church has a role of trailblazer in a holistic mission.

2.3   In parts of the world the Church has actively helped to transform society. But in order for the Church to pursue its prophetic calling, it needs to serve as a model for society. It therefore constantly needs to examine its own structures and consider whether they are helpful in realising the Kingdom. An ongoing review of Church programmes, outreach and ministry is necessary if the Church is to be an effective witness and service to people.

2.4   Suggestions for action

- The Section urges Churches to find ways to release bishops and clergy from their administrative work, to free them to pursue their role as prophets, pastors and spiritual leaders.

- The Church should consider ways in which the Church can review its structures so that it can help realise the Kingdom.

- The Section recommends that the Church explores ways to create a more effective co-operation with government agencies in their social services and in the formation of government policy.

3 .   Responding to the particular issues of today

3.1   The Church is living at a time of great technological and social change. Questions of religious fundamentalism, secularism, and inter-church conflict all present challenges to Christian understanding. Diverse understandings of questions of sexuality, divorce, suicide, euthanasia and family relations may seem to undermine traditional Church teachings. The multicultural composition of the Anglican Communion may heighten the complexity of finding meaningful responses to these questions.

3.2   The Anglican understanding of a Christian life based on Scripture, tradition and reason needs to be realised afresh for today's Church.

3.3   Dialogue with people of other faiths or other beliefs is essential and has to be promoted. Mutual respect and tolerance needs to be encouraged and developed and is essential for world peace.

3.4   In order to enter into dialogue with people of other faiths, Anglicans need a clear and confident understanding of their own faith and an openness to God's revelation.

3.5   Anglicans have a responsibility to promote dialogue where there is conflict between Churches.

3.6   Dialogue between Christians and other faiths and between different Church groups needs to find a practical expression in action and mutual co-operation.

3.7   The need for cultural integrity is a major concern of the indigenous peoples. These peoples challenge the Church to organise its life within different cultures, whilst maintaining a common understanding of what it means to be Church.

3.8   The Church's response to questions of sexuality, divorce, suicide, euthanasia and family relations must be based upon an understanding of God's love and forgiveness and an appreciation of the different cultural settings in individual provinces.

3.9   Suggestions for action

> •   Churches are asked to support and give financial help to the Anglican Peace and Justice Network, the Anglican Indigenous Network, the Anglican Observer at the UN office and the Inter-Faith Network.

> •   The complexities of the multicultural nature of the Anglican Communion can be diminished by the Church committing itself to:
> > a)   organising its affairs within each culture;
> > b)   diligently keeping open all avenues which lead to a common ground between cultures;
> > c)   maintaining the right of everyone to chose a particular cultural expression of the faith;
> > d)   ensuring that, through each culture, the ministry of worship and service is accessible to all.

4.   Empowering and equipping the laity

4.1   The Anglican Consultative Council is unique amongst the instruments of unity of the Communion in its lay representation. The Kingdom of God is for all people, lay and ordained. By empowering and equipping the people of God to be more confident and effective in the mission of the Church, the Church will release new energies and initiatives to help realise God's Kingdom.

4.2   Suggestions for action

•   Churches need to ask the Primates' Meeting, Lambeth, an Anglican Congress and Bishops' Councils to discuss the potential and implications of investing in a greater empowerment of the laity. These bodies should encourage experimentation in individual dioceses and parishes and ask and listen to the laity about how they can be equipped for their ministry.

•   Churches should ensure that clergy training includes provisions for equipping and empowering the laity.

•   The Section urges Churches to use networking to facilitate the exchange of ideas, information and 'models that work,' etc, for bishops, clergy and laity.

•   Churches need to support local laity cells where, through regular meetings, action and reflection, this empowerment can be realised.

5.   Prayer for the Church in the world

God the Father,
Lord of creation,
help us to remember
that we live in a world alienated from you,
torn apart by strife,
plundered by human selfishness
and divided by greed.
Our failure at stewardship constantly
threatens the wholeness of your creation.

God the Son,
We have belittled your salvation.
Help us to reclaim the privileges of your victory,
and to share them with others,
that we may all dwell in your joy,
your peace, your freedom and your fullness of life.

God the Holy Spirit,
enable us to turn away from our sin.
By your mercy forgive us.
O Holy Spirit transform and renew us,
that we may be true lights in the midst of evil,

temptations and weakness.
Help us to stand firm and be a true and living Church.

God, Father, Son, and Holy Spirit,
may we show your love
in our care and solidarity with the poor,
the oppressed and the displaced of the world.
May your Kingdom come O God,
through Christ our Lord.
Amen

Section 4 Report
Looking to the Future in
Communicating Our Belief in God

CHAIR: The Revd Canon Lovey Kisembo, Uganda
SECRETARY: The Rev Roger Chung Po Chuen, Indian Ocean

COMMUNICATOR: Mr Steve Jenkins, England

MEMBERS: Mrs Margaret Bihabanyi, Rwanda
The Rt Revd J. Mark Dyer, USA
The Rt Revd Kenneth Fernando, Sri Lanka
The Rt Revd Richard D. Harries, England
The Most Revd Samir Kafity, Jerusalem &
  the Middle East
The Rt Revd Michael S. Lugor, Sudan
Mr W. Luyaben, Phillipines
The Rt Revd Dr Alexander John Malik, Pakistan
The Revd Nelson Koboji Nyumbe, Sudan
Mrs Lenore Parker, Australia
The Most Revd S. Stewart Payne, Canada
Mr Samuel Sarkar, Bangladesh
Ms Maureen Sithole, Southern Africa
The Ven. Alvin E. Stone, West Indies

OBSERVERS: The Revd George Tavard,
  Roman Catholic Church
Prof. Roger Nostbakken,
  Lutheran World Federation

*"Lead us on, Great Holy Spirit, as we gather
from the four corners of the earth;
enable us to walk together in trust,
from the hurt and shame of the past,
into the full day which has dawned in Jesus Christ.*

Amen!"

(Australian Aboriginal prayer)

Preamble

Jesus is the Word through whom God communicates with us. If communication fails, it is not God's fault but ours. At times, we communicate well as Christians, putting our faith and the love of God before ourselves. At others, we confuse the message or allow it to come second to our own self-interest.

Communication is more than merely sending out a message; it must also be received. More than that, for communication to be successful, it must be acted upon. Jesus calls us to be disciples (Matthew 28:19) in the same way. If we fail to make disciples of others, or if those we help come to faith fail to make disciples, then Jesus' message has been cut off. The communication has failed.

Communication is more then mere words. We communicate just as strongly, often more so, by our lives and our actions. We are called to be Christians in everything we say and everything we do. *"By this shall all men know that you are my disciples, if you have love one for another"* (John 13.35). If what we do denies what we say, then God's message is stifled. Disciples are called to be channels through whom the Gospel is made available to God's people. By our very actions, we can either open up the channel or close it.

Communication is not one-way. Those who communicate must also listen to those the message is aimed at. Jesus spoke to people as one of them. He used messages that related to people's everyday lives. If we try to communicate the Gospel in ways that have no meaning to those we hope to touch, then there will be no communication. The message will appear irrelevant and not worth listening to.

Similarly, our message, God's message, can be stifled, like the sower's seed (Luke 8:1ff), by the environment we live in. The world is increasingly dominated by the media and the media is dominated by commercial interests. Many such interests may see the Gospel as a barrier to their own aims.

If we are to communicate our belief in God in the third millennium, we will have to find ways to overcome such barriers and address people in their own lives.

The Virginia Report speaks of the need for attentiveness, interdependence and subsidiarity. Without those, the Church can communicate neither with its own members, nor with those its message is yet to touch.

HOPES AND VISIONS

1. Views on a changing world

1.1   Secularisation is a disputed concept; but two characteristics may be noted. First, in some countries, the Christian Church has lost power and influence in the public sphere. There may be some residual belief in the population or new forms of spirituality, but the Christian Churches are no longer the dominant force they once were. Secondly, the forces that increasingly shape these societies are economic and financial. Behind the media, which influences so many of our attitudes and so much of our behaviour, are commercial interests. Of their nature, these encourage commercialism and support political policies that buttress it. They work to marginalise any dissent from the prevailing ideology, including the Church. Although the process of secularisation is advanced in Europe and North America, its effect is increasingly being felt in every country in the world.

1.2   The Gospel of Jesus Christ, the Son of God, has been for centuries proclaimed with the power of the Holy Spirit to change human hearts, to give new life.

1.3   Today, in some parts of the world, the Gospel needs to be proclaimed in a culture that has been named 'post-modern.' A whole generation of people has been brought up with symbols and words which proclaim the message that there is no such reality as objective truth, no unified centre to human experience and existence, no foundational truth. That is to say, universal truth and ultimate reality do not exist. The only truth and goodness that one might experience is to be found in what any individual community decides works for them, here and now.

1.4   The challenge to evangelism that post-modernism presents is not simply the rejection of objective, universal truth, but it is especially the fact that post-modernism claims there is no unified centre to reality, to human existence.

1.5   As Christians, we must proclaim that the focus of universal truth and the unifying centre of all reality is found in the Word of God, Jesus Christ, the incarnate Son of God, our Saviour and Lord.

1.6   Post-modernism challenges us also to set ourselves free from the individualism inherited in the Enlightenment culture. The Gospel speaks to the whole human person as person in community. Hence, all evangelism must be freed from individualism and become personal. Evangelism needs to be an invitation to people to accept Jesus Christ as Lord and Saviour and become members in the community of those whose life is committed to God, the Holy Trinity, and whose mission it is to bring Gospel life to all humanity.

1.7   In the cities and suburbs of affluent communities, alongside the homes and dwellings of the poor, one sees the growing presence of satellite dishes. People receive thousands of images and words calling them to follow, offering the promise of a better life. The Church needs to optimise its use of the media in all its forms, including print, broadcast and the internet.

1.8   In the future we would like to see a Church that is able to discern the value of contemporary media, use the media effectively to communicate the Gospel and offer a prophetic critique of the media's dehumanising influence.

1.9   Looking to the future in a changing world, we would like to see a Church that:

•   has the confidence to profess its faith in the face of antagonism, witnessing to the Gospel through its social and political action, as well as its teaching; portraying the love and grace of God in all it says and all it does;

•   affirms individual's choice, while challenging a postmodern world to recognise the love and grace available through community, tradition and history;

•   speaks loudly of all that binds it together, shows by example that diversity does not mean conflict, and faces, on its own terms, a worldwide media that thrives on conflict and is increasingly antagonistic to Christianity;

•   takes the Gospel to people in their own lives, listens to them and is willing to learn from their tradition and culture so that all might be transformed.

2.   Views on a searching world

2.1   We are indigenous minority peoples living in our own lands. We are committed to the Anglican tradition while affirming our own traditional spirituality. We have discovered that we have many things in commona common spirituality, common concerns, common gifts and common hopes. We believe that God is leading the Church to a turning point in this history and that the full partnership of indigenous peoples is essential. Therefore, we pledge to work together to exercise our leadership in contributing our vision and gifts to transform the life of the Christian community *(Anglican Indigenous Network Mission Statement 1992).*

2.2   The sacrifice of God's own Son made us one with the Father. Our sons also died, their blood too is shed as sacrifice and offering. The Father weeps for us all, white and black who suffered, and comforts us with the promise of the Resurrection brought about by the great sacrifice of love.

2.3   We are all sons and daughters of the sacred sacrifice and the fire and the blood, who are the spirit and the Christ.

2.4   The mystical 'Dreaming' is union with God, when our response is to invite Him into our being, to be the 'I in you' within us. We are then united in him, reconciled in him, and at one with all creation.

2.5   Looking to the future in a searching world, we would like to see a Church that:

- •   takes its authority from Jesus Christ and the scriptures, while listening to tradition and reason;

- •   talks openly and freely about its faith, growing in its understanding and teaching its children a faith that is strong and lifelong;

- •   encourages enquirers into the faith, welcomes them and travels with them on their journey of faith to true discipleship;

- •   is confident in its belief and alive to the different situations of those to whom it wishes to speak;

- •   affirms the progress in the Decade of Evangelism and takes it forward into the dynamic life of the Church.

3.   Views on a world of faiths and creeds

3.1   More emphasis needs to be put on the Holy Spirit and his gifts as the source of power for the Lord's ministry (Acts 1:8), bearing in mind that a living Church is a charismatic Church—a Church sensitive and open to the moving of the Holy Spirit, responding to his call to check and revise our methods of ministering to the community.

3.2   The Anglican Communion needs to note that the biggest loophole through which it has lost members in some Provinces has been due to neglecting Baptism by immersion, as offered by some evangelical Churches as 'a more complete Baptism.' This way of administering the sacrament of Baptism needs to be recovered and practiced where necessary in the Communion. Renewal of Baptismal vows should be made as significant as possible, while in no way confusing it with a once and for all Baptism.

3.3   Plurality of religions is a characteristic of many of our societies. Interfaith understanding and respect that is reciprocated must be the basis for building true community among all our people. Dialogue among people of different faiths about our respective beliefs, a dialogue of life, shared spirituality and working together for the common good are prerequisites for harmony and peace.

3.4   Such relationships will enable us to share the insights of the Gospel and the saving work of Jesus Christ with others.

3.5   Looking to the future in a world of faiths and creeds, we would like to see a Church that:

•   confident in its own beliefs, listens to other interpretations of the Gospel and shares its own;

•   is so strong and confident in its own beliefs that it can work alongside those of other faiths, listen to their stories and gain new insights, while offering its own.

4.   Views on a world of inequality

4.1   As reflected in the Archbishop of Canterbury's address to ACC-10, the Church, in communicating its belief in God, looking to the future, ministering to a generation we can no longer call dark, ignorant and sick, should examine carefully the contents of W. B. Yeats' poetic stanza:

> "Things fall apart, the centre cannot hold,
> Mere anarchy is loosed upon the world,
> the blood-dimmed tide is loosed, and everywhere
> the ceremony of innocence is drowned."

4.2   The Church must challenge, with witnessing proof the excuses given by media, that conflict is deeply seated in the hearts of people when there is material proof that causes other than hatred, race, tribe and colour have been paramount.

4.3   In the new millennium, the Church should come clearly out to be involved in international trouble spots, putting the words of comfort into action for the weak, the poor, the oppressed and the refugees; and give them bread!

4.4   In the new millennium, the Church of God must speak out first, without counting the cost. Then, if the world cannot hear, we may begin to see the recurrence of martyrdom. Or do we keep silent because we are scared of imminent death?

4.5   Every Province in our Anglican Communion needs to put in place a central world relief and development fund, in its own name or that of its Primate. This would strongly communicate the Church's commitment to justice for the poor, weak and oppressed. Programmes to develop such funds would speak loudly of every Christian's love for their fellow men and women.

4.6   Looking to the future in a world of inequality, we would like to see a Church that:

•   is not afraid to speak up for what is right, supports the poor, defends the weak and stands by those that are oppressed;

•   in a world of increasing conflict, seeks reconciliation and peace for all.

Conclusion

5.1   When Jesus hung on the tree, you heard the cries of your people and became one with your wounded ones: the convicts, the hunted and the dispossessed.

5.2   The sun sets on our sorrow, but the promise of the Resurrection tells us that the Son will rise and come again.

5.3   Our vision for the future is of a Church witnessing to the Gospel in everything it says and everything it does; strong in the diversity of its beliefs; confident in its ministry to all people; and alive to the challenge of a growing worldwide media.

"May the Lord Jesus who loves with a wounded heart
Be your love for evermore.
May the Lord Jesus who serves with wounded hands
Help you serve others.
May the Lord Jesus who walks on wounded feet
Walk with you to the end of the road.
Look for the face of the Lord Jesus in everyone you meet."

RESOLUTIONS

No world-wide meeting is complete without an array of resolutions that speak to the unified agreement of a diverse community on various issues that face individual members, provinces, and the world at large. Care was taken in Panama not to try to speak in an inadequate way on issues on which the group was not informed, while still meeting the need for people around the Communion to make their individual concerns known and shared. Thus, the Resolutions are smaller in number and even those that did not make it to the final vote at least stimulated members to work and pray about the various matters that arose or were presented by ACC members.

Resolutions of ACC-10

Resolution 1:   Welcome to new Provinces—Province of Mexico

Resolved that the Primates having assented, this ACC-10 meeting in Panama welcomes to membership the Province of Mexico.

Resolution 2:   Welcome to new Provinces—Province of South-East Asia

Resolved that the Primates having assented, this ACC-10 meeting in Panama welcomes to membership the Province of South-East Asia.

Resolution 3:   Cessation of membership of the CCEA

Resolved that in consequence of the Province of South-East Asia having been admitted to membership of the ACC, at this, the 10th meeting of this Council, membership of the Council of Churches of East Asia shall, with effect from the date of this meeting, lapse.

Resolution 4:   Anglican contribution to the development of Bethlehem

Resolved that this Anglican Consultative Council requests the Secretary General to respond positively to the request to the Anglican Communion from the people of the municipality of Bethlehem, to assist in a millennium project to establish a town planning design for the city. This project will first provide a feasibility study, for consideration by the Standing Committees of ACC and the Primates and the Anglican Bishop in Jerusalem and the Middle East, concerning the renovation of Manger Square. Such a study would secure information regarding personnel and finance, as well as possible ecumenical involvement, to complete such a programme to celebrate the dawn of the new millennium for world Christianity. A support group, made up of members from around the Communion, should be established to assist in this development task. To ensure ownership of the project by the wider Church, the Secretary General is asked to keep the Provinces informed and to invite responses and indications of commitment.

Resolution 5:   On Korea

Resolved that this Council expresses its concern for the Churches and people of North and South Korea in their efforts to achieve the re-unification of their motherland on the basis of mutual acceptance and respect.

Resolution 6:   Proposal to increase the size of the ACC Standing Committee

Resolved that in view of:

a)   The increasing size of the ACC;

b)   The recent practice of joint meetings of the ACC Standing Committee and the Primates' Standing Committee; and

c)   The suggestion contained in paragraph 6.26 of the (draft) *Virginia Report* this Council requests the ACC Standing Committee to consider proposing an increase in the size of the Standing Committee to allow an appropriate balance of bishops, clergy and laity, with consideration to age and gender, on the Standing Committee.

Resolution 7:   Network Guidelines

That the following guidelines for Networks be substituted for the guidelines for Networks adopted by the ACC in 1987, namely:

Guidelines for Networks

The Anglican Consultative Council may recognise Networks addressing particular themes and concerns throughout the Anglican Communion on application, in accordance with the following guidelines. The Networks shall be identified in the published edition of the minutes of the meeting of the Council.

1.   a)   The subject matter of the Network shall be consistent with and supportive of the initiatives of the Provinces and member Churches of the Communion.

b)   The Network shall identify an acceptable process of accountability to the Anglican Consultative Council.

c)   Through the Secretary General the Network may propose subjects for consideration by the Anglican Consultative Council and shall be available whenever possible to consult on subjects on which its members hold expertise.

d)   The Secretary General of the Anglican Consultative Council shall call meetings of representatives of the Networks for mutual consultation from time to time and may on occasion invite representatives of the Networks to meet with the Joint Standing Committees.

2.   a)   Networks are encouraged to seek funding for their budgets from any appropriate source, in consultation with the Secretary General.

b)   Networks receiving funds from the budget of the Anglican Consultative Council shall account for their use, as required by the Standing Committee of the Council.

c)   Networks seeking all or part of their budget by general appeals to the Provinces and member Churches of the Anglican Communion should obtain permission of the Secretary General of the Anglican Consultative Council.

Resolution 8:   Provisions of the Constitution—Amendments (Handbook)

Resolved that the provisions of the Constitution as contained in a handbook entitled *"The Anglican Communion,"* shall be referred for detailed analysis and consideration, with a view to such amendment and revision as may be deemed necessary for the removal of doubt, to a Committee on the Constitution (appointed by the Secretary General) which shall, as soon as practicable, report with recommendations to the Standing Committee.

Resolution 9:   Youth co-opted members

Resolved that this Council requests the Standing Committee

a)   to review the principle and purpose of having any co-opted members and to report to ACC-11;

b)   on the basis that some members be co-opted, to prepare for ACC-11 a constitutional change to permit co-options of up to 10% of the elected membership and in making appointments the Standing Committee take into account factors such as age, gender, geography and special skills and experience.

Resolution 10: Climate Changes

Resolved that at its tenth meeting, held in Panama in October 1996, the ACC expresses its support for the International Petition initiated by the WCC earlier in 1996 and which will be submitted to governments of industrialised countries concerning climate changes and encourages member Churches in the industrialised world to circulate the petition through their networks.

Resolution 11: Article 3 (a) of the Constitution Amendment to final sentence

Resolved

1.   That, subject to the necessary approvals, in Article 3(a) of the Constitution for the final sentence there shall be substituted "Primates for the purposes of this Article shall mean the principal Archbishop, Bishop or Primate of each of the bodies listed under paragraphs (b), (c) and (d) of the Schedule of Membership;" and

2.   Requests the Secretary General to refer this amendment to the Provinces appearing on the schedule for ratification under Article 10.

Resolution 12: Creation of new Provinces

Resolved that this Council

1.   affirms its commitment to assisting in the creation of new Provinces, where conditions indicate that such a development is appropriate in the Anglican Communion;

2.   urges those involved in promoting the creation of new Provinces to consult the Council through its Secretary General and other officers from the earliest stages in their discussions;

3.   affirms the guidelines set out in previous Council resolutions;

4.   adopts the additional guidelines as set out in the appended Schedule;

5.   requests the Secretary General to publish as a separate document a summary of the Council's views for circulation to Primates, Provincial Secretaries and all others concerned with promoting the creation of a new Province; and

6.   requests the Secretary General to keep these matters under review and to report to the next meeting.

Schedule (Additional Guidelines)

1.   For the Primate, or any other Council or body having metropolitical authority for the relevant dioceses, to make contact with the ACC as soon as a proposal for formation of a new Province is under serious consideration.

2.   This referral might (and ideally would normally) be accompanied by an invitation to the ACC for a visit by the Secretary General, or by someone nominated by the Secretary General, to the dioceses or region, if possible to co-incide with some other activity of the Anglican Communion requiring the Secretary General's presence in the area. The purpose of the visit would be to discuss the application of the ACC's guidelines to the specific situation in the local area.

3.   Once initial consultation had taken place, and it was agreed in principle that it would be expedient to form a new Province in the region, the promoters would appoint a drafting committee, to consider the outline draft constitution set out by the ACC. They would address any issues arising from it that had not yet been considered by the promoters, and set up clear lines of communication and a timetable for consultation with the dioceses concerned, with their metropolitical authority, and with the ACC.

4.   The drafting process in itself is likely to take some considerable time, but the ACC can provide significant assistance in advising both on the content of constitutions (by comparison with those used elsewhere in the Communion), and on the arrangements that may need to be made for that stage of the discussion.

5.   On receipt of the first (and any subsequent) draft constitution by the ACC, the Secretary General may, in consultation

with the Standing Committee as appropriate, appoint a committee, or call upon individual consultants, to make observations on its behalf for further consideration by the promoters and their advisors.

6.   Having agreed on the form of the new constitution, the proposers are asked to submit their application for revision of the scheduled list to the ACC not less than 15 months ahead of the next meeting of the full Council.

7.   The Secretary General in accordance with Article 3(a) will then consult with the Primates, either at their next scheduled meeting or individually, to seek the two-thirds majority approval required by its constitution.

8.   The proposal of revision of the schedule (to add the new Province to the scheduled list) will be put on the agenda for approval at the next full meeting, subject to any outstanding consents of Primates.

9.   The Secretary General will be charged with informing the Archbishop of Canterbury at every stage as to the ACC's view on the eligibility of the applicant body for recognition as an autonomous Province of the Anglican Communion.

Resolution 13: Anglican Women's Network

Resolved that this Council supports the action of the Secretary General in calling together representatives of women's organisations throughout the Communion to

i)   discover ways in which stronger links among women may grow; and

ii)   develop responses to the challenges coming from the Fourth Conference on Women in Beijing and requests that a report of the Beijing event be sent to the Joint Standing Committees of the Primates and the ACC for their 1997 Meeting.

Resolution 14: Article 3(a) of the Constitution Amendment to second sentence

Defeated

Resolution 15: On Rwanda

Resolved that trusting in God's reconciling power and giving thanks for repentance and spiritual renewal within the Episcopal Church of Rwanda, this Council:

1.   urges the Anglican Communion to continue its prayer for the people, Government and Church in Rwanda;

2.   in the quest for peace, we urge the Episcopal Church of Rwanda never to abandon its call to be God's instrument of justice and reconciliation, without which no peace in Rwanda can be lasting;

3.   in the light of steps taken both by the Provincial Synod of EER, and the Archbishop of Canterbury, to persuade the bishops in exile to return to their dioceses, or to resign, and given that these bishops have not responded to these calls, we recognise that those sees are now vacant, and request the authorities in those dioceses to communicate this to their respective bishops, and to record this action in their records [In this respect, we refer to the Dioceses of Cyangugu, Kibungo, Shyira and Shyogwe.];

4.   we urge the Church leadership, in consequence, in consultation as necessary with the secular authorities, to set in motion legal procedures to elect bishops to those four vacant sees; and as soon as possible after these elections and consecrations, to call a Provincial Synod meeting in order to finalise a Provincial Constitution;

5.   not only do we applaud and support the initiatives which have been taken by the Archbishop of Canterbury, the Secretary General, and the Archbishop's special envoy to Rwanda, the Right Reverend David Birney, but we offer our continued support and encouragement to them to take such future initiatives as they think necessary, consulting where possible the Primates of the Communion, the ACC Standing Committee, and other representatives of the Communion whose specialist knowledge of the situation may aid the process.

Resolution 16: Agros Report: Replacement of the Ecumenical Advisory Group by an Inter-Anglican Standing Commission

Resolved that this ACC endorses the proposal contained in the *Agros Report* that the Ecumenical Advisory Group be replaced by an Inter-Anglican Standing Commission on Ecumenical Relations following the Lambeth Conference, whose tasks would be:

a) to monitor and enable Anglican participation in multilateral and bilateral dialogues;

b) to monitor and encourage the process of reception, response and decision;

c) to ensure theological consistency in dialogues and conversations by reviewing local, regional and provincial proposals with ecumenical partners and when an agreement affects the life of the Communion as a whole, to propose, after consultation with the ACC and the Primates' Meeting, that the matter be brought to the Lambeth Conference before the Province votes to enter the new relationship;

d) to address issues of terminology; and

e) to facilitate the circulation of documents and ecumenical resources throughout the Communion.

Resolution 17: Publication of the Agros Report as a companion

Resolved that this Council:

a) expresses its thanks to the Ecumenical Advisory Group who drafted the *Agros Report* and looks forward to its completion at the St Augustine's Seminar in April 1997, in preparation for the Lambeth Conference 1998; and

b) requests that the Report be published in study form as a companion booklet to the Report of ACC-10.

Resolution 18: On Tibet

Withdrawn.

Resolution 19: On Cuba

Resolved that whereas it is the duty of the Christian Church to proclaim the liberating Good News as enunciated in Holy Scripture, and that whereas the suffering and deprivation of human beings anywhere in the world demeans those who are created in the image of God:

>   1.   this 10th meeting of the Anglican Consultative Council, convened in Panamá City, Panama, hereby calls upon the Government of the United States to lift its embargo against Cuba; and

>   2.   calls upon its observer at the United Nations to convey our concern to that gathered body of nations; and

>   3.   recommends that copies of this resolution be forwarded to the President of the United States, both Houses of Congress, the Presiding Bishop of the Episcopal Church, the President of the House of Deputies of the General Convention, and the Bishop, clergy and people of the Episcopal Church in Cuba.

Resolution 20: Timber Harvesting in Papua New Guinea and the Solomon Islands

Withdrawn.

Resolution 21: Anglican Peace and Justice Network resolutions

Resolved that this ACC

>   1.   encourages all Anglicans to work for strict controls and safeguards on personal firearms and to set an example by their own renunciation of firearms except when needed for a legitimate livelihood;

>   2.   encourages all Anglicans to engage in the "Turning Swords into Ploughshares" programme;

>   3.   challenges all Governments not to engage in the manufacture, import, export, storage, sale or purchase of landmines; and

4.   encourages all people of goodwill to engage in supporting financially programmes to rid countries of land-mines.

Resolution 22: MISSIO: Promoting the spirit of jubilee for the year 2000

Resolved that the ACC endorses the request of MISSIO that the Anglican
Communion and its member Churches promote the spirit of the jubilee
for the year 2000 by:

a)   co-operating with other churches, agencies and governments in support of international movements for the cancella-
tion of international debt of developing countries by the year
2000; and

b)   seeking, under the leadership of their bishops, concrete
actions in the local church and in their local context which
reflect the spirit of forgiveness and reconciliation implicit in
the Biblical jubilee motif.

Further, this meeting of the ACC appeals to the IMF, and the World Bank,
and other such institutions, to take steps to cancel the debts of the third
world countries by the year 2000.

Resolution 23: MISSIO: Mission given top priority

Resolved that the ACC endorses the challenge of MISSIO that the
Churches of the Communion move beyond maintenance thinking by giving mission the top priority it deserves in their budgets.

Resolution 24: MISSIO: Report on the Mid-Point Review of the Decade of Evangelism (G-CODE 2000)

Resolved that this ACC

a)   welcomes the MISSIO Report on the Mid-Point Review
of the Decade of Evangelism (G-CODE 2000), held in Kanuga
in September 1995;

b)   recommends the circulation of that decade report
throughout the Communion, in translation where necessary;
and

c)   urges Provinces to take forward the 10 'Emerging Issues and Future Directions' which were identified as priorities for the Communion as a result of the Decade Review.

Resolution 25: Jerusalem Endorsement of President Bishop's Statement

Resolved that this meeting of ACC, ACC-10, having received, through the President Bishop of the Province of Jerusalem and the Middle East, the Statement of all the Heads of Christian Churches in Jerusalem dated November 14, 1994, on the significance of Jerusalem for Christians, endorses this statement and commends it to the Provinces of the Anglican Communion and to the Lambeth Conference.

Resolution 26: ACC: Equal Representation

Withdrawn and tabled to Standing Committee

Resolution 27: ACC: Contributions from Provinces

Resolved that this ACC applauds the many Provinces which continue to contribute, fully and sacrificially, to the core activities and budget of the Anglican Communion Office; and calls upon all Provinces to make their full contribution to the Anglican Communion rather than by their actions restrict the constructive, Communion-wide contribution of the Anglican Communion Office in relation to priorities determined by its worldwide membership.

Resolution 28: Lambeth Conference Feasibility Study for beyond 1998

Resolved that this ACC asks the Standing Committees of ACC and the Primates to set up a feasibility study to look at the questions which have been raised in connection with the Lambeth Conferences beyond 1998, so that the Lambeth bishops may have a working paper on which to base their considerations in Lambeth 1998 regarding future meetings.

Resolution 29: Anglican Refugee Network

Resolved that this meeting of ACC, recognising that 1997 is to be observed as 'The Year of Uprooted Peoples':

1.   affirms the importance of the work of the Anglican Refugee network; and

2.   asks the ACC Standing Committee to take steps to ensure the continuance of this work, whether as a distinct Network, or in association with another Network, or through our UN Observer, or by other means.

Resolution 30: Liturgy

Resolved that this Anglican Consultative Council

1.   receives the Principles and Recommendations on the renewal of the Eucharist of the Fifth International Anglican Liturgical Consultation, Dublin, Republic of Ireland, 1995, and commends them to the Provinces for study, together with the statements of the working groups of the Consultation;

2.   urges the Primates to commend these documents for study to appropriate committees, colleges, and networks which will guarantee their wide dissemination among all who are concerned with the renewal of liturgical practice and the revision of the liturgical texts; and

3.   asks the Provincial offices to report on the reception of these documents to the Coordinator for Liturgy by the end of 1997.

Resolution 31: Anglican Congress

Resolved that this ACC desires to have an International Anglican gathering after the 1998 Lambeth Conference (perhaps in 2001) and asks the Standing Committees of ACC and the Primates:

a)   to set up a group to conduct a feasibility study;

b)   gives authority to the Standing Committees to decide to proceed with such a gathering if the feasibility study suggests this is wise;

c)   to write to ACC members to inform them of progress in this matter.

Resolution 32: Minutes of ACC meetings

Resolved that at the Meeting of ACC-11 and at all meetings of ACC thereafter full written minutes of all proceedings be taken.

Resolution 33: Anglican Investment Agency

Resolved that this Council, gratefully acknowledging the enormous amount of time and effort which has been given to the proposal to form an Anglican Investment Agency, by a small group of lay people led by Mrs Marion Dawson Carr:

1.   supports this initiative to raise money for the special initiatives of the international ministry of the Archbishop of Canterbury and the Anglican Communion, as set out in the introductory document;

2.   accepts the invitation to nominate three of its members to the Disbursement Trust and asks the Standing Committee to implement this; and

3.   requests a regular report of the activities of the Agency to be made available to its full Council meeting, and to meetings of the Joint Standing Committees of the ACC and the Primates.

Resolution 34: Resolutions of thanks

Resolved that the 10th meeting of the Anglican Consultative Council gives thanks to God for the ministry of so many whose commitment and service have enabled the Council to do the work of the Church and the will of God:

for our President, Archbishop George Carey, whose personal commitment, clear proclamation and pastoral compassion inspire us;

for our Chairman, Canon Colin Craston, whose wisdom and experience have been a grace and a strength to us;

for our Vice-Chairman, Bishop Simon Chiwanga, with assurance of our prayers and support as he moves to further service in our midst;

for our Secretary General, Canon John Peterson, whose enthusiasm excites us, whose initiative strengthens us and whose energy empowers us;

for the Design Group, led by Dr Diane Maybee, who enabled us to work with diligence and responsibility for all that we faced;

for the Nominations Committee, led by Bishop Mark Dyer, who steered us through complex procedures and helped us discern our future leaders;

for the Resolutions Committee, led by Lady Brenda Shiel, who helped us express our mind and will clearly;

for the Bible studies, prepared by Bishop Dinis Sengulane, which drew us closer to our Lord and to each other;

for the worship team, led by the Chaplain, Bishop Roger Herft, who gathered our hearts and spirits in common prayer and fellowship;

for the Communications team, led by Canon Jim Rosenthal, who have enabled us to speak to the world those words we share with each other;

for our partners, Roger Nostbakken from the Lutheran World Federation and Fr George Tavard from the Roman Catholic Church, whose presence and encouragement have raised our eyes to the ecumenical horizon;

for the translators, led by the Revd Diana Luz Parada, who opened the meeting to Spanish and French speakers;

for the members of the office staff, Mrs Christine Codner, Miss Clare Dell, Miss Fiona Millican and Mrs Rosemary Palmer, whose work behind the scenes have given us the tools to do our work;

for Senor Miguel Franco and the staff of the Hotel Riande Continental Ciudad, who have laboured mightily to cope with our diverse needs and wants;

for the local committees on arrangements and the countless volunteers, whose availability and service have supported us at every step;

for the Bishop of Panama and Mrs Connie Hayes, the Dean and people of St Luke's Cathedral and Senor Biron Daniels and the staff of the diocesan office, who have opened their hearts and their arms to offer us unforgettable hospitality and witness;

for all who have participated in our common search to know the will of God and to do it.

Resolution 35: Prayers and Greetings

Resolved that this 10th meeting of the Anglican Consultative Council sends its greetings and assurances of prayer to the following:

the Presiding Bishop of the Episcopal Church of the United States of America, the Most Revd Edmond Lee Browning;

and the President of Province IX, the Right Reverend Neptali Larrea, in whose Province we have met;

the Eglise Episcopale du Burundi, and their member of this Council, the Reverend Bernard Ntahoturi, with regret that present troubles make it impossible for them to be represented here and with assurance of our continuing prayers and support;

the Bishop of Rome, His Holiness Pope John Paul II, with prayers for his continued restoration to health and in anticipation of his meeting with our President and Secretary General;

the Ecumenical Patriarch, His All Holiness Bartholomeos I, with prayers for the patriarchate in Istanbul;

the Moderator of the World Council of Churches, His Holiness Aram I, and the Secretary General, Dr Konrad Raiser, with thanks for their work on behalf of all of us who pray for growth among Christians in faith and order, in life and work;

the Pontifical Council for Promoting Christian Unity and its President, Cardinal Cassidy;

and the Lutheran World Federation and its President, Dr Ishmael Noko, for enabling ecumenical partners to be with us;

other church leaders closely associated with the Anglican Communion and its work:

The Most Reverend Antonius Jan Glazemaker, Archbishop of Utrecht, and the Old Catholic Union of Utrecht

His Holiness Karekin II, Catholicos of the Armenian Orthodox Church

The Reverend Dr Milan Opocensky, General Secretary of the World Alliance of Reformed Churches

Dr Joe Hale, General Secretary of the World Methodist Council

His Holiness Moran Basileos Mar Thoma Mathew II

His Holiness Ignatius Zakka I Ivas, Patriarch of Antioch and All the East of the Syrian Orthodox Church

The Roman Catholic Archbishop of Panama, Monsenor Dimas Cedeno, and other ecumenical Church leaders in Panama

The President of Panama, SE Ernesto Perez Balladares

The Mayor of Panama City, Senora Mayin Correa

The Ambassador of the United Kingdom in Panama and Mrs Sinton.

GENERAL BUSINESS

The expectations are high from around the Communion when it comes to the work of the London Secretariat. The elected officers, coming from their own Provinces with their own monumental tasks to accomplish, are called upon increasingly to be more active in affairs of the Communion. The Secretariat is being bombarded with requests for assistance in every aspect of ministry and administration. The budget for the ACC presents a stark reality that our resources must increase if the demands that are being made upon the ACC and its staff are to be met. The listing of the elected officers and members of the ACC continued to point us to that great gift we have as a worldwide Church as being "God's rainbow people," the wonderful phrase attributed to Archbishop Tutu.

Officers and Members of the ACC
Participants and Staff at ACC-10

OFFICERS

President
>The Most Revd and Rt Hon. Dr George L. Carey
>>Archbishop of Canterbury

Chairman
>The Revd Canon Colin Craston (England)

Vice Chairman
>The Rt Revd Simon Chiwanga (Tanzania)

Secretary General
>The Revd Canon John L. Peterson

JOINT STANDING COMMITTEE OF ACC AND THE PRIMATES

>The Revd Roger Chung Po Chuen (Indian Ocean)
>The Most Revd Brian Davis (Aotearoa, New Zealand & Polynesia)
>The Most Revd Robin Eames (Ireland)
>Mr Tutik Garuda (Council of Churches of SE Asia)
>>(unable to attend)
>The Most Revd Alwyn Rice Jones (Wales)
>>(unable to attend)
>The Most Revd Samir Kafity (Jerusalem & the Middle East)
>The Most Revd Orland Lindsay (West Indies)
>The Rt Revd Dr Alexander Malik (Pakistan)
>Dr Diane Maybee (Canada)
>Revd Bernard Ntahoturi (Burundi)
>>(unable to attend)
>Mr John Rea (Scotland)
>The Rt Revd Fernando Soares (Lusitanian Church)

FINANCE COMMITTEE

>The Most Revd Michael Peers, Chairman
>The Revd Canon Colin Craston
>The Most Revd Robin Eames

Dr Diane Maybee
The Rt Revd Fernando Soares

MEMBERS OF THE COUNCIL

The Anglican Church in Aotearoa, New Zealand and Polynesia
The Rt Revd John C. Paterson (ACC-8,9,10)
Prof. Whatarangi Winiata (ACC-10,11,12)

The Anglican Church of Australia
The Rt Revd Philip K. Newell (ACC-10,11,12)
The Very Revd David J. L. Richardson (ACC-9,10,11)
Mr Robert Tong (ACC-10, 11)

The Church of Bangladesh
Mr Samuel Pronoy Sarkar (ACC-10,11,12)

The Episcopal Anglican Church of Brazil
The Rt Revd Sumio Takatsu (ACC-8, 9, 10)

The Church of the Province of Burundi
The Revd Bernard Ntahoturi (ACC-9, 10, 11)
(unable to attend)

The Anglican Church of Canada
The Most Revd S. Stewart Payne (ACC-10)
The Revd Barbara Clay (ACC-9, 10, 11)
Dr Diane Maybee (ACC-8, 9, 10)

The Church of the Province of Central Africa
The Rt Revd Bernard A. Malango (ACC-9, 10)
Mr Michael M. Kututwa (ACC-9, 10, 11)

The Church of Ceylon (Sri Lanka)
The Rt Revd Kenneth Fernando (ACC-10, 11, 12)

The Council of Churches of East Asia
The Rt Revd Datuk Yong Ping Chung
(unable to attend)

The Church of England
The Rt Revd Richard D. Harries (ACC-10, 11, 12)
The Revd John Broadhurst (ACC-9, 10)
(unable to attend; represented by the Very Revd Robert Jeffrey)
Dr Christina A. Baxter (ACC-9, 10, 11)

The Church of the Province of the Indian Ocean
The Revd Roger Chung Po Chuen (ACC-8, 9, 10)

The Church of Ireland
The Rt Revd Michael H. G. Mayes (ACC-8, 9, 10)
Lady Brenda Sheil (ACC-9, 10, 11)

The Holy Catholic Church in Japan
The Revd Samuel I. Koshiishi (ACC-10, 11, 12)

The Episcopal Church in Jerusalem and the Middle East
The Rt Revd Ghais Malik (ACC-10, 11, 12)
    (unable to attend)

The Church of the Province of Kenya
Mr Samuel Arap Ng´eny (ACC-9, 10, 11)
The Rt Revd Joseph O. Wasonga (ACC-10, 11, 12)

The Anglican Church of Korea
The Revd Dr John Jae-Joung Lee (ACC-10, 11, 12)

The Church of the Province of Melanesia
The Rt Revd James Mason
    (attended ACC-9 and ACC-10 to fill a casual vacancy)

The Church of the Province of Mexico
Mr Antonio R. Ortega (ACC-10, 11, 12)

The Church of the Province of Myanmar (Burma)
The Rt Revd Samuel San Si Htay (ACC-8, 9, 10)

The Church of the Province of Nigeria
The Rt Revd Maxwell S. C. C. Anikwenwa
    (attended ACC-9 and ACC-10 to fill a casual vacancy)
The Very Revd Vincent O. Muoghereh (ACC-8, 9, 10)
Chief Ajaji (ACC-10, 11, 12)
    (unable to attend)

The Church of North India
The Most Revd D K Mohanty (ACC-10, 11, 12)
    (unable to attend; represented by the Rt Revd Vinod A. Peter)
Dr Vidya Lall (ACC-10, 11, 12)

The Church of Pakistan
The Rt Revd Dr Alexander Malik (ACC-8, 9, 10)
Mr Theodore Phailbus (ACC-8, 9, 10)

The Anglican Church of Papua New Guinea
     The Rt Revd Tevita Talanoa (ACC-8, 9, 10)

The Philippine Episcopal Church
     Mr Warren Luyaben (ACC-10, 11, 12)

The Episcopal Church of the Province of Rwanda
     The Rt Revd Jonathan Ruhumuliza (ACC-9, 10, 11)
          (unable to attend)
     The Revd Athanase Ngirinshuti (ACC-9, 10, 11)
          (unable to attend; represented by the Revd Prudence Ngarambe)
     Mrs Margaret Bihabanyi (ACC-10, 11, 12)

The Scottish Episcopal Church
     Mr John Rea (ACC-10, 11, 12)

The Church of the Province of Southern Africa
     The Rt Revd Dinis S. Sengulane (ACC-8, 9, 10)
     The Revd Canon Malusi Mpumlwana (ACC-9, 10, 11)
          (unable to attend)
     Ms Maureen Sithole (ACC-10, 11, 12)

The Church of the Province of South East Asia
     The Venerable Bolly Lapok (ACC-10, 11, 12)

The Church of South India
     The Rt Revd B. Peter Sughandar (ACC-10, 11, 12)
     The Revd J Prabhakar Rao (ACC-10, 11, 12)
     Prof. George Koshy (ACC-10, 11, 12)

The Anglican Church of the Southern Cone
     The Revd Hector T. V. Zabala (ACC-10, 11, 12)

The Episcopal Church of the Sudan
     The Rt Revd Michael S. Lugor (ACC-10, 11, 12)
     The Ven. Nelson K. Nyumbe (ACC-9, 10, 11)
     Mr Is-hag Kodi Kodi Kannedy (ACC-10, 11, 12)

The Church of the Province of Tanzania
     The Rt Revd Charles Mwaigoga (ACC-8, 9, 10)
     The Revd Canon Mkunga H.P. Mtingele (ACC-9, 10, 11)

The Church of the Province of Uganda
     The Most Revd Lingstone Mpalanyi-Nkoyoyo (ACC-10, 11, 12)
     The Revd Canon J. Wilson Baganizi (ACC-9, 10)
     Mr Edward S. Mungati (ACC-9, 10, 11)

The Episcopal Church of the United States of America
>The Rt Revd Prof. Mark Dyer (ACC-9, 10, 11)
>The Revd Austin R. Cooper (ACC-8, 9, 10)
>Ms Judith G. Conley (ACC-10, 11, 12)

The Anglican Church in Wales
>Ms Suzie Cole (ACC-10, 11, 12)
>>(unable to attend; represented by Miss Sylvia D. Scarf)
>The Revd Canon David G. Williams (ACC-9, 10, 11)

The Church of the Province of West Africa
>Prof. Adrian DeHeer Amissah (ACC-10, 11, 12)
>>(unable to attend)

The Church of the Province of the West Indies
>Mr Bernard S. A. Turner (ACC-10, 11, 12)
>The Ven. Alvin E. Stone (ACC-8, 9, 10)

The Province of the Anglican Church of Zaire
>The Rt Revd S. Mugerta Tibafa (ACC-9, 10, 11)
>The Revd Basimaki Byabasaija (ACC-10, 11, 12)

Co-opted Members
>The Rt Revd Fernando Soares (ACC-9, 10, 11)
>>Representing the Lusitanian Church
>Mr Ghazi Musharbash (ACC-10, 11, 12)
>>Representing the laity of the Church in Jerusalem and the Middle East
>The Revd Canon Lovey Kisembo (ACC-10, 11, 12)
>>Representing women
>Mrs Lenore Parker (ACC-10, 11, 12)
>>Representing women
>Miss Rachel B. Beleo (ACC-10, 11, 12)
>>Representing youth
>Mr J. J. Tabane (ACC-10, 11, 12)
>>Representing youth; unable to attend

OBSERVERS FROM OTHER CHURCHES

Prof. Roger Nostbakken, Lutheran World Federation
The Revd George Tavard, Roman Catholic Church
The Rt Revd Pedro Arauz, World Methodist Council

CHAPLAIN

The Rt Revd Roger Herft, Bishop of Newcastle, Australia

PRIMATES' PERSONAL STAFF

The Revd Canon Andrew Deuchar, England
The Revd David Hamid, Canada

STAFF

The Revd Dr Donald Anderson, Director of Ecumenical Relations
Mrs Christine Codner, Secretariat
Miss Clare Dell, Secretariat
The Revd Paul Gibson, Liturgical Officer
The Revd Dr Johncy Itty, Office of UN Observer
Mr David Long, Lambeth Conference Manager
Miss Fiona Millican, Secretariat (Lambeth Palace)
Mr Michael Nunn, Director of Finance
The Revd Dr Cyril Okorocha, Director of Mission & Evangelism
The Rt Revd James Ottley, Anglican Observer at the United Nations, New York
Canon James Rosenthal, Director of Communications
Ms Rosemary Palmer, Finance & Administration
Mr Ajay Sodha, Key Travel Agent

SECONDED INTERNATIONAL COMMUNICATIONS TEAM

The Revd Dr Robert Browne, USA
Mrs Nicola Currie, England
The Revd Dorothy Curry, USA
Mr Todd Fitzgerald, USA
The Revd Dr Joan Ford, USA
Mrs Liz Gibson Harries, Ireland
Mr Stephen Jenkins, England
Ms Jackie Kraus, USA
Revd Clement Lee, USA
The Dss. Margaret Rodgers, Australia
The Ven. Lynn Ross, Canada

ADVISERS

The Rt Revd David Birney, USA (on Rwanda)
Ms Marion Dawson Carr, Anglican Investment Agency
The Revd John Rees, Solicitor, Winkworth and Pemberton

HOST PROVINCE CO-ORDINATORS

The Rt Revd Clarence Hayes, Bishop of Panama, and Mrs Connie Hayes
Mr Biron Daniels, Administrator, Diocese of Panama,
    leading team of volunteers
The Revd Diana Luz Parada, leading team of interpreters

Annual Audited Accounts of the Council

Every year, following approval of the ACC Standing Committee, Council members are sent copies of the audited accounts. These include information about the income and expenditure related to the core budget as well as the various designated and special funds held. The report for 1995 was circulated with the papers for this Council meeting.

The Audited accounts for 1993, 1994, and 1995 are laid before this meeting. Extra copies can be made available if individual delegates need them.

Report to the Council

This report focuses firstly on the financial position in relation to the core budget for the current Triennium and then on the core budget for 1997.

The Triennium 1994 to 1996

Figures for the current Triennium are summarised on page 205, with highlight comments on page 206. The figures for 1996 are an estimate of the outturn for the year.

Details of contributions from Member Churches are given on page 207. Each year shows contributions actually credited in that year. In some cases the figures may include arrears paid for prior years. The figures for 1996 show only the actual amounts paid to date.

1997 Core Budget

In order to give ACC-10 the opportunity to determine priorities for the next Triennium, the Joint Standing Committees of the Primates and Council agreed that the Triennium should span the years 1998 to 2000. It has therefore been necessary to prepare a one-year core budget for 1997.

The figures for the 1997 Core Budget are summarised on page 205 in the column at the right-hand side of the page. Highlight comments are given in the last frame of page 206.

Contribution requests are listed on page 207 in the right-hand column of the page.

Pages 208 to 211 set out the 1997 budget and contributions request list in chart form.

UN Observer's Office

The 1997 budget includes a contribution towards this. An explanation of the background is given on page 212.

Michael Nunn, *Treasurer*
4 October 1996

Inter-Anglican Budget Outturn 1994 to 1996 and Budget 1997

	1994 Budget £	1994 Actual Results £	1994 Variation £	1995 Budget £	1995 Actual Results £	1995 Variation £	1996 Budget £	1996 Estimated Results £	1996 Variation £	1997 Budget £
INCOME										
Interest on deposits	5,000	27,401	(22,401)	10,000	30,895	(20,895)	14,000	20,080	(6,080)	15,000
Publications income	9,000	5,849	3,151	7,750	4,108	3,642	5,000	1,150	3,850	5,000
Anglican World	4,500	16,940	(12,440)	6,000	67,006	(61,006)	9,000	99,500	(90,500)	50,000
Services to other bodies	500	2,510	(2,010)	550	2,500	(1,950)	550	500	50	500
Rent receivable	10,750	10,276	474	11,000	7,775	3,225	11,300	5,435	5,865	4,600
Grants for equipment	2,000	2,709	(709)	2,000	3,506	(1,506)		1,750	(1,750)	
Donations & miscellaneous income	750	235	515	700	2,273	(1,573)	650	2,200	(1,550)	500
Special Fund Raising								134,290	(134,290)	175,350
	32,500	**65,920**	**(33,420)**	**38,000**	**118,063**	**(80,063)**	**40,500**	**264,905**	**(224,405)**	**250,950**
Contributions from member churches	917,500	841,952	75,548	962,000	855,392	106,608	1,009,500	853,720	155,780	926,830
Inter-Church Conversations 1996										11,000
Property depreciation recovered					39,873	(39,873)				
	950,000	**907,872**	**42,128**	**1,000,000**	**1,013,328**	**(13,328)**	**1,050,000**	**1,118,625**	**(68,625)**	**1,188,780**
EXPENDITURE										
Secretary General's office	184,400	162,138	22,262	162,750	146,458	16,292	174,350	163,150	11,200	172,335
Communications department	85,500	90,316	(4,816)	89,085	102,887	(13,802)	98,775	106,375	(7,600)	170,400
Anglican World	32,000	56,443	(24,443)	35,600	122,487	(86,887)	34,500	125,000	(90,500)	131,000
Mission and Evangelism	72,375	74,225	(1,850)	77,635	74,991	2,644	83,250	83,930	(680)	82,494
Liturgical co-ordinator	6,600	2,791	3,809	6,950	3,325	3,625	7,300	5,040	2,260	7,300
Ecumenical relations	50,575	43,554	7,021	53,835	55,772	(1,937)	57,750	67,760	(10,010)	73,283
Administration department	97,000	91,922	5,078	103,650	100,120	3,530	111,750	136,390	(24,640)	131,168
Office overheads (rents,fees etc)	121,750	110,734	11,016	131,550	135,612	(4,062)	137,100	138,480	(1,380)	148,300
Contingencies	32,500		32,500	35,000	1,000	34,000	40,000	6,000	34,000	
	682,700	**632,123**	**50,577**	**696,055**	**742,652**	**(46,597)**	**744,775**	**832,125**	**(87,350)**	**916,280**
Provision for meetings etc:										
Inter-Church conversations	40,000	40,000	0	40,000	40,000	0	40,000	40,000	0	40,000
Missio	10,000	10,000	0	12,000	15,000	(3,000)	12,000	21,000	(9,000)	15,000
Council and Standing Committee	60,000	60,000	0	60,000	45,000	15,000	60,000	60,000	0	60,000
Primates	40,000	40,000	0	45,000	30,000	15,000	50,000	50,000	0	20,000
Lambeth Conference	100,000	100,000	0	110,000	110,000	0	120,000	120,000	0	130,000
UN Observer's Office										5,000
Research	2,200	2,200	0	2,300	2,300	0	2,500	2,500	0	2,500
	934,900	**884,323**	**50,577**	**965,355**	**984,952**	**(19,597)**	**1,029,275**	**1,125,625**	**(96,350)**	**1,188,780**
Surplus/(Deficit)	**15,100**	**23,549**	**(8,449)**	**34,645**	**28,376**	**6,269**	**20,725**	**(7,000)**	**27,725**	**0**

Anglican Consultative Council

Inter Anglican Budget Outturn 1994 to 1996 and Budget 1997

1994

Comments:

Contributions shortfall of £75,548 is covered by a combination of extra income in other categories (£33,420 overall) and savings on expenditure (£50,577 overall).

The expansion of 'Anglican World' had commenced and the 'Actual' figures reflect a net cost to the budget of £39,503 (i.e. expenditure £56,443 less income £16,940).

The bottom line shows a surplus of £23,549 for the year.

1995

Comments:

Contributions shortfall is £106,608. This is substantially covered by:

- £39,873 property depreciation written back. Part of the profit on the sale of property.
- £34,000 of the contingencies provision.
- £27,000 net reduction in the meetings provisions.

Interest income exceeded the budget by £20,895.

'Anglican World' expansion continued with a net cost to the budget of £55,481 (i.e expenditure £122,487 less income £67,006. The income included £30,000 from special funds raised for promotion of the magazine.).

The bottom line shows a surplus of £28,376 for the year.

1996

Comments:

Contributions shortfall is projected at £155,780.

Aside from the 'Anglican World' items, variations on normal income heads cancel each other out, as do the expenditure heads (which include an allowance for an additional provision of £9,000 for Missio).

The net 'Anglican World' budget cost is projected at £25,500 (£125,000 expenditure less £99,500 income. The income figure includes £49,000 special funds raised for the promotion of the magazine.).

Allowing for a sustainable deficit of £7,000, this leaves £134,290 to be covered from special fund raising, of which £100,000 is still to be found, in order to secure the position for the year.

1997

Comments:

The 1997 budget allows for contributions based mainly on previous payment patterns. This makes the total requests (£926,830) lower than the amounts requested in 1995 and 1996.

At the same time, expenses are projected to be higher than previously, a major element being the cost of new posts in the Communications department.

A net cost to the budget of £81,000 is allowed for 'Anglican World' (£131,000 expenditure less £50,000 income).

In order to balance the budget, it is proposed to reallocate £11,000 anticipated savings on the 1996 Ecumenical programme and seek £175,350 as special donations.

Report dated 14 October 1996

Inter-Anglican Budget
Contributions History 1994 to 9 October 1996 and Requests for 1997

	1994			1995			1996			1997
	Request	Total Paid	Variation	Request	Total Paid	Variation	Request	Total Paid	Variation	Request
Australia	96,338	69,638	26,700	101,010	91,788	9,222	105,997	60,545	45,452	94,000
Brazil	4,588	4,108	480	4,810	0	4,810	5,048	0	5,048	4,500
Burundi	138	138	0	144	144	0	150	0	150	200
Canada	100,925	67,841	33,084	105,820	62,536	43,284	111,044	32,421	78,623	72,000
CCEA	6,147	2,762	3,385	6,445	5,675	770	6,764	1,091	5,673	6,500
Central Africa	11,469	0	11,469	12,025	11,876	149	12,619	0	12,619	13,120
Ceylon	917	1,956	(1,039)	962	962	0	1,010	1,010	0	1,100
ECUSA	250,019	241,188	8,831	262,145	221,438	40,707	275,088	168,715	106,373	225,490
England [inc Dio in Europe]	258,276	290,000	(31,724)	270,803	290,000	(19,197)	284,173	288,000	(3,827)	295,600
Indian Ocean	2,294	2,284	10	2,405	2,405	0	2,524	2,524	0	2,700
Ireland	20,644	20,644	0	21,645	21,645	0	22,714	22,714	0	23,740
Japan	11,469	12,585	(1,116)	12,025	12,025	0	12,619	6,310	6,309	13,120
Jerusalem & M.E.	3,211	6,855	(3,644)	3,367	3,367	0	3,533	3,177	356	3,680
Kenya	13,763	10,351	3,412	14,430	10,018	4,412	15,143	0	15,143	8,000
Korea	3,028	3,443	(415)	3,175	1,215	1,960	3,331	1,960	1,371	3,500
Melanesia	917	917	0	962	962	0	1,010	1,010	0	1,100
Mexico [from 1995]				0	852	(852)	1,000	1,000	0	1,200
Myanmar [Burma]	917	1,039	(122)	962	917	45	1,010	1,972	(962)	1,100
New Zealand	27,525	27,525	0	28,860	28,860	0	30,284	33,645	(3,361)	33,645
Nigeria	13,763	360	13,403	14,430	7,833	6,597	15,143	200	14,943	15,250
Papua New Guinea	917	917	0	962	962	0	1,010	1,063	(53)	1,100
Philippines	4,588	4,478	110	4,810	5,297	(487)	5,048	4,945	103	5,250
Rwanda	1,220	0	1,220	1,280	0	1,280	1,343	1,343	0	1,000
Scotland	13,763	13,763	0	14,430	14,430	0	15,143	15,143	0	15,500
South East Asia	0	0	0	0	0	0	0	0	0	20,000
Southern Africa	16,056	16,056	0	16,835	11,959	4,876	17,666	0	17,666	12,480
Southern Cone of S. America	2,294	1,660	634	2,405	948	1,457	2,524	0	2,524	2,630
Sudan	2,294	0	2,294	2,405	1,202	1,203	2,524	2,000	524	2,630
Tanzania	4,588	4,880	(292)	4,810	4,810	0	5,048	5,048	0	5,250
Uganda	6,881	1,000	5,881	7,215	0	7,215	7,570	400	7,170	1,000
Wales	20,644	20,644	0	21,645	21,645	0	22,714	22,714	0	23,740
West Africa	3,211	1,434	1,777	3,367	3,000	367	3,533	0	3,533	2,000
West Indies	9,175	9,175	0	9,620	9,620	0	10,095	10,095	0	10,500
Zaire	293	0	293	307	600	(293)	323	323	0	500
United Churches										
Bangladesh	459	459	0	481	481	0	505	24	481	525
Church of North India	917	917	0	962	962	0	1,010	653	357	1,100
Church of Pakistan	917	0	917	962	1,879	(917)	1,010	505	505	1,100
Church of South India	1,376	1,376	0	1,443	1,443	0	1,514	1,514	0	1,600
Extra-Provincial Dioceses										
Hong Kong										10,000
Bermuda	917	917	0	962	962	0	1,010	1,010	0	1,500
Lusitanian Church	321	321	0	337	337	0	353	526	(173)	500
Spanish Rfmd Episcopal Church	321	321	0	337	337	0	353	0	353	500
	917,500	**841,952**	**75,548**	**962,000**	**855,392**	**106,608**	**1,010,500**	**693,600**	**316,900**	**926,830**

Anglican Consultative Council

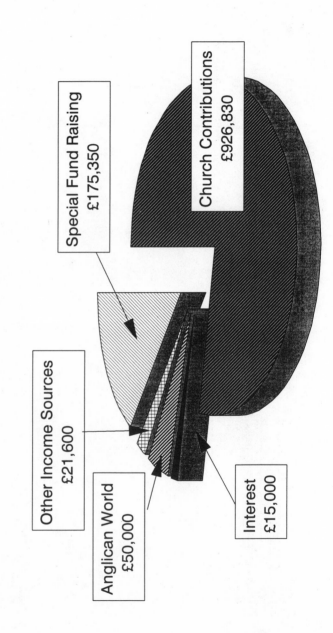

ANGLICAN CONSULTATIVE COUNCIL
INCOME BUDGET 1997

(Total Budget £1,188,780)

Special Fund Raising
£175,350

Church Contributions
£926,830

Other Income Sources
£21,600

Anglican World
£50,000

Interest
£15,000

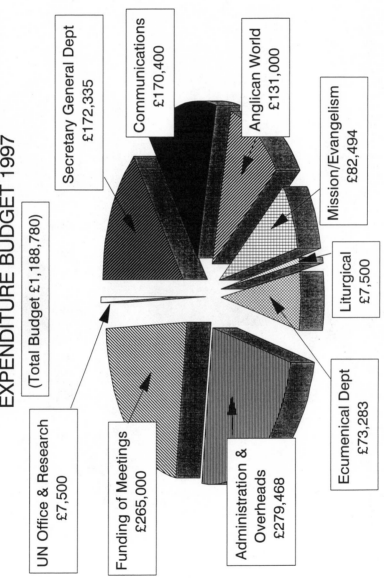

ANGLICAN CONSULTATIVE COUNCIL
EXPENDITURE BUDGET 1997

(Total Budget £1,188,780)

UN Office & Research
£7,500

Funding of Meetings
£265,000

Administration &
Overheads
£279,468

Secretary General Dept
£172,335

Communications
£170,400

Anglican World
£131,000

Mission/Evangelism
£82,494

Liturgical
£7,500

Ecumenical Dept
£73,283

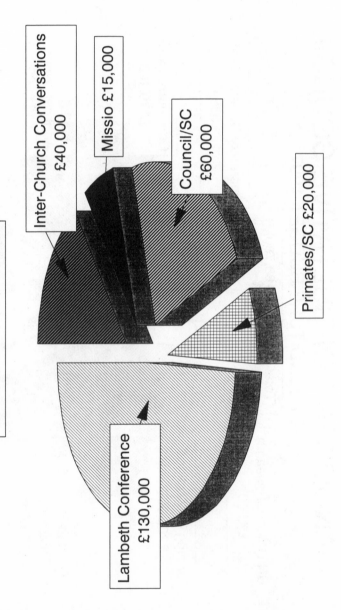

ANGLICAN CONSULTATIVE COUNCIL
MEETINGS ALLOCATIONS 1997

(Total Allocations £265,000)

Inter-Church Conversations £40,000

Missio £15,000

Council/SC £60,000

Primates/SC £20,000

Lambeth Conference £130,000

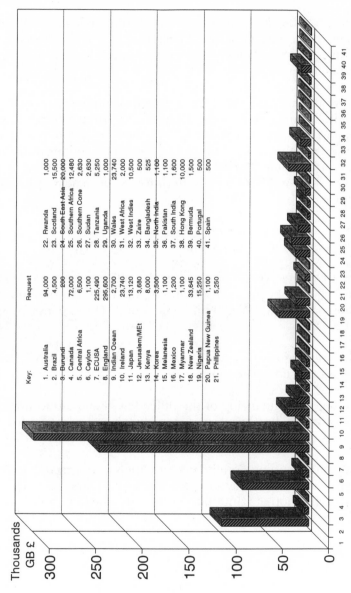

ANGLICAN CONSULTATIVE COUNCIL
Contributions Requests 1997

Key:	Request
1. Australia	94,000
2. Brazil	4,500
3. Burundi	800
4. Canada	72,000
5. Central Africa	6,500
6. Ceylon	1,100
7. ECUSA	225,490
8. England	295,600
9. Indian Ocean	2,700
10. Ireland	23,740
11. Japan	13,120
12. Jerusalem/MEt	3,680
13. Kenya	8,000
14. Korea	3,500
15. Melanesia	1,100
16. Mexico	1,200
17. Myanmar	1,100
18. New Zealand	33,645
19. Nigeria	15,250
20. Papua New Guinea	1,100
21. Phillipines	5,250

22. Rwanda	1,000
23. Scotland	15,500
24. South East Asia	20,000
25. Southern Africa	12,480
26. Southern Cone	2,630
27. Sudan	2,630
28. Tanzania	5,250
29. Uganda	1,000
30. Wales	23,740
31. West Africa	2,000
32. West Indies	10,500
33. Zaire	500
34. Bangladesh	525
35. North India	1,100
36. Pakistan	1,100
37. South India	1,600
38. Hong Kong	10,000
39. Bermuda	1,500
40. Portugal	500
41. Spain	500

Thousands
GB £

Churches - See Key list above

United Nations Observer Office

The UN Observer's Office was started some years ago with the appointment of the first Observer. In discussions about the financial arrangements, ACC-8 in Wales (1990) determined that the funding should be extra-budgetary.

Up to the current year, 1996, substantial funding has been provided by Trinity Church, Wall Street. However, as Trinity Church has a policy of support for a limited period only, their provision is scheduled to be phased out this year. Additional funding has been provided through various fund-raising efforts based on an advisory committee in the United States. The Archbishop of Canterbury has been actively involved in these efforts.

These contributions covered the costs of the office up to the end of 1995, but, at that point, funds for the office were exhausted.

For 1996, the expense budget for the office is £238,000. To date, about £148,000 has been raised (including the final contribution from Trinity Church), leaving £90,000 still to be found. The expense budget for 1997 is £260,000.

The ongoing work of this office, therefore, depends on the continuing provision of adequate funds.

Although the financing of the office has always, up to now, been extra-budgetary, it has been suggested that it is important for prospective donors to be aware that ACC has a financial commitment towards it.

The Joint Standing Committees have therefore agreed that £5,000 should be provided in 1997 as a contribution. This amount was chosen because the Archbishop of Canterbury contributes the same amount annually.

PHOTOGRAPHS

Scenes from Anglican Consultive Council X, Panama City
and
from throughout the Anglican Communion

Procession at ACC 10 in Panama.

The Rt. Revd. James H. Ottley, UN Office and former Bishop of Panama, leads the procession.

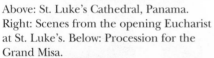

Above: St. Luke's Cathedral, Panama.
Right: Scenes from the opening Eucharist
at St. Luke's. Below: Procession for the
Grand Misa.

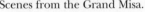

Scenes from the Grand Misa.

Bishops from Province IX, USA., meet with Archbishop Carey.

Traditional Panamanian dress.

St. Christopher's Episcopal School.
(Photo: J. Krause)

Panamanian dancing at diocesan dinner.

Westminster Abbey in
London.

The new Archbishop of Capetown, The Most Revd.
Njongonkulu Winston Ndungane.

Archbishop Carey with the bishops of
Mozambique on a pastoral visit.

Scene from an Anglican Religious
Order.

Canterbury Cathedral, England.

An Anglican choir in Sudan.

Anglicans in Mexico at Holy Cross Church.

Church of the Nativity, Bethlehem.

Archbishop Carey and Pope John Paul II in Rome, December 1996.

The Primus of Scotland on the Via Dolorosa (Way of the Cross) in Jerusalem.

Women priests in Wales at Bangor Cathedral.

(Photos by James Rosenthal/*Anglican World*)

Archbishop Carey visits orphanage in Rwanda.

APPENDICES

The following pages contain some of the most important documents available for the Anglican Communion as we look to the challenges of the next millennium and our own life within the one holy catholic and apostolic Church of Jesus Christ. We have much to share, we have much to learn. Our resources are vast and can gather momentum if we learn to share from South-to-North, South-to-South, and North-to-North. Communication is key; where there is lack of communication and lack of compassion there is lack of trust and confidence. These reports speak of a confident Anglican Christianity that can lead us to celebrate Jesus Christ at the millennium with a new vigour and fervour.

Can we be true to the spirit of Anglicanism? Can we be faithful followers of the Gospel of Jesus Christ? Can we support with our time, talent, and treasure the work of the world-wide Church? Can we rejoice and be thankful for our diversity? These are the questions we bring with us as we welcome the next century of proclaiming Christ.

Anglican Communion Office

THE VIRGINIA REPORT

*The Report
of the Inter-Anglican Theological
and Doctrinal Commission*

Contents

Preface

This Report is the work of the Inter-Anglican Theological and Doctrinal Commission which comprises theologians and church leaders who themselves represent the diversities of the Anglican Communion. Their task was to respond to the call of the Lambeth Conference of 1988 to consider in some depth the meaning and nature of communion. This response was to be set within the context of the doctrine of the Trinity, the unity and order of the Church and the unity and community of humanity. At the heart and centre of the Anglican pilgrimage lies the concept of communion. From it we derive so much of our belief and practice. It is not itself a static concept. It has become with our pilgrimage a living and developing reality. Yet that fact alone demands understanding which cannot be tied to any one period of our history or to any single cultural approach.

This Report is offered to the Anglican Communion as one more step in the process of seeking greater understanding of what communion means to the Body of Christ. In particular it seeks to suggest ways in which our Communion can respond in practical ways which touch and concern how we order our corporate life and lives as individuals.

I wish to acknowledge with sincere gratitude the generosity and support given to the Commission by the Right Reverend Peter Lee, Bishop of Virginia, the Diocese of Virginia and the staff of the Virginia Theological Seminary. Their practical assistance and encouragement made the production of this Report possible.

It has been a great privilege to chair the Commission and I acknowledge the support and work of all its members.

Robert Eames
Archbishop of Armagh

Members of the Inter-Anglican Theological and Doctrinal Commission

The Revd Victor R Atta-Baffoe, The Church of West Africa

The Rt Revd Colin Bazley, Iglesia Anglicana del Cono Sur de America

The Most Revd Peter F Carnley, Anglican Church of Australia

The Rt Revd J Mark Dyer, The Episcopal Church, USA

The Revd Dr Milton B Efthimiou, Orthodox Participant

The Rt Revd Penelope A B Jamieson, Church of Aotearoa,
New Zealand & Polynesia

The Very Revd Colin Jones, The Church of Southern Africa

The Rt Revd Dr Samuel B Joshua, The United Church of North India

The Revd Dr Patricia G Kirkpatrick, Anglican Church of Canada

The Revd Samuel I Koshiishi, Nippon Sei Ko Kai

Professor Dr Michael Root, Lutheran Participant

The Rt Revd Stanford S Shauri, Church of Tanzania

The Rt Revd Stephen Sykes, The Church of England

Dr Mary Tanner, The Church of England

Dr Fredrica Harris Thompsett, The Episcopal Church, USA

The Most Revd Robert H A Eames, The Church of Ireland (Chairman)

The Revd Dr Donald Anderson, Anglican Communion Office
(Secretary to November 1996)

The Revd Canon David Hamid, Anglican Communion Office
(Secretary from November 1996)

Mrs Christine Codner, Anglican Communion Office
(Administrative Secretary)

The Revd Professor David Scott, Virginia Theological Seminary
(Observer)

Introduction

Origin and Mandate of the Commission

In 1988 the Lambeth Conference was faced with a question that challenged the unity of the Communion: the proposal by the Episcopal Church of the United States of America to consecrate a woman to the episcopate. In the light of its deliberations, the Lambeth Conference passed Resolution 1 on the ordination or consecration of women to the episcopate. In response to this resolution of the Conference, the Archbishop of Canterbury, in consultation with the Primates, established a Commission on Communion and Women in the Episcopate under the leadership of the Most Revd. Robert Eames, Archbishop of Armagh

> (a) to provide for an examination of the relationships between Provinces of the Anglican Communion and ensure that the process of reception includes continuing consultation with other Churches as well;

> (b) to monitor and encourage the process of consultation within the Communion and to offer further pastoral guidelines (*The Truth Shall Make You Free*, The Lambeth Conference 1988. Resolution 1, page 201).

The Eames Commission, as it came to be known, met five times and produced four reports which were published together in December 1994. Its last meeting was in December 1993 and its report will be presented to the 1998 Lambeth Conference. During its lifetime the Commission engaged in theological reflection on the nature of *koinonia*. It offered guidelines on how Anglicans might live together in the highest degree of communion possible, while different views and practices concerning the ordination of women continued to be held within the Communion. The Eames Commission saw this as a way of enabling an ongoing process of reception both within the Anglican Communion and the wider ecumenical fellowship. Its guidelines are intended to support graceful and charitable relationships and to ensure proper pastoral care for one another. Before its last meeting, five women had been consecrated as bishops. Also in that period the ordination of women to the priesthood had received the necessary consents in the Church of England and over 1000 women were ordained as priests, and by then, women had also been ordained as priests in Australia, Aotearoa, New Zealand and Polynesia, Brazil, Burundi,

Canada, Hong Kong and Macao, Ireland, Kenya, the Philippines, Scotland, Southern Africa, Uganda, the USA and West Africa.

The Eames Commission between 1988 and 1993 provided a model of how Anglicans can remain together in the highest degree of communion possible while endeavouring to come to a common mind on a matter which touches the fundamental unity of the Communion.

The 1988 Conference recognized that there was a need to describe how the Anglican Communion makes authoritative decisions, while maintaining unity and interdependence in the light of the many theological issues that arise from its diversity. To address this need, the Conference resolved that there should be:

> As a matter of urgency further exploration of the meaning and nature of communion with particular reference to the doctrine of the Trinity, the unity and order of the Church, and the unity and community of humanity (Lambeth Conference 1988, Resolution 18, page 216. See Appendix I).

Resolution 8 on the Final Report of the Anglican-Roman Catholic International Commission also had a direct bearing on the exercise of authority in the Church. It encouraged ARCIC to explore the basis in Scripture and tradition of the concept of a universal primacy, in conjunction with collegiality, as an instrument of unity, the character of such primacy in practice, and to draw upon the experience of other Christian Churches in exercising primacy, collegiality and conciliarity.

In implementing Resolution 18 of Lambeth 1988, and at the request of the Primates of the Communion, the Archbishop of Canterbury invited a group of representative church leaders and theologians to meet in December 1991 at the Virginia Theological Seminary at Alexandria, USA, to begin the exploration. The Consultation's report was called *Belonging Together.* The Report was circulated widely within the Communion between 1992 and 1994, with a request for critical comment. A number of Anglican member churches responded officially. There were also responses from theological institutions and individuals.

All the responses were considered by the Inter-Anglican Theological and Doctrinal Commission, the successor of the 1991 Consultation, when it met in December 1994, and again in January 1996, on both occasions at the Virginia Theological Seminary. This report is the product of its consideration and further reflection on the issues.

Chapter One
The Context

1.1 Our Lord Jesus Christ prayed that his followers might be one, as He and the Father are one, so that the world might believe (Jn 17:20-21). Christians of every tradition struggle to respond in faith, life and witness to the vision of unity expressed in the prayer of Jesus. At every level of Christian life, the call to graceful interdependence and unity in faith and doctrine challenges us.

1.2 From the earliest time in the history of the Christian community, an admonishing voice has been heard exhorting believers to maintain agreement with one another and thereby to avert divisions. From an almost equally early date they have found consensus, even on apparently major matters, singularly difficult to achieve. When the second century Churches evolved a collection of early Christian documents, which came to be called the New Testament, they had a few documents which did not attest and reflect deep disagreements, and the formation of the collection itself was the product of controversies. Nevertheless, the controversies themselves were stages on a road towards greater consensus.

1.3 What makes unity and interdependence particularly difficult today? In the last 200 years the world has seen extraordinary development in the political, scientific, economic and psychological spheres. These developments have brought many blessings to the peoples of the world. At the same time there has been the disintegration of traditional cultures, values and social structures and unprecedented threats to the environment. The tension between blessing and disintegration creates a challenge to the unity and interdependence that the peoples of the world face.

1.4 The authority of nineteenth and twentieth century notions of progress, economic growth and the free market economy, the omnipotence of scientific method and technology, and competitive individualism is no longer accepted without question. In many places there is a search for cultural, personal and social identity which honours the integrity and value of cultural roots.

1.5 Within this context Anglicans strive to be faithful to the Gospel in their particular cultural contexts and to face moral, doctrinal, social and economic exigencies which demand discernment and response, if identity as the Christian community is to be maintained. For example, issues of justice and human rights, including human sexuality, the family and the status of women, racial equality, religious freedom and the use and distribution of resources, demand attention. Our response to these issues is conditioned by our particular cultural context, our way of interpreting the Bible, our degree of awareness of being part of a wider human community, and our attentativeness to the response of other ecumenical partners and to the concerns of those of other faiths.

1.6   The churches of the Anglican Communion struggle with these concerns within a life of communion and interdependence. Discernment has to be exercised about which concerns are best addressed by the local church, by the province, and by the whole Communion. An added burden is placed on decision making when churches are separated from one another.

1.7   New challenges to unity press impatiently upon all churches, and not least of all are those of the Anglican Communion. Today we might cite divisive issues in, for example, the Indian Ocean and Europe, Rwanda, Northern Ireland, Nigeria and the Middle East, the United States, Australia and South East Asia.

1.8   When Christians find themselves passionately engaged in the midst of complex and explosive situations, how do they avoid alienation from those who by baptism are their brothers and sisters in Christ, who are embraced in the communion of God the Holy Trinity, but who disagree? How do they stay in communion with God and each other; how do they behave towards each other in the face of disagreement and conflict? What are the limits of diversity if the Gospel imperative of unity and communion are to be maintained?

1.9   In addressing issues raised by the complexities of contemporary life, solutions will in some cases be necessarily provisional. There are times when the path ahead is insufficiently clear for categorical claims to be made. Forming a mind entails learning from those within the Anglican Communion and being in partnership and dialogue with ecumenical and interfaith colleagues. There is merit in the Anglican approach of listening to others, of holding each other in the highest degree of communion possible, with tolerance for deeply held differences of conviction and practice.

1.10   While we are aware of significant challenges to our unity as a Communion, we recognise that we have received the gracious gift of God the Holy Trinity, the resources of our life in Christ in word and sacrament, and the determination to develop appropriate and more effective structures for maintaining unity in service and mission.

1.11   The Commission has centred its study on the understanding of trinitarian faith. It believes that the unity of the Anglican Communion derives from the unity given in the triune God, whose inner personal and relational nature is communion. This is our centre. This mystery of God's life calls us to communion in visible form. This is why the Church is called again and again to review and to reform the structures of its life together, so that they nurture and enable the life of communion in God and serve God's mission in the world.

1.12 The references in the Lambeth resolution to the trinitarian doctrine and the unity and community of the whole human family make it clear that the concern of the Lambeth Conference was not simply for strengthening the peace and unity of the Anglican Communion, but also for the faithful and effective engagement of the Communion in God's mission of love and reconciliation in the world.

1.13 The mission and ministry of reconciliation entrusted by God to the Church are given in baptism to the whole people of God, the *laos*. While this report necessarily dwells on the structures of ministry in the processes of oversight, and their interdependence and accountability, it does so in the conviction and hope that this reflection will open up the possibility of creative change, which will strengthen the ministry and mission of the whole people of God.

1.14 The instruments of communion, which are a gift of God to the Church, help to hold us in the life of the triune God. These are the instruments which we seek to renew within the Anglican Communion. They are also the structures we seek to share with all those who have been baptised into the life of the Triune God. Our hope is that this theological reflection may contribute not only to the Anglican Communion but to the ecumenical goal of full visible unity.

1.15 In reflecting on the structures of Anglican unity and authority, we are aware that discernment, decision making and teaching with authority are today, sadly, in the context of separated Churches, and are therefore only partial reflections of the One, Holy Catholic and Apostolic Church. This requires Anglicans to listen to the experience of other ecclesial communities and to continue to deepen the work of ecumenical dialogue on the nature of authority and its exercise in the Church and to renew our Anglican structures in line with the emerging ecumenical convergence.

1.16 Having referred in this chapter to the context and the challenges that face Christians today, the report goes on in **Chapter Two,** to a theological reflection on the gracious gift of love in the triune God and how the Church responds to that gift in the ministry that the Church has received from Christ. **Chapter Three** examines the bonds of interdependence, or what holds Anglicans together. **Chapter Four** explores the principle of subsidiarity, indentifying the ways in which the bonds of unity are appropriately expressed at the different levels the Church's life. **Chapter Five** identifies the principles which undergird our life together and **Chapter Six** offers some observations about how Anglican international institutions of unity might be strengthened and improved, in order to strengthen our life together for the sake of God's mission in the world.

Chapter Two

Theology of God's Gracious Gift: the Communion of the Trinity and the Church

I. The Understanding of Gracious Gift

2.1   God's gracious gift of steadfast loving kindness was from the beginning known by the people of God in the form of covenant. From the prophets came the conviction that God's faithfulness was never ending, even when God's people were forgetful and betrayed the divine trust.

2.2   God's love and faithfulness were understood as having been an act of creation. God's promise to remember the everlasting covenant between God and every living creature on the earth (Gen 9:17) was a promise which was renewed again and again through the ages.

2.3   God's word to Moses in Exodus 3:14 expresses the divine promise which forever grounds the hope of inter-relational communion between God and the people of God in an everlasting and personal relationship, even in the midst of tragedy.

2.4   The people of God interpreted the memory of the Sinai Covenant in words remembered as spoken by Moses, words which would forever define God's sacred relationship with his chosen people:

> For you are a people holy to the LORD your God; the LORD your God has chosen you out of all the peoples on earth to be his people, his treasured possession. It was not because you were more numerous than any other people that the LORD set his heart on you and chose you - for you were the fewest of all peoples. It was because the LORD loved you and kept the oath that he swore to your ancestors. (Deut. 7:6-8a).

2.5 God's chosen, the people of Israel, would tell the story of God's never failing love in intimate longing and passion. So the prophet is moved to proclaim:

> You shall no more be termed Forsaken,
> and your land shall no more be termed Desolate; but you shall
> be called My Delight is in Her,and your land Married; for the
> LORD delights in you, and your land shall be married.
>
> For as a young man marries a young woman, so shall your

builder marry you, and as the bridegroom rejoices over the
bride, so shall your God rejoice over you (Is 62:4-5).

And in the midst of despair and anguish Jeremiah speaks of God's loving
act of restoration:

> But this is the covenant that I will make with the house of Israel
> after those days, says the LORD: I will put my law within them,
> and I will write it on their hearts; and I will be their God, and
> they shall be my people (Jer 31:33).

2.6   Jesus spoke of this God of steadfast loving kindness and faithfulness,
as his Father. He prayed: "I thank you, Father, Lord of heaven and earth,
because you have hidden these things from the wise and the intelligent
and have revealed them to infants; yes, Father, for such was your gracious
will. All things have been handed over to me by my Father; and no one
knows the Son except the Father, and no one knows the Father except the
Son and anyone to whom the Son chooses to reveal him" (Matt. 11:25-27).

2.7   The good news of the Christian Gospel is that Jesus' life among us is
God's life—God breaking down the barriers of our bondage and sinfulness. In Jesus, God is with us in all our human helplessness, in our life and
in our death. In Jesus, God is faithful to us even on a cross. In the risen
Jesus, God is with us to transfigure and set free all those who are bound
by fear and sin. Jesus is God with us, and to know Jesus is to be with God.
God has shared our human world with us, and through the great events
of cross and resurrection, we are empowered and invited to share God's
life, to share God's glory and freedom, and to proclaim God's holiness
and mercy in word and act. We know God as we live with Jesus, so that we
can and must say that Jesus' life is the act and expression of God (The
Lambeth Conference 1988, page 82).

2.8   The climax of the Son's revelation of the Father occurs in the passion, death and resurrection of Jesus. On the night before he died Jesus
revealed that the communion of love he shared with the Father would be
shared by the community of his disciples. John's Gospel remembers the
intimate moment of God's gracious gift of love.

> As the Father has loved me, so I have loved you; abide in my
> love. No one has greater love than this, to lay down one's life
> for one's friends. I have called you friends, because I have
> made known to you everything I have heard from my Father.
> You did not choose me but I chose you. And I appointed you
> to go and bear fruit, fruit that will last, so that the Father will
> give you whatever you ask him in my name. I am giving you

these commands so that you may love one another (John 15, 9, 13, 15-17).

2.9   The love with which the Father loves Jesus is the love with which Jesus loves us. On the night before he died, Jesus prayed (Jn 17) that all who follow him should be drawn into that love and unity which exists between the Father and the Son. Thus our unity with one another is grounded in the life of love, unity and communion of the Godhead. The eternal, mutual, self-giving and receiving love of the three persons of the Trinity is the source and ground of our communion, of our fellowship with God and one another. Through the power of the Holy Spirit, we are drawn into a divine fellowship of love and unity. Further, it is because the Holy Trinity is a unique unity of purpose, and at the same time a diversity of ways of being and function, that the Church is called to express diversity in its own life, a diversity held together in God's unity and love (The Lambeth Conference 1988, page 130).

2.10   At the Last Supper with his disciples, Jesus promised the outpouring of God's Holy Spirit. He prayed that God would come to the community as the gift of the Holy Spirit. The Spirit would bear witness to the truth of all that Jesus said and did.

> I will ask the Father, and he will give you another Advocate, to be with you forever. This is the Spirit of truth, whom the world cannot receive, because it neither sees him nor knows him. You know him, because he abides in you, and he will be in you.

Jesus goes on,

> On that day you will know that I am in my Father, and you in me, and I in you. They who have my commandments and keep them are those who love me; and those who love me will be loved by my Father, and I will love them and reveal myself to them (John 14:16-17; 20-21).

2.11   The sending of the Holy Spirit at Pentecost created the Church, the community of Jesus Christ. The Holy Spirit lifted up the community into the very life of God: Father, Son and Holy Spirit. The Spirit empowered the community to pray "Abba, Father" as free, adopted, children of God (Romans 8:15-17, Gal 4:4-7). "Clothed with power from on high" (Luke 24:49), the community is empowered to go forth to proclaim the Good News of God to all peoples and nations. The Holy Spirit is the unifying force of God in the community. The unity of the Church which is given, and yet which it seeks to deepen, is grounded in the very unity of God, Father, Son and Holy Spirit (Ephesians 1:3-14, 4:1-6).

2.12 Every act of God is an act of the undivided Holy Trinity. The very being of the Church is thus dependent upon the outpouring of God's gracious love, the love of Father, Son and Holy Spirit. The experience of the truth of the revelation of God in Jesus Christ came to the disciples as a gracious gift. What the disciples experienced at Pentecost in Jesus Christ was that communion of life with God which was present at creation and which will be perfected in the fullness of time.

II. The Communion of the Trinity and the Life of the Church

2.13 By the power of the Holy Spirit, the Church is born into history as the Body of Christ (1 Cor. 12:27). The Church is called the temple of God (1 Cor. 3:16), a chosen race, a royal priesthood, a holy nation, a people God claims as his own (1 Pet 2:9). These images of the Church speak of a communion with God: Father, Son, and Holy Spirit. Christians are participants in the divine nature. This communion also determines our relationship with one another. "We declare to you what we have seen and heard so that you also may have fellowship with us; and truly our fellowship is with the Father, and with his Son, Jesus Christ" (I John 1:3). Communion with God and one another is both gift and divine expectation for the Church (Eames I, Koinonia and the Mystery of God, 21-22).

2.14 Because the Church as communion participates in God's communion of Father, Son and Holy Spirit, it has an eschato-logical reality and significance. The Church is the advent, in history, of God's final will being done "on earth as it is in heaven." That will was revealed in the life and ministry of Jesus Christ and is continually inspired by the work of the Spirit in the life and mission of the Church. The Church is the icon of the future, toward which God is directing the history of the world. A faithful church signifies by its life that it is the living promise of God's purpose in the midst of today's history. The Church lives in the present, remembering again and again (making *anamnesis*) the Christ event and receiving in hope the promise of the Kingdom. In this way, the saving events of Christ's death and resurrection and the foretaste of the Kingdom are brought into the present experience of the Church.

2.15 The Church looks forward in Christ, through the power of the Holy Spirit, to that day when God's name will be made holy, God's Kingdom come, when God's will is done on earth as it is in heaven. The seventh century theologian St. Maximus the Confessor put it this way: "The things of the past are shadow; those of the present icon; the truth is to be found in the things of the future" (Scolion on the ecclesiastical hierarchy, 3,3:2). Faithful Christian community with God, the Holy Trinity, is focused in a vision of the final and ultimate reign of God. Its mission is to be the living and visible sign of that divine reign, when He will dwell with them as their

God; "they will be his peoples, and God himself will be with them; he will wipe every tear from their eyes. Death will be no more; mourning and crying and pain will be no more; for the first things have passed away" (Revelation 21:3-4).

III.   The Communion of the Trinity and Mission and Ministry

2.16 A living faith in the God of Jesus Christ draws us into the life of the Holy Trinity. This means living as Jesus understood and lived his life, empowered by God's Spirit:

> The Spirit of the Lord is upon me, because he has anointed me to bring good news to the poor. He has sent me to proclaim release to the captives and recovery of sight to the blind, to let the oppressed go free, to proclaim the year of the Lord's favour (Luke 4:18-19).

2.17 The same Spirit of the Lord rests upon the Church and dwells in the hearts of the believers, empowering the community to go forth as Christ did to proclaim the reign of God. The mission of the Church is to be the icon of God's life. By prayer and praise, mercy and peace, justice and love, constantly welcoming the sinner, the outcast, the marginalised into her sanctuary, the Church is revealed as communion and is faithful to its mission. As Body of Christ (1 Cor. 12:27), Temple of the Holy Spirit (1 Cor. 1:16), God's own people (1 Pet 2:9), the Church lives in mutual love and is sent forth as a missionary community to gather all of creation into God's reconciling love, restore and renew it in the life of the triune God (Rom 8:19-25).

2.18 The mission of Christ and the Church is celebrated and proclaimed in the liturgy which shapes the trinitarian faith of the people of God and empowers them for a life of ministry and mission. This is especially true of holy baptism and holy eucharist.

2.19 As the sacrament of initiation into the life of the Church, baptism is related not only to a single experience, but to life-long growth in Christ and participation in his ministry. Those who are baptized are called upon to reflect the glory of the Lord with ever increasing splendour, as they are transformed by the power of the Holy Spirit into his likeness. As they grow in the Christian life of faith, baptized believers demonstrate that humanity can be regenerated and liberated. They have a common responsibility to bear witness in the Church and the world to the Gospel of Christ, "the Liberator of all human beings" (BEM, Baptism 9,10).

2.20 The eucharist also embraces all aspects of life. It is a representative act of thanksgiving and offering on behalf of the whole world. The eucharistic celebration demands reconciliation and sharing among those who are brothers and sisters in the one family of God, and constantly challenges those who participate to search for appropriate relationships in social, economic and political life (Matt 5:23f. I Cor 10:16f; 11:20-22. Gal 3:28). All injustice, racism, separation and denial of freedom are radically challenged when Christians share in the body and blood of Christ. Through the eucharist the grace of God penetrates, restores and renews human personality and dignity. The eucharist involves believers in the central event of the world's history, the passion, death and resurrection of Christ, and sends them into the world in peace to love and serve the Lord (BEM, Eucharist 20).

2.21 Jesus Christ manifests and carries out for us God's creative, reconciling and perfecting mission and ministry to the world. All Christian ministry is rooted in that unique ministry of Jesus Christ. The centre of Jesus's ministry is his self-offering on the cross for the reconciliation of God and humanity and the healing of the whole human family (Colossians 1:19; 2 Cor. 5:19). Christ's passion, death and resurrection brings into relationship those who had become alienated, both individually and corporately. The reconciling work of Christ, the very heart of the Christian good news, brings those who receive him into the trinitarian life of sharing and inter-relationship.

2.22 Christ calls human beings to share in that loving and redeeming work of God and empowers them for that ministry with his Spirit. Jesus prayed, "As you have sent me into the world, so I have sent them into the world" (John 17:18). Christ called and equipped his disciples and sent them to reflect his own ministry of healing, teaching, leading, feeding and proclaiming. Through the varied aspects of the Church's one ministry, the Kingdom which Jesus proclaimed is brought into historical expression.

2.23 To be baptized and to participate at the Table of the Lord is to be entrusted with Christ's one, continuing mission through the Church. The baptised are called to unity and interdependence. United to Christ, each member of the Body relates to the other members; they are interdependent with and through Christ. To celebrate the eucharist together reveals and builds this mutuality; "we who are many are one body for we all partake of the one bread." In eucharist the Spirit affirms and renews communion in Christ and the gifts given us to participate in the divine mission.

2.24 The Holy Spirit bestows on the community diverse and complimentary gifts (cf BEM, Ministry 5). God the Creator blesses people with many talents and abilities. The Holy Spirit graces individuals with special gifts.

The outworking of one person's gift in the Church is unthinkable apart from all the others. The mutuality and interdependence of each member and each part of the Church is essential for the fulfilment of the Church's mission. In the early Church, those who spoke in tongues needed interpreters of tongues; Paul's mission to the Gentiles complemented Peter's mission to the Jews. The ministry of serving tables in the early Church freed the other disciples to preach God's word. The gifts of all contribute to the building up of the community and the fulfilment of its calling.

2.25 But the one mission of the Church, the Body of Christ, must always find its motivation, its intelligibility and its integrity in the one ministry of the Church's Lord, Jesus Christ. The variety and difference among Christian charisms would quickly become incoherent and disabling if it were to become eccentric, without a reference to its centre in Christ. An important function of life in communion is always to remain attentive to one another, particularly when conflict arises, so that the centre may never be forgotten. Seen in the framework of God's mission of love in Christ and the Spirit, the variety of gifts, which may appear to be potentially divisive, is seen to be necessary, mutually enriching, and a cause for thanks and praise to God.

2.26 God invites his people to enjoy diversity. As Christ's body, the Church must affirm that variety of gifts and use them faithfully, both for the building up of the body "until all of us come to the unity of the faith and of the knowledge of the Son of God, to maturity to the measure of the full stature of Christ" and "to equip the saints for the work of ministry" (Eph 4:12-13).

Chapter Three
Belonging Together
in the Anglican Communion

3.1   Anglicans are held together in a life of visible communion. Baptism is God's gift of unity, the means by which an individual participates in the life of God, Father, Son and Holy Spirit and is brought into a living community of faith. The confession of a common faith, the celebration of the eucharist, a life of common prayer, the service of an ordered ministry, conciliar structures, shared service and mission sustain a life of Anglican belonging. These elements belong to the universal Church and are not unique to Anglicans. They are, nevertheless, lived out in a recognisable and characteristically Anglican way.

3.2   In the sixteenth century, members of the Church of England continued to understand themselves as the local embodiment of the Catholic Church, continuing to live in England with the same faith, sacraments and ministry of the Church through the ages. And yet, they developed a family likeness which today characterises Anglicans who live not only in England but in the 36 provinces of the Anglican Communion.

3.3   One feature of Anglican life is the way it holds together diversities of many kinds. From the Reformation, Anglicans endeavoured to hold together people of different temperaments, convictions and insights, including the puritans who wanted more radical reform and the conservatives who emphasized their continuity with the pre-reformation Church. Today, for example, evangelicals, catholics, liberals, and charismatics bring a diversity of insights and perspectives, as Anglicans struggle to respond to the contemporary challenges to faith, order and moral teaching. Bound up with these groupings are the differences which arise from a variety of reactions to critical study of the Bible, particular cultural contexts, different schools of philosophical thought and scientific theory. The Reformation's insistence on providing the Scriptures in the vernacular opened the possibility that the faith is expressed in the language, symbols and imagery of the different cultural contexts.

3.4   At best, the Anglican way is characterised by generosity and tolerance to those of different views. It also entails a willingness to contain difference and live with tension, even conflict, as the Church seeks a common mind on controversial issues. The comprehensiveness that marks the Anglican Communion is not a sign of weakness or uncertainty about the central truths of the faith. Neither does it mean that Anglicans accept that there are no limits to diversity.

I.   The Anglican Way: Scripture, Tradition and Reason

3.5   Anglicans are held together by the characteristic way in which they use Scripture, tradition and reason in discerning afresh the mind of Christ for the Church in each generation. This was well described in the *Report of the Pastoral and Dogmatic Concerns* section of Lambeth 1988.

3.6   Anglicans affirm the sovereign authority of the **Holy Scriptures** as the medium through which God by the Spirit communicates his word in the Church and thus enables people to respond with understanding and faith. The Scriptures are "uniquely inspired witness to divine revelation," and "the primary norm for Christian faith and life."

3.7   The Scriptures, however, must be translated, read, and understood, and their meaning must be grasped through a continuing process of interpretation. Since the seventeenth century Anglicans have held that Scripture is to be understood and read in the light afforded by the contexts of "tradition" and "reason."

3.8   In one sense **tradition** denotes the Scriptures themselves, in that they embody 'the tradition,' 'the message,' and 'the faith once delivered to the saints.' Tradition refers to the ongoing Spirit-guided life of the Church which receives, and in receiving interprets afresh God's abiding message. The living tradition embraces the ecumenical creeds and the classical eucharistic prayers, which belong with the Scriptures as forming their essential message. Tradition is not to be understood as an accumulation of formulae and texts, but as the living mind, the nerve centre of the Church. Anglican appeal to tradition is the appeal to this mind of the Church carried by the worship, teaching and the Spirit-filled life of the Church.

3.9   Properly speaking, **"reason"** means simply the human being's capacity to symbolise, and so to order, share and communicate experience. It is the divine gift in virtue, of which human persons respond and act with awareness in relation to their world and to God, and are opened up to that which is true for every time and every place. Reason cannot be divorced either from Scripture or tradition, since neither is conceivable apart from the working of reason. In another perspective, reason means not so much the capacity to make sense of things as it does "that which makes sense," or "that which is reasonable." The appeal to reason then becomes what people—and that means people in a given time and place—take as good sense or "common" sense. It refers to what can be called "the mind of a particular culture," with its characteristic ways of seeing things, asking about them, and explaining them. If tradition is the mind that Christians share as believers and members of the Church, reason is the mind they share as participants in a particular culture.

3.10 Anglicanism sees reason, in the sense of the "mind" of the culture in which the Church lives and the Gospel is proclaimed, as a legitimate and necessary instrument for the interpretation of God's message in the Scriptures. Sometimes Scriptures affirm the new insights of a particular age or culture; sometimes they challenge or contradict those insights. The Word of God is addressed to the Church as it is part of the world. The Gospel borne by the Scriptures must be heard and interpreted in the language that bears the "mind" and distils the experience of the world. Tradition and reason are therefore, in the Anglican way, two distinct contexts in which Scriptures speak and out of which they are interpreted.

3.11 The characteristic Anglican way of living with a constant dynamic interplay of Scripture, tradition and reason means that the mind of God has constantly to be discerned afresh, not only in every age, but in each and every context. Moreover, the experience of the Church as it is lived in different places has something to contribute to the discernment of the mind of Christ for the Church. No one culture, no one period of history has a monopoly of insight into the truth of the Gospel. It is essential for the fullest apprehension of truth that context is in dialogue with context. Sometimes the lived experience of a particular community enables Christian truth to be perceived afresh for the whole community. At other times a desire for change or restatement of the faith in one place provokes a crisis within the whole Church. In order to keep the Anglican Communion living as a dynamic community of faith, exploring and making relevant the understanding of the faith, structures for taking counsel and deciding are an essential part of the life of the Communion.

II. The Anglican Way: Sacrament and Worship

3.12 Fundamental to the Anglican way of living with and responding to diversity is the constant interplay and influence of Scripture, tradition and reason. The Scriptures are read and interpreted in the round of common daily prayer and in the celebration of the sacraments. In worship the faith is encountered in the hearing of the word and in the experience of the sacrament. In the sacrament of baptism Christians die and rise again with Christ through the waters of baptism to new life in him. In the eucharist they encounter the central mysteries of the faith in the *anamnesis,* the making present of those past events and the experience of future glory, through the power of the Holy Spirit. Word and sacrament are fundamental to the life of the Anglican Communion, as it seeks to teach the faith and to give guidance for the right conduct in human life, expressing this in doctrine and moral guidance. A family likeness in common prayer expressed in many languages is a precious heritage, which is significant in forming Anglican identity and maintaining unity. A commitment to daily prayer, to systematic scripture reading, to praying the psalms and canticles, to regular credal confession of the faith, and to intercessory prayer for one another and for the needs of the world is an integral part of Anglican belonging.

3.13 All of these resources keep Anglicans living together in fidelity to the memory and hope of Jesus under the guidance of the Holy Spirit, who leads into all truth. In the present they are bound together as they remember the past and anticipate the reconciliation of all things in Christ at the end of time.

III.   Interdependence of Charisms in the Life of the Church

3.14 All who are baptised into the life of God and live out their calling as members of the Anglican Communion are given a charism of the Holy Spirit for the life of the Communion and for the service of others. The vocation of the laos is exercised in a broad context of social and communal life in civil society, at work and in recreation and within the family, as well as within the life of the community of the Church. By virtue of their baptism, all members are called to confess their faith and to give account of their hope in what they do and what they say.

3.15 The calling of lay persons is to represent Christ and his Church, to bear witness to him wherever they may be and according to the gifts given to them, to carry out Christ's work of reconciliation in the world, and to take their place in the life, worship and governance of the Church.

3.16 To enable the community of faith to respond to Christ's call, God has given to the Church the charism of ordered ministry: the episcopate, the presbyterate, and the diaconate. The ordained ministry is exercised with, in, and among the whole people of God.

3.17 The calling of a bishop is to represent Christ and his Church, particularly as apostle, chief priest, teacher and pastor of a diocese; to guard the faith, unity and discipline of the whole Church; to proclaim the word of God; to act in Christ's name for the reconciliation of the world and the building up of the Church; and to ordain others to continue Christ's ministry.

3.18 The calling of a priest or presbyter is to represent Christ and his Church, particularly as pastor to the people; to share with the bishops in the overseeing of the Church; to proclaim the gospel; to administer the sacraments; and to bless and declare pardon in the name of God.

3.19 The calling of a deacon is to represent Christ and his Church, particularly as a servant to those in need; and to assist bishops and priests in the proclamation of the Gospel and the administration of the sacraments (ECUSA, BCP, page 855-856).

3.20 The complementary gifts bestowed by the Holy Spirit on the community are for the common good and for the building up of the Church and the service of the world to which the Church is sent.

IV. The Ministry of Oversight

3.21 The continuation of a ministry of oversight (episkopç) at the Reformation exercised by bishops, by bishops in college and by bishops in council is what is referred to in the current ecumenical writing as "the personal, collegial and communal" ways of exercising the ministry of oversight. These forms of ministry help to hold Anglicans together in a community of discernment and reflection.

3.22 Every diocese in the Anglican Communion knows something of the exercise of the personal ministry of oversight of the bishop (or bishops); of collegiality in the coming together of bishops and clergy; and of the communal dimension of oversight which brings together the bishop with clergy and laity in the meeting of synods. These dimensions of the ministry of oversight are expressed in different ways in the different regions of the world and are affected by local circumstance and custom.

3.23 The bishop presides over the gatherings, collegial and communal, in the diocese. Sometimes the bishop shares the presiding over meetings with a member of the laity. In most places at the level of a Province, the collegial and synodical gatherings are presided over by an archbishop or presiding bishop. Collegiality and primacy are thus part of the Anglican experience at diocesan, Provincial and Communion-wide levels. Within the Communion, Provincial primacy, influenced by the different cultural contexts, varies in perception and practice.

V. Structures of Interdependence

3.24 The life of belonging together, with its characteristic ethos within the Anglican Communion, is supported by a web of structures which hold together and guide a common life of belonging. These structures owe something to their continuity with the western catholic Church and also to the Reformation of the sixteenth century. They have undergone considerable development since the sixteenth century and continue to be subject to change and development today.

3.25 At the Reformation the Church of England maintained the three-fold order of ministry in continuity with the early Church. Bishops in their dioceses continued to be the personal focus of the continuity and unity of the Church. There was no attempt to minimise the role of bishops as ministers of word and sacrament, nor to stop a collegial relation between bishops and presbyters in the diocese or bishops together at the level of Province. Conciliar life continued to be part of the Church of England's experience. The role of Parliament and the Royal Supremacy ensured that the role and place of the laity were embedded in the structuring of the life of the Church of England. In time this developed into synodical structures which bring together ordained and lay for discernment, decision making and authoritative teaching.

3.26 The expansion of the Church of England as a result of British colonisation led to the formation of Provinces, each with its own episcopal and synodical structures for maintaining the life of the Church. In the post colonial period of the twentieth century, the various independent Anglican Churches are governed by synods which recognise bishops' authority in some form as crucial and distinct, but which include, not only presbyteral representation, but also lay representation. Each Province, too, has developed some form of primatial office in the role of archbishop or presiding bishop.

3.27 The expression of episcopacy and the form of synodical and collegial government are not identical in each place. The experience and exercise of authority in the local context has played a part in shaping the different Provincial structures and processes. In some places the increasing emphasis on democratic forms of representation in modern secular governments has also affected church government.

3.28 In the development of the Anglican Communion, there is no legislative authority above the Provincial level. (How far this is a result of the Royal Supremacy in the Church of England is a matter for reflection. Other historical factors in other Provinces have also affected the questions of autonomy and interdependence.) There has been an insistence upon the autonomy of the Provinces of the Anglican Communion. However, while autonomy entails the legal and juridical right of each Province to govern its way of life, in practice, autonomy has never been the sole criterion for understanding the relation of Provinces to one another. There has generally been an implicit understanding of belonging together and interdependence. The life of the Communion is held together in the creative tension of Provincial autonomy and interdependence. There are some signs that the Provinces are coming to a greater realisation that they need each other's spiritual, intellectual and material resources, in order to fulfil their task of mission. Each Province has something distinctive to offer the others and needs them in turn to be able to witness to Christ effectively in its own context. Questions are asked about whether we can go on as a world Communion with morally authoritative, but not juridically binding decision-making structures at the international level. A further question is the relationship between the autonomy of a Province and the theological importance of a diocese, which is reckoned to be the basic unit of Anglicanism.

3.29 The interdependence of the Provinces has come to be maintained by certain ministries, structures and relationships which continue to develop. The first of these is the **Archbishop of Canterbury.**

3.30 While the request for first Lambeth Conference in 1867 came from the Communion and not from Canterbury, it assembled at the invitation of the Archbishop of Canterbury, who also presided over it. The continuing role of Canterbury, as a focus of the unity of the Anglican Communion and the "first among equals" in the Anglican college of bishops, came to clear expression in this way. The primacy of Canterbury and the international collegiality and conciliarity of Anglicanism are inextricably interrelated.

3.31 The primacy of the See of Canterbury and its key role in the Communion clearly emerged in many of the resolutions of the first Lambeth Conference. However, at the Conference of 1897 the role of the Archbishop of Canterbury in gathering the Communion was explicitly acknowledged and affirmed, when he was urged to foster the maintenance and development of the Communion by calling the Conference of bishops every ten years.

3.32 Today Anglican identity and authenticity of belonging is generally determined by the outward and visible test of communion with the See of Canterbury. The 1930 Lambeth Conference explicitly defined Anglicanism in this way:

> It is part of the Holy Catholic and Apostolic Church. Its centre of unity is the See of Canterbury. To be Anglican it is necessary to be in communion with that See.

Resolution 49 added further:

> The Anglican Communion is a fellowship, with One, Holy, Catholic and Apostolic Church... in communion with the See of Canterbury... (Lambeth Conference 1930, Resolution 49).

3.33 Lambeth 1968 described the role of the Archbishop of Canterbury in more detail:

Within the college of bishops it is evident that there must be a president. In the Anglican Communion this position is at present held by the occupant of the historic See of Canterbury, who enjoys a primacy of honour, not of jurisdiction. This primacy is found to involve, in a particular way, that care of all the churches which is shared by all the bishops.

3.34 The Lambeth Conference of 1978 in a further statement on the basis of Anglican unity said *inter alia:*

Its [unity] is personally grounded in the loyal relationship of each of the churches to the Archbishop of Canterbury who is freely recognised as the focus of unity.

3.35 Being in communion with the See and Archbishop of Canterbury has been a visible sign of the membership of bishops and of their Churches in the Anglican Communion. The Archbishop of Canterbury's task has been described as involving "in a particular way, that care of all the churches which is shared by all the bishops," and also as a task "not to command but to gather" the Communion. Clearly, the emphasis is upon service and caring and not upon coercive power.

3.36 **The Lambeth Conference** of bishops first met in 1867. It arose from the missionary concern of the Provinces, particularly the bishops of Canada, but the first moves to establish a meeting of all bishops of the Anglican Communion did not go unopposed. What was said about the identity and role of the first Lambeth Conference in 1867 was cautious:

It has never been contemplated that we should assume the functions of a general synod of all the Churches in full communion with the Church of England, and take upon ourselves to enact canons that should be binding upon those represented. We merely propose to discuss matters of practical interest and pronounce what we deem expedient in resolutions which may serve as safe guides (Lambeth Conferences 1867-1930, SPCK [1948], page 9).

3.37 The consultative rather than legislative role of the Conference was reiterated clearly in 1920:

The Lambeth Conference does not claim to exercise any powers of control. It stands for the far more spiritual and more Christian principle of loyalty to the fellowship. The Churches represented in it are indeed independent, but independent with the Christian freedom which recognizes the restraints of truth and love. They are not free to ignore the fellowship... the Conference is a fellowship in the Spirit (Lambeth Conference 1920, SPCK (1920), Evangelical Letter, page 14).

3.38 A balance is held between denying any power of compliance or control while upholding the need for loyalty to the fellowship expressed in restraint imposed by virtue of belonging to the Communion. No one part should act without regard for the others.

3.39 In 1958, the Lambeth Conference recognised the need for an executive officer who would serve both the Lambeth Consultative Body and the Advisory Council on Missionary Strategy. It was out of the tireless efforts of the Rt. Rev'd. Stephen F. Bayne, Jr. that communication within the Communion was strengthened and a new vision of interdependence and mutual accountability in Anglicanism was shaped. From his work, and that of his successor, Archbishop Ralph Dean, came the vision of a Consultative Council.

3.40 **The Anglican Consultative Council** (ACC) was established by a resolution of the 1968 Lambeth Conference. The Conference recognised that there was a need for more contact between the Churches of the Anglican Communion than that provided by the Lambeth Conference every ten years, by bringing together bishops, presbyters and laity, under the presidency of the Archbishop of Canterbury, to work on common concerns. The Council met for the first time at Limuru, Kenya in 1971.

3.41 Resolution 69 of the 1968 Lambeth Conference set out 8 areas of ministry belonging to the Anglican Consultative Council:

1. To share information about developments in one or more provinces with the other parts of the Communion and to serve as needed as an instrument of common action.

2. To advise on inter-Anglican, provincial, and diocesan relationships, including the division of provinces, the information of new provinces and regional councils, and the problems of extra-provincial dioceses.

3. To develop, as far as possible, agreed Anglican policies in the world mission of the Church and to encourage national and regional Churches to engage together in developing and implementing such policies by sharing their resources of personnel, money, and experience to the best advantage of all.

4. To keep before national and regional Churches the importance

of the fullest possible Anglican collaboration with other
Christian Churches.

5.   To encourage and guide Anglican participation in the ecu-
      menical movement and the ecumenical organisations; to co-
      operate with the World Council of Churches and the world
      confessional bodies on behalf of the Anglican Communion;
      and to make arrangements for the conduct of pan-Anglican
      conversations with the Roman Catholic Church, the
      Orthodox Churches, and other Churches.

6.   To advise on matters arising out of national or regional
      Church union negotiations or conversations and on subse-
      quent relations with united Churches.

7.   To advise on problems of inter-Anglican communication and
      to help in the dissemination of Anglican and ecumenical
      information.

8.   To keep in review the needs that may arise for further study
      and, where necessary, to promote inquiry and research.

3.42 The Anglican Consultative Council meets every three years and its
Standing Committee meets annually. Its constitution and functions have
been clearly set out and agreed to by the Provinces, and it has been incorporated as the legal entity for the Communion. In 1988, the members of
the ACC were invited participants without vote at the Lambeth
Conference. They have been invited to Lambeth 1998.

3.43 Its most vital purpose, however, like the Lambeth Conference, is to
establish a communion of mutual attentiveness, interdependence and
accountability to serve the unity and interdependence in mission of the
Anglican Communion. The mutual attentiveness required when members from various parts of the Communion share the richness of their
experiences also helps to form the mind of the Communion and is a
reminder of the rich diversity of gifts which God has given us. The sharing of stories enhances and deepens the Communion's experience of
interdependence at all levels.

3.44 Important to this process are representatives who are able not only
to bring the concerns and stories of their Provinces with them but carry
the proceedings of the council back to their communities, at the
Provincial, national and diocesan levels. Only this constant interchange
will provide the basis on which member Churches are able to develop and
maintain constant relations and full communion with their sisters and

brothers around the world. Each Provincial Church has a responsibility to assist their representatives to carry out this task.

3.45 The gathering of bishops, priests and laity at the meetings of the Anglican Consultative Council since Kenya 1971 provides a much needed opportunity for the opinions and experiences of the Communion to be shared.

3.46 The 1978 Lambeth Conference approved a proposal that the Archbishop of Canterbury convene a regular **Meeting of the Primates.** At that Conference Archbishop Coggan said:

> "...I am coming to believe that the way forward in the coming years—and it may be a slow process—will be along two lines: first, to have meetings of the Primates of the Communion reasonably often, for leisurely thought, prayer and deep consultation. There have been such meetings, but on very informal and rare bases. I believe they should be held perhaps as frequently as once in two years. But if that meeting now on some fairly regular basis is to be fruitful, those primates would have to come to such meetings well informed with a knowledge of the mind and will of their brothers whom they represent. Then they would be channels through which the voice of the member Churches would be heard, and real interchange of mind and will and heart could take place. That's the first thing.
>
> The second line, I think, on which we might make progress would be to see that the body of Primates, as they meet, should be in the very closest and most intimate contact with the ACC."

3.47 The minutes of the 1979 Meeting of the Primates comment that:

> The role of a Primates' meeting could not be, and was not desired as a higher synod... Rather it was a clearing house for ideas and experience through free expression, the fruits of which the Primates might convey to their Churches.

3.48 Since then, meetings of the Primates have become occasions of debate and discussion of personal and Provincial matters in the context of eucharist, prayer and study, in which the primates have achieved, in spite of the constantly changing membership of the group, a deep sense of fraternity that has nourished the unity of the Communion. At a meeting of the Primates at Newcastle, Northern Ireland in 1991, the Primates considered that the primary importance of meeting is the building and maintenance of personal relationships:

(a) as a sign of the unity and catholicity of the Church;

(b) to give high profile to important issues;

(c) for mutual support and counsel.

3.49 The Primates also expressed the opinion that there appears to be no issue which is the exclusive preserve of the Primates alone; all issues, doctrinal, ecclesial and moral, are the concern of the whole baptised community.

3.50 What has yet to be given serious consideration is Resolution 18 Section 2(a) of Lambeth 1988:

> This conference urges that encouragement be given to a developing collegial role for the Primates' Meeting under the Presidency of the Archbishop of Canterbury, so that the Primates' meeting is able to exercise an enhanced responsibility in offering guidance on doctrinal, moral and pastoral matters.

3.51 The episcopate is the primary instrument of Anglican unity, but *episcopé* is exercised personally, collegially and communally. The emergence of the Lambeth Conference and more recently, the Primates' Meeting and the Anglican Consultative Council, together with the primacy of the Archbishop of Canterbury, have become effective means of keeping the Provinces in touch with each other and of binding the Anglican Communion together. Apart from the episcopate these instruments were not given from the beginning but have gradually developed and are still developing. The instruments, while having no legislative authority, provide the means of consultation and go some way to helping to form a Communion-wide mind on issues that affect the whole Communion. In these developments we see the conciliar nature of modern Anglicanism which is one of its least recognised yet most characteristic features. However, the Provinces remain autonomous. They are governed and regulated by synods which recognize the authority of bishops in some form as crucial and distinct, but which also include representation from the ordained clergy and the laity.

3.52 This complex and still evolving network of structures within Anglicanism has developed and serves to keep Anglicans in a life of belonging together, a life of relationship. These structures are both formal and informal and interrelate and affect one another in subtle ways. They involve personal, collegial and communal relationships at the parochial, diocesan, regional and international levels. Each contributes towards a web of interdependence and serves to guard against isolation.

3.53 This complex network of structures gives expression to the fundamental bond of Anglican life which is that unity given in the life of God, Father, Son and Holy Spirit. That life of divine communion is made visible in a characteristic way within the ordered life of the Anglican Communion. The combination of allegiance to Scripture, tradition and reason, the life lived within the gifts of Scripture, creeds, sacraments, and ordained ministry, the essential inter-relatedness of lay and ordained and the structured, conciliar life contribute each in their particular way to a life of interdependence and belonging. The life of the Communion is dynamic as the fellowship seeks to respond to new insights, challenges and threats.

3.54 At the end of the decade, one question for Anglicans is whether their bonds of interdependence are strong enough to hold them together embracing tension and conflict while answers are sought to seemingly intractable problems. In particular the call for more effective structures of communion at a world level will need to be faced at Lambeth 1998 for the strengthening of the Anglican Communion and its unity into the next millennium. A further question concerns the wider ecumenical community. Is there a need for a universal primacy exercised collegially and respecting the role of the laity in decision-making within the Church? This question was referred to the Anglican-Roman Catholic International Commission (ARCIC) by Lambeth 1988 and is also raised by the Bishop of Rome's invitation in *Ut Unum Sint*.

Chapter Four

Levels of Communion—
Subsidiarity and Interdependence

4.1   The Churches of the Anglican Communion belong to the one, holy, catholic and apostolic Church. That is to say, they understand themselves as an integral part of the mystery of God's reconciling work and an embodiment of the presence of God in the world. The task and aims of the Church are given by divine commission. The Church is commanded to go to all nations and make them disciples of the Lord (Mt.28: 19f). His followers are sent by Christ into the world, as he was sent by the Father into the world (Jn 17). God has entrusted the Church's ministers with the task of being ambassadors, and makes an appeal for reconciliation through them (2 Cor. 5:18ff). In the most fundamental way, therefore, the Church is for mission, by commission.

4.2   As the Church reflected on the nature of this mission it formulated four classic "marks" or "attributes" which ought to characterise its life at all times, and in all places. These it confesses in the words of the Nicene Creed. It is to be **one,** as the Body of Christ, to proclaim and to embody the reconciliation of all things in Christ. It is to be **holy,** that is, to have about it the marks of the sanctifying presence of the Holy Spirit; it is to be **catholic,** that is, to be, as Christ was, for all people, at all times, in all places; and it is to be **apostolic,** to witness courageously and unceasingly to the authentic and liberating gospel of Christ, as taught by the apostles.

4.3   Together with these marks goes the presupposition that the Church must be a receptive and learning community. It can manifest none of these attributes unless Christians are encouraged corporately "to go to school" with Christ, to be nourished by teaching and the sacraments, and to grow up into his likeness (Eph 4:11-16). So the Church is a school in which the gift of teaching is acknowledged, but in which all the teachers are themselves learners, enjoying mutuality of encouragement and correction. This enables the Church to be a teaching community not simply for its own sake, but for the sake of its mission to the world.

4.4   Although the **aims** of the Church have been given to it, nonetheless the Church has continually to formulate and reformulate its specific **objectives** with a view to their being consistent with these fundamental aims, and also appropriate and relevant to the given conditions of a particular place and time. The gospel has to be proclaimed afresh in each generation. New challenges and opportunities constantly arise to be addressed; new threats have to be resisted.

I.   The Levels of the Church's Life

4.5   This raises the question of where and at what levels decisions are to be made. Characteristically, questions arise in the Communion in a particular place at a particular time. To respond appropriately and effectively the Church needs to be clear that there is a diversity of levels on which the God-given mission of the Church is carried out. The word "level" is used in this context neutrally; the more local is not "lower" in a pejorative sense, nor is the more international "higher" and for that reason more important. Each level has its own integrity and its own demands. Some matters concern a single parish; some relate to a diocese; some would be appropriately addressed by a national or Provincial assembly; a very few would be better approached at a regional or international level; and some are matters for the Communion as a whole as a part of the universal Church.

4.6   There is no simple way of separating levels, or of assigning the consideration of particular matters to particular levels without controversy. An ethnic matter, for example, may be divisive at parish level, and be relevant at every intermediate stage to the international level. No one guideline can be invoked to determine where responsibility for a decision lies.

4.7   The character of the Christian faith from its early days has given it a profound investment in the quality of personal, face-to-face relationships. Christians are called to embody in daily life God's reconciliation of all things in Christ, living newly in the light of God's justice and forgiveness. It is through the personal witness of Christians to the reality of that new life that the attractiveness of the gospel becomes apparent. And the gifts of the Holy Spirit, which are various to different people, are given precisely so that used together in humility and love and with attentiveness to one another's interests, they may contribute to the building up of the whole body.

II.   The Principle of Subsidiarity

4.8   The principle of "subsidiarity" has been formulated to express this investment in the local and face-to-face. Properly used, subsidiarity means that "a central authority should have a subsidiary function, performing only those tasks which cannot be performed effectively at a more immediate or local level" (Oxford English Dictionary).

4.9   Subsidiarity may properly be applied to the life of the Church in order to resist the temptation of centralism. But in the life of the Church the local level was never seen as simply autonomous. Because the work of Christ was itself a reconciliation of humanity, there is evidence from the first days of the churches of concern for the unity of the communities, both in their internal relationships and in their inter-relationships. St. Paul, for example, writes of his anxiety for the continuity of preaching and teaching the authentic apostolic gospel, and for the effectiveness of the united witness of the Church to the gospel of reconciliation. Care was taken, as the Church grew, to preserve the continuity of its witness across time and its coherence and effectiveness in different places.

4.10 It is important to clarify the principles which should govern the relationship of the different levels of the life of the Church to one another. Clarity on this matter makes for creative, sustainable and transparent partnerships in the Body of Christ. Every "higher" authority ought to encourage the free use of God's gifts at "lower" levels. There must be clarity on what has to be observed and carried out at that level, and also on the limits of its competence. As much space as possible should be given to personal initiative and responsibility. For example, in the relationship between a bishop and a parish priest and congregation, there is initially a giving of responsibility to the latter for the task of worship, witness and service within its geographical boundaries or area of immediate influence. The priest and parish will be given a set of tasks which they are obliged to fulfil. These will be few in number and general in character. The limits of their authority and responsibility will also be explained to priest and parish. These will essentially reflect agreements made previously by church synods, and expressed in canons and other ways. They will be honoured by all unless and until they are changed by the due processes of agreement. Subject to such boundaries the priest and parish will be encouraged to use all their gifts, energy and commitment to enable the gospel to go forward in that area. The bishop and parish priest will maintain the highest level of communication possible so that encouragement, advice, and, where necessary, correction can be given, together with new tasks as occasion arises.

4.11 Anglicans may properly claim that the observation of different levels and the granting of considerable freedom to the lowest possible level has been a feature of their polity. In Anglicanism today canonically binding decisions can only be made at the level of a Province or in some Provinces at the level of a diocese.

4.12 Decision-making by Provinces on appropriate matters has proved a source of strength to the Anglican Communion. Thereby, Provinces take responsibility in clear and bold ways for what they do.

4.13 However, when decisions are taken by Provinces on matters which touch the life of the whole Communion without consultation, they may give rise to tension as other Provinces or other Christian traditions reject what has been decided elsewhere. The Eames Commission has stressed the need for consultation prior to action, and for charity and patience in this situation, insisting that discernment and "reception is a continuing process in the life of the Church, which cannot be hurried" (Eames III, Reception 43-4).

4.14 The proclamation of the gospel to all humanity must embody its universal coherence. Care needs to be taken to prevent a Province from becoming bound by its culture. The corrosive effects of particular environments are often not perceptible to those who are immersed in them. The principle articulated here of a relationship between Provinces and the worldwide Communion applies at other levels also. At each interface the aim is to free the people of God to use their God-given gifts responsibly and cooperatively, in every way compatible with the gospel and its effective proclamation in word and deed.

4.15 The move to ordain women to the priesthood and the episcopate provides a recent example of the process by which Anglicans have struggled together to form a mind on a matter which affects the ministry and therefore the unity of the Communion. It is a story which throws into sharp relief some of the emerging questions concerning both the structures of Anglican interdependence and the processes by which we come to take decisions together.

4.16 The story illustrates, for particular historical reasons, how binding decisions can only be made at the level of a Province or in some places at the level of a diocese. However, it also reveals a struggle to honour the interdependence of Anglicans through reference to the international organs of consultation. When, in the 1960's, the matter of the ordination of women became urgent for the mission of the Church in Hong Kong, Hong Kong first brought the matter to the Lambeth Conference. The Conference asked that every regional church should study the matter. In this way consultation was initiated. But in spite of an attempt to listen to one another, in fact no written responses had been received by the time the Provincial representatives met for the first meeting of the Anglican Consultative Council. The Council adopted the following resolution:

> In reply to the request of the Council of the Church of South-East Asia, this Council advises the Bishop of Hong Kong, acting with the approval of his Synod, and any bishop of the Anglican Communion acting with the approval of his Province, that, if he decides to ordain women to the priesthood, his action will be acceptable to this Council; and that this Council will use its good offices to encourage all Provinces of the Anglican Communion to continue in communion with

these dioceses (Resolution 28(b) *The Time is Now* Anglican Consultative Council First Meeting Limuru, Kenya, 23 February-5 March, 1971. London: SPCK [1971], page 39).

4.17 In a similar way in 1985, after the General Convention of ECUSA had expressed its intention not to withhold consent to the election of a bishop on the grounds of gender, it also sought the advice of the newly created Primates Meeting. Through its working party the Primates sought the advice of Provinces. It was that Communion-wide reflection from 17 provinces that formed the background to resolution 1 of Lambeth 1988:

> That each province should respect the decision and attitudes of other provinces... without such respect necessarily indicating acceptance of the principles involved, maintaining the highest degree of communion with the provinces that differ.

4.18 In much the same way as a juridical decision made at Provincial level has to be received, so the expressed 'mind of the Communion' given in resolutions of Lambeth Conferences, still has to undergo a process of 'open reception' in the life of the Anglican Communion and the whole Church. Much emphasis was placed by the Eames Commission on the need for an open process of reception following the Lambeth 1988 Resolution (see *The Eames Commission*, pp. 54-5).

4.19 There has been an increasing awareness that certain issues arise that affect the unity of the universal Church. Issues of faith, the sacraments, the ordering of the ministry, fundamental changes in relationships with another World Communion and ethical issues have implications for the life of communion. These need a Communion-wide mind if a life of interdependence is to be preserved.

4.20 Matters which touch the unity of the whole Communion can rarely be decided without argument and therefore must always be brought to the life of prayer. The Church needs to be tolerant and open enough to conduct its arguments with charity and attentiveness to the wisdom and guidance of the Holy Spirit. Care needs to be taken to ensure that complex matters are fairly and appropriately considered. Different cultures have differing traditions in the matter of consultation and decision-making.

4.21 Anglican theologians, such as Richard Hooker, have spoken of the need for consent, without which the mere exercise of authority can amount to tyranny. But there is no one way of establishing what constitutes consent. Where there is disparity and diversity of traditions there is need for great care with communication. As long ago as 1888 the Chicago-Lambeth Quadrilateral asserted the appropriateness of different styles of episcopal authority, appropriate to different cultures: "The Historic Episcopate, locally adapted in the methods of its administration to the varying needs of the nations and peoples called of God into the Unity of His Church" (Report on Home Reunion, Article 4, pages 159f).

III.   The Particular Church and the Church Catholic

4.22 The life and mission of the Church is at its most authentic and vibrant in a particular context, that is a cohesive geographical region or an area covered by a people, tribe or group with its own traditions and customs. 'Local' can mean different things in different places. A single parish can be a locality, and that place can be as small as a village, or as big as a city. A cohesive geographical region can be a local entity, or an area covered by a people, tribe or group with its own traditions and customs. Styles and ways of living, received wisdom, social customs or rituals, clan structures and inter-relationships can all contribute to a sense of particularity. The Church is effective when it is embedded a local place, challenging wrongs, healing relationships, standing with the vulnerable and marginalized, and opening up new possibilities for mutual service, respect and love. In such a context what the word "church" stands for is a rich, many-sided reality embodying God's saving and reconciling presence within a particular context. It is a richly referential term, culturally resonant, and locked into an established symbolic system or network of meanings.

4.23 It is important that the Church in its particular embodiment is not the 'translation' of an abstract ideal into a merely temporary or transitory vehicle. The life of the Church, particularly developed, would show respect for the history of the Church of past centuries, including the early centuries and the biblical communities, noting both their failings and faithfulness. It would also be ready to be helped and challenged by the contemporary Church in other places, and use the experience of fellow Christians as a way of discerning truth within the ambiguities of local tradition and culture.

4.24 Dependent upon such embodied ecclesiologies is the expression of a catholic doctrine of the Church, which attempts to express what is, or should be, true of the Church in all places. Our trinitarian theology (Chapter 2) provides the basis of such an ecclesiology. It is no accident that it is rooted not just in the doctrines and experiences of the churches of the Anglican Communion, but in the convictions of the vast preponderance of Christians who have ever lived, and of the public witness of their churches. In no sense is this ecclesiology untried or flimsy. Like certain forms of highly sophisticated modern metals, it is thin and exceptionally tough, proved in vast numbers of stresses. It is a vital resource, and to draw upon it is to show a wholly appropriate respect for the Church catholic. We have also spoken of the "marks" or "attributes" of the Church (para 4.2) as providing its general aims. These are true, but likewise unspecific. Nor do they prevent disputes from breaking out as to their precise interpretation. What, for example, does it mean to be a "holy" Church in the context of a hedonistic culture? St Paul himself had to work hard to interpret the Christian's responsibility in relation to the ramifications of idolatry in pagan society.

4.25 At all times the theological reflection and *praxis* of the local church must be consistent with the truth of the gospel which belongs to the universal Church. The universal doctrine of the Church is important especially when particular practices or theories are locally developed which lead to disputes. In some cases it may be possible and necessary for the universal Church to say with firmness that a particular local practice or theory is incompatible with Christian faith. This was said, for example, to those churches in South Africa which practised and justified racial discrimination at the eucharist. Similarly if a church were to develop a different baptismal formula than that delivered in Scripture and used throughout the world, a comparable situation would arise. The Chicago-Lambeth Quadrilateral is a list of norms and practices which must characterise the Church at all times everywhere. However, it is not a complete ecclesiology; nor is it free from interpretative ambiguity.

4.26 Elizabethan Anglican ecclesiology, for example as developed by Richard Hooker (c.1544-1600) or Richard Field (1561-1616), is a locally embodied ecclesiology for a particular time and place. It is not a 'translation' of a universal ecclesiology, which can then be (as it were) 'retranslated' into different times and places. It is, as ecclesiologies should be, a whole-hearted attempt to embody the saving presence of God in a given culture. It is a rendering of biblical ecclesiology, which is itself particular and local. Elizabethan Anglicans, however, acknowledged the authority of the Nicene creed and sought to show how the Church of England belonged to the one, holy, catholic and apostolic Church. The contemporary churches of the Anglican Communion also need locally embodied ecclesiologies, not pale imitations of Elizabethan Anglicanism, but full, rich, and relevant embodiments of God's saving presence within a locality. Nor will they be mere 'translations' of a universal ecclesiology, but a confident and whole-hearted seeking of God's way for the Church in transforming relationships with particular traditions, structures and institutions.

4.27 But no local embodiment of the Church is simply autonomous and it is plain from the history of the Church that local churches can make mistakes. A care for reconciliation and unity is implicit in the catholicity of Jesus' unique, atoning work. The apostolicity of a particular church is measured by its consonance with the living elements of apostolic succession and unity: baptism and eucharist, the Nicene and Apostles' creeds, the ordered ministry and the canon of Scripture. These living elements of apostolic succession serve the authentic succession of the gospel and serve to keep the various levels of the Church in a communion of truth and life.

Chapter Five

Koinonia: Purpose and Principles for Developing Structures

5.1   The purpose of all structures and processes of the Church is to serve the *koinonia,* the trinitarian life of God in the Church, and to help all the baptised embrace and live out Christ's mission and ministry in the world. Through baptism each person is called to live the new life in Christ in the power of the Holy Spirit and is anointed with grace to do so in communion with all members of the same Body of Christ.

5.2   As we have seen in the Anglican Communion today the structures of unity and communion at a world level are still developing. This development needs now to be inspired by a renewed understanding of the Church as *koinonia;* a recognition of God's gift to the whole people of God of a ministry of *episcopé,* exercised in personal, collegial and communal ways within and by the whole company of the baptised; by principles of subsidiarity, accountability and interdependence; and by an understanding of the Spirit led processes of discernment and reception.

I.   The Communion of the Trinity

5.3   In chapter two we explored an understanding of the Church as communion, participating in and called to manifest in its own life, the life of God, Father, Son and Holy Spirit. Those who are baptised, through the power of the Holy Spirit, die with Christ and rise to new life in him and are joined with all the baptised in the communion of God's own life and love. Through baptism and through participation at the Table of the Lord the baptised are called to a life of unity and interdependence and using all their diverse charisms entrusted with carrying out God's mission in the world. The structures of the Church, at every level, are to serve this vocation of the Church. In the way they are ordered as well as in the way they inter-relate and function they are to reflect and embody the fundamental reality of the Church's life—its communion in the life and love of God, Father, Son and Holy Spirit.

5.4   This means that the personal and relational life of the Church is always prior to the structural. But without enabling structures the Church's life is weakened and the relational and personal life unsupported. Right structures and right ordering provide channels by which, through the power of the Holy Spirit, the mind of Christ is discerned, the right conduct of the Church encouraged and the gift of the many are drawn upon in the service and mission of the Church.

II.   *Episcopé*, Personal, Collegial and Communal

5.5   A ministry of oversight *(episcopé)* of interdependence, accountability and discernment is essential at all levels of the Church's mission and ministry, and for the sake of the Church's wellbeing, must be exercised at every level in a way that is personal, collegial and communal. A bishop's authority is never isolated from the community; both the community of the Church and the community and unity of all humankind.

i.   Personal

5.6   The ministry of oversight should be *personal* because the presence of Christ among his people can most effectively be pointed to by the person ordained to proclaim the gospel and to call the community to serve the Lord in a unity of faith and witness. Bishops have a special responsibility for maintaining and focusing the internal unity and communion of the local Church. In the diocese where they have oversight they represent, focus and have a care for the unity of the Church. Bishops also relate the local church to the wider Church and the wider Church back to the local church.

5.7   Bishops are called by God, in and through the community of the faithful, to personify the tradition of the gospel and the mission of the Church. As the one with special responsibility to ensure that the proclamation of the word and the celebration of the sacraments is faithful to the gospel and the tradition of the Church, the bishop has specific responsibilities for the calling of all humanity into the unity of the Church. This specific responsibility is exercised in partnership with other bishops, clergy and laity, with members of other ecclesial bodies and leaders of the local community. Thus episcopal ministry is no authoritarian ministry above and separate from the community, but is a ministry, based in the grace of God, always exercised in relation to the community and always subject to the word of God.

5.8   By virtue of ordination, bishops are called and empowered to represent Christ to the community of the faithful and to the wider local community. This is the personal ministry of *episcopé*. While this is the unique responsibility of the diocesan bishop, it is at the same time always shared with others. At a regional level Primates exercise a personal ministry of oversight and at the level of the whole Communion the Archbishop of Canterbury exercises a personal ministry of *episcopé*.

ii.   Collegial

5.9   Bishops share in a collegial relation with those whom they commission to serve with them in the diocese, in the priestly ministry of word and sacrament and in the pastoral work of the Church. Bishops also share collegially with other bishops of the same Province representing the concerns of the local church and community to the wider Church, and bringing back the concerns and decisions of the wider Church to their local community. The Lambeth Conference and the Primates' Meeting are wider expressions of collegiality.

iii.   Communal

5.10   Bishops exercise their office communally. The community's effective participation is necessary in the discovery of God's will, under the guidance of the Spirit. In their communal relationships, bishops meet with representatives of those who hold office, or those who exercise responsibility within the community of the local churches. This accords with the principle of subsidiarity, keeping the bishop in touch with the concerns and decisions which belong properly to the more parochial levels of diocesan life. As representative persons, bishops have a moral duty to reflect the concerns of the whole community, especially those whom society pushes to the margins.

5.11   The practical expression of the personal, collegial and communal ministry of the bishop is to be seen in synodical government. The churches of the Anglican Communion may be said to be episcopally led and synodically governed. The task of synods is properly consultation, deliberation and legislation. Episcopal leadership is, however, always in accountable relation to the whole Church, both local and universal.

5.12   There is a proper place for the communal expression of the Church's life and ministry at levels other than the diocesan. Every Province has its communal synodical gathering. At the world level the Anglican Consultative Council (ACC) currently embodies the communal dimension of the church life, reminding the Communion of the shared episcopal, presbyteral, diaconal, and lay vocation in the discovery of the mind of Jesus Christ. At the world level, however, the meetings of the Anglican Consultative Council (ACC) are consultative, not legislative in character.

5.13   Primacy and collegiality are complementary elements within the exercise of *episcopé*. One cannot be exercised without reference to the other in critical and creative balance. Further, both in turn must be open to the Christian community in a way that is both transparent and accountable, and in the decision-making of the Church, upholds a reception process in which critique, affirmation and rejection are possible.

5.14 The role of primacy is to foster the communion by helping the bishops in their task of apostolic leadership both in their local church and in the Church universal. A Primate's particular role in _episcopé_ is to help churches to listen to one another, to grow in love and unity, and to strive together towards the fullness of Christian life and witness. A Primate respects and promotes Christian freedom and spontaneity; does not seek uniformity where diversity is legitimate, or centralize administration to the detriment of local churches.

5.15 A Primate exercises ministry not in isolation but in collegial association with other bishops. If there is a need to intervene in the affairs of a diocese within the Province, the Primate will consult with other bishops, and if possible act through the normal structures of consultation and decision-making. The Primate will strive never to bypass or usurp the proper responsibility of the local church. ARCIC I spoke of the ministry of primacy in this way:

> Primacy fulfils its purpose by helping the churches to listen to one another, to grow in love and unity, and to strive together towards the fullness of Christian life and witness; it respects and promotes Christian freedom and spontaneity; it does not seek uniformity where diversity is legitimate, or centralise administration to the detriment of local churches. (_The Final Report_, Authority I, para 21)

5.16 The primacy of the Archbishop of Canterbury and the meeting of Primates reflects at the Anglican Communion level the primacy and collegiality exercised at Provincial level. There is a difference, however, in that distance and infrequency of meeting add difficulty to the process of consultation and decision. Discernment, decision and action at this level will normally depend only upon the consensus of the Primates' meeting or a part of it and demands great sensitivity.

III.   Subsidiarity, Accountability and Interdependence

5.17 The Holy Catholic Church is fully present in each of its local embodiments. Decisions about the life and mission of the Church should be made in that place and need only be referred to wider councils if the matter threatens the unity and the faithfulness of teaching or practice of the Church catholic, or where the local church encounters genuinely new circumstances and wishes advice about how to respond.

5.18 The various levels of the Church are accountable to each other. This will be expressed by openness to dialogue, by attentiveness to the particularity of people, times and places, by acceptance of interdependence on both the personal and corporate levels and by honouring plurality and diversity as gifts of God.

5.19 Attentiveness, in the Christian community, is a specific quality of interacting among members of Christ's body. Christian attentiveness means deciding to place the understanding of others ahead of being understood. It means listening and responding to the needs and the hopes of others, especially when these differ from one's own needs, agendas and hopes. Further, Christian attentiveness means keeping these needs and agendas in mind, when making one's own decisions and developing one's own practices. Such attentiveness is consonant, we said, with the quality of God's love known in Christ and shared in the Holy Spirit. This divine love is imaged beautifully in John's Gospel, where the Father and Son glorify and affirm the identity of one another. It is mirrored further in our Lord's acute awareness of and compassionate responsiveness to the needs of others.

5.20 The worldwide Anglican assemblies are consultative and not legislative in character. There is a question to be asked whether this is satisfactory if the Anglican Communion is to be held together in hard times as well as in good ones. Indeed there is a question as to whether effective communion, at all levels, does not require appropriate instruments, with due safeguards, not only for legislation, but also for oversight. Is not universal authority a necessary corollary of universal communion? This is a matter currently under discussion with our ecumenical partners. It relates not only to our understanding of the exercise of authority in the Anglican Communion, but also to the kind of unity and communion we look for in a visibly united Church.

IV.   Discernment and Reception

5.21 The faith of the Church is always in need of fresh interpretation, so that the living Christ can be realised in the lives of contemporary men and women. Discerning the mind of Christ for the Church is the task of the whole people of God, with those ordained for a ministry of oversight guiding and leading the community. Authority is relational. Some matters are properly determined at a local or regional level, others which touch the unity in faith need to be determined in the communion of all the churches.

5.22 When a matter is raised by a local church processes of discernment, decision making and reception all have their part to play. It is the responsibility of the local church to consider the implication of taking decisions for the wider Communion. Anglicans agree that the Great Ecumenical Councils of the fourth and fifth centuries were the highest conciliar authority. However, no ecumenical council possesses final authority simply as an institution. Even with these early councils there was no guarantee that the guidance of a council was free from error of judgement or distortion of the truth. Its words were accepted as true and binding, not because a particular council spoke, nor because it has been convened by a particular authority, but because its decisions came to be received and recognised by the faithful in the local churches as expressing the truth of the gospel. This is not to say that certain councils of the Church in the past and in the Anglican Communion today should not command the respect of the faithful and be taken with all due seriousness in the response and discernment process.

5.23 Anglicans hold that the universal Church will not ultimately fail. Through the leading of the Holy Spirit, truth is gradually discerned. However the discernment of truth is never an uncomplicated and straightforward matter. There are always setbacks along the way.

5.24 Within the Anglican Communion matters which touch the communion of all the churches need to be discerned and tested within the life of the interdependence of the Provinces, through the meeting of bishops in the Lambeth Conference and through the consultative process of the Anglican Consultative Council and the Primates' Meeting. Beyond that lies the process of open reception within the life of the local churches. The maintenance of communion both within and between churches, in the process of testing the truth of a decision needs great sensitivity, and adequate space needs to be found for clearly expressed dissent in testing and refining truth. In the process of discernment and reception relationships need to be maintained, for only in fellowship is there opportunity for correcting one-sidedness or ignorance. Though some of the means by which communion is expressed may be strained, the need for courtesy, tolerance, mutual respect, prayer for one another and a continuing desire to know and be with one another, remain binding upon us as Christians. The reception process involves the preparation of appropriate and informative study materials and the preparation of occasions for conversations, bringing together those on both sides of the particular issue.

5.25 In a divided Christendom there is no possibility of making decisions today in a General Council. Nevertheless, at this stage of the ecumenical movement any decisions which touch the faith or order of the universal Church need to be offered for testing within the wider ecumenical fellowship.

5.26 In the matter of discussing the mind of Christ for the Church, under the guidance of the Holy Spirit, discernment, conciliar debate and decision making followed by a process of reception each have a part to play. It is not a matter of weakness that the Church is unable to make instant decisions in relation to the complex matters of faith, order and morals which come before it, but the way it lives in the process of discernment, decision making and reception may give profound witness and provide a model for other communities.

V. Theological Coherence

5.27 The mission of the Church is to embody and proclaim Christ's gospel of love and reconciliation, healing and freedom. This must be transparent not only in the words it speaks and in its advocacy of justice and peace, but also in its visible structures and processes. The theology implicit in the Church's structures and processes must be one with the explicit theology of its words.

5.28 It is with the principles we have explored in this chapter that we turn now to reconsider the instruments of Anglican belonging at a world level and raise questions about how they might develop in the light of these principles.

Chapter Six
The Worldwide Instruments of Communion: Structures and Processes

6.1   In this chapter we raise a number of questions about the future development of the worldwide instruments of communion, the way they function and their inter-relation, one with the other. The Commission was not asked to give specific proposals for future developments. It simply seeks to ask questions which the bishops at Lambeth will need to address if they are to give direction for the future interdependence and coherence of the Anglican Communion.

I.   The Archbishop of Canterbury

6.2   In our historical section we noted that to be in communion with the See of Canterbury is an important ingredient of Anglican interdependence, yet each of the Provinces is autonomous. The Archbishop of Canterbury is neither a supreme legislator nor a personification of central administrative power, but as a pastor in the service of unity, offers a ministry of service, care and support to the Communion. The interdependence of the Anglican Communion becomes most clearly visible when the Archbishop of Canterbury exercises his primatial office as an enabler of mission, pastoral care and healing in those situations of need to which he is called. This pastoral service of unity is exercised by invitation. For example, at the request of Provincial leaders, the Archbishop has exercised a pastoral role and mediation in the Sudan and Rwanda.

6.3   The Archbishop of Canterbury exercises his ministry in relationship with his fellow Primates. In considering how to respond to a request for assistance from a Province, he wisely consults all the appropriate resources in the region, the Province and the local diocese. Here, as elsewhere in the exercise of primacy, subsidiarity is important. So too is the exercise of an *episcopé* in which personal, collegial and communal elements are held together.

6.4   Together with a ministry of presence and teaching, there is also a certain administrative primacy. Historically this has found its unique expression when the Archbishop of Canterbury calls and presides at the Lambeth Conference, where the relationship of the Archbishop of Canterbury to the Communion, and the bishops to each other, is most clearly seen. It is also visible in his chairmanship of the regular meetings of the Primates, and also exercised within the life of the Anglican Consultative Council where the Archbishop of Canterbury acts as its president and as an active participant in its meetings.

6.5   It is nevertheless most often the personal pastoral element in the exercise of this office which has become the most visible evidence of the Archbishop of Canterbury as an instrument of unity. Given the magnitude of this ministry, there must be concern that pastoral and spiritual care, beyond the prayers of the Communion, be made available to the Archbishop.

6.6   The special position of the Archbishop of Canterbury in the Communion raises questions that need to be addressed. **Are there mechanisms by which tasks may be shared within the fellowship of the Primates, without weakening the symbol of unity provided by one person? Is the Archbishop of Canterbury adequately resourced as Primate of the Communion? Is there sufficient coherence and consultation between the Anglican Communion Secretariat and the staff of Lambeth Palace? Does the role of the Archbishop mean that the Church of England must be more cautious in its decisions than other Provinces? Does an Archbishop of Canterbury necessarily have to be a member of the Church of England? Does the Primate of the Anglican Communion need to be the occupant of the see of Canterbury?**

II.   The Lambeth Conference

6.7   The Lambeth Conference plays an important role in strengthening the unity of the Anglican Communion by expressing the collegiality of bishops in a clear and concrete way at the international level and in symbolising the relatedness in bonds of spiritual communion of each of the dioceses from which the bishops come.

6.8   Though the Conference is not legislative it offers the opportunity to bishops who come from churches in different cultures and social and political contexts, and with different agendas and problems, to live together, to worship together, to join in Bible study together and to listen to each other. Through these means each bishop may share the difficulties and joys of every other church. This indicates that each church in the Anglican Communion is a partner in mission and a part of the body of Christ. In this way the Conference embodies the Pauline concept of the Church as a body. As Paul writes "when one part of the body suffers the rest of the body suffers". Each part of the body is different, but every part is necessary to the body.

6.9   The Conference also signifies the fundamental importance of face to face communication for the healthy life of the Communion. The personal encounters that it facilitates and the relationships that grow from them sig-nify one aspect of the servanthood of bishops who bring the reality of each diocese to the whole Communion as a whole back to their own diocese.

6.10 The Lambeth Conference thus helps to define the bishop's role as one who represents the part to the whole and the whole to the part, the particularity of each diocese to the whole Communion and the Communion to each diocese.

i.   Attentiveness at the Lambeth Conference

6.11 In the context of the Lambeth Conference, Christian attentiveness entails in the first place, that individual bishops and groups of bishops will heed the voice of other bishops when these express the needs and hopes of the Church in their place. Such respecting of the voice of others, espe-cially when such respect requires taking into account needs and agendas that are not one's own, can mean that bishops from one part of the world make their own an agenda they did not bring originally to Lambeth. And this can result in a bishop or group of bishops leaving the Lambeth Conference committed to a quite new programme.

6.12 A special concern of Lambeth 1998 will need to be how the college is attentative to, and integrates the insights of women bishops attending the Conference for the first time.

6.13 Christian attentiveness at Lambeth should mean giving special heed to those bishops whose first language is not English, and to those bishops who do not come from politically, culturally and economically powerful Provinces in the Communion. Attentiveness becomes distinctively Christian when the bishops assembled give ear to, and make space for, the voices of those Christians who are seldom, if ever, heard.

6.14 One example of such Christian attentiveness in the past is western bishops' heeding of, and being responsive to, the deep concern of African bishops regarding polygamy. A second example, from the Lambeth Conference, 1988, is western bishops acknowledging the legitimacy of a call from Asian and African bishops for a renewed commitment to evan-gelism. All the bishops left Lambeth 1988 committed to a Decade of Evangelism which they had not anticipated before the Lambeth Conference process began.

6.15 Increasing the opportunities for, and occasions of, Christian atten-tiveness should be promoted and protected at the Lambeth Conference. This will allow the bishops gathered at Lambeth to share in, to be shaped by, and to show forth, the attentiveness of God the Father's love as we know it in Jesus Christ through the Holy Spirit.

ii.   Interdependence at the Lambeth Conference

6.16 The principle of communal interdependence, if brought to bear on the Lambeth Conference, might be thought to demand its reform so as to introduce priests and deacons and lay people into its structure. This was in fact suggested in 1871 before the second Lambeth Conference, when the presiding bishop of the Episcopal Church, USA suggested that the Lambeth Conference should be transformed into a "Patriarchal Conference" of world bishops, representative clergy and laity, under the presidency of the Archbishop of Canterbury. This would tend, however, to confuse Lambeth with the synodical structures of the local and national churches and move it in the direction of a "world synod". The calling of a World Anglican Congress from time to time may be a more appropriate opportunity for presbyters, deacons and lay people to meet together with bishops at an international forum. We explore this proposal in Appendix II.

6.17 An alternative approach would be to suggest that the gathering of bishops should continue to be seen collegially, but in the context of the life of the Church as a whole. Insofar as bishops are representative persons they should understand Lambeth as an opportunity to bring the issues and concerns of their own dioceses to the consideration of brother and sister bishops. Few issues are entirely peculiar to a particular diocese, and the sharing of experiences and approaches to the resolution of difficulties makes for the easing of the burden of decision making.

6.18 At the last Lambeth Conference the Archbishop of Canterbury invited participating bishops "to bring their dioceses with them". At the same Lambeth Conference bishops voted on resolutions in the light of a preceding consultative process that had already occurred in their home dioceses and Provinces and at ACC-7. One obvious example was the resolution on the *Final Report of ARCIC I* which expressed a "Communion-wide mind" on the consonance of ARCIC with the faith of Anglicans. This resolution did not just express the mind of the bishops acting entirely alone, but as spokespersons who reflected the mind of their Provinces and were together expressing the mind of the Communion.

6.19 The bishops acting collegially can speak prophetically to the Church and to the world. On some issues such as, for example, ordination, the Church itself should expect the advice of those to whom the responsibility to ordain has been given. When the bishops speak to the Church, however, this should not be in an autocratic way, but in a manner that makes a positive contribution to, and stimulates, a continuing conversation in the wider life of the Church. True leadership demands consultation and partnership.

iii.   Accountability at the Lambeth Conference

6.20 Bishops are accountable for their words and actions at Lambeth, before God and the whole Church. The bishops at Lambeth are to represent those who have no voice: those who can rely on no one else to tell their story and plead their case; those whose concerns society and/or the Church have chosen, sometimes deliberately, sometimes forgetfully to address. It is when the bishops consider themselves to be accountable to those who have the least that they discover the way of God's Kingdom.

6.21 The diocese is to be brought with the bishop to Lambeth, and Lambeth through the bishop back to the diocese. It is an important way of involving the entire membership of the people of God in the concerns and thinking of the worldwide communion. Post-Lambeth educational programs may dictate that, in addition to the usual publication of a report of its proceedings, educational resources, audiotapes and videos should be made available so as to assist the bishops in the sharing of the Lambeth experience.

6.22 There are again questions worth asking. **Is a Conference every ten years too frequent to allow for adequate preparation, consultation and reception? What is the nature of the authority of the Conference? How binding are the resolutions of the Conference? How should issues be selected and prepared; what concerns should be addressed? What form of report or pastoral letter would best strengthen the communion of the Church? If the Lambeth Conference is an effective instrument of unity of the Anglican Communion, what is its special vocation in relation to the movement for the visible unity of the Church? What part should ecumenical participants play? How might the Lambeth Conference encourage the development of shared oversight with other Christian traditions? How does the authority of the Lambeth Conference relate to the authority of other churches, in particular to those churches which claim to be *the* Church?**

III.   The Anglican Consultative Council

6.23 Unique among the international Anglican instruments of unity, the ACC includes laity among its members. The inclusion of the laity in decision-making bodies has long been a principle of Anglican life. Thus, the royal priesthood of the entire people of God (1 Peter 2:9), and the mutuality and interdependence of the various ministries within the Church, are witnessed to and affirmed. Means must be found to honour the specific experience and expertise that various lay members bring and also to provide them with whatever further resources and experiences they might need to participate fully and responsibly in the life of God's Church.

6.24 It is important that these rich experiences of being in community not be lost through either infrequency of meeting or too large a gathering. Significant too is the participation of members from the two-thirds world who represent a growing majority in the Communion and whose issues increasingly occupy the Communion's concern. Every effort needs to be made to enable people whose first language is not English to communicate freely and effectively so that there be no feeling of exclusion.

6.25 The mission of the Anglican Consultative Council is to represent the concerns of the Communion, in the Communion and for the Communion. Most of this work is effected day by day through the General Secretary and the Secretariat. However, to be effective and credible, the Secretariat must be governed by a reference group which is informed, has continuity and is also representative of the Communion's diversity. It must be adequately staffed.

6.26 There are two possible ways in which change might be effected in order to enhance the representative nature of the ACC and its effectiveness: first, by creating a smaller council which would meet more frequently, or alternatively, by enlarging the Standing Committee and leaving the size and frequency of the ACC as it presently is. It is important that the representation be balanced between laity and clergy, with greater continuity of membership than at present. Representatives should have entrée to the councils of their own church and be knowledgeable about its concerns and interests.

6.27 The existence of the Anglican Consultative Council raises questions of a general nature. What is the relationship of this body to the Lambeth Conference and to the Primates' Meeting? **What part should the ACC play in contributing to the major issues that are to come before the Lambeth Conference and the reception of the Lambeth resolutions? Should the ongoing tasks of the Communion be done by an expanded secretariat, or through meetings of the ACC, or a combination of both? Who is responsible for the continuity of membership in the ACC; is it the members themselves, is it the Primates, who makes this decision? What is the nature of the responsibility and accountability of those elected to serve on the ACC?**

IV.   The Primates' Meeting

6.28 The Primates' Meeting provides the opportunity for mutual counsel and pastoral care and support of one another and of the Archbishop of Canterbury. Their meetings have an inherent authority by virtue of the office which they hold as chief pastors. The Meeting provides a place between Lambeth Conferences for each to share the burning or persistent issues of their Province and their own primatial ministry. It is the context in which Primates can identify common issues and resolve outstanding concerns. It also provides for a broader horizon than the Provincial which makes it possible for a Primate to consider a regional matter in a worldwide context. There is an opportunity to take responsibility together in the concern for the wellbeing of all the churches.

6.29 The Primates have in fact found it easier to affirm collegiality for the sake of consultation, study and mutual support than for the exercise of pastoral, moral and doctrinal guidance. This experience raises in yet another context the theological and practical importance of holding together the personal, collegial and communal modes of *episcopé*.

6.30 Each Primate exercises his personal primatial ministry with fellow bishops and the synod of his Province. Similarly, the Archbishop of Canterbury exercises this Communion-wide ministry both collegially and communally. In the same way, the collegiality of the Primates' Meeting is exercised in relation to the personal and communal elements of the *episcopé* at the Communion-wide level.

6.31 The exercise of collegiality with one another and with the Archbishop of Canterbury, as well as the exercise of collegiality with all the bishops at the Lambeth Conference, raises the question of the relation of the Primates' Meeting to the communal gatherings of the Anglican Consultative Council. It is to be noted that while the Standing Committee of the Primates' Meeting meets with the Standing Committee of the ACC, this has hardly enhanced relations with the ACC. As an instrument of worldwide unity within the Communion, the Primates' Meeting has responsibility to maintain a living relationship with the ACC, so that the collegial and communal exercise of oversight are held together. Archbishop Donald Coggan commented at the 1978 Lambeth Conference that the Primates' Meeting should be in the very closest and most intimate contact with the ACC. What in fact this would mean in practice still has to be worked out.

6.32 **How far should the task of the Primates' Meeting be that of responsibility for monitoring the progress of recommendations and resolutions which come from the Lambeth Conference in the interim between**

Conferences? For example, in the period following Lambeth 1988, the Primates received and promulgated the recommendations of the Eames' Commission to the Communion. The Primates' Meeting also referred to the Provinces the *Porvöo Common Statement* and the *Concordat of Agreement.*

6.33 In chapter 3 (paragraph 3.50) it was noted that the Primates have been reluctant to give serious consideration to resolution 18 Section 2(a) of Lambeth 1988 which asks the Primates to exercise greater responsibility in offering guidance on doctrinal, moral and pastoral matters. **Should Primates be expected to make authoritative statements, or should the Primates' Meeting be encouraged to exercise a primarily pastoral role, both for their own numbers, but also for the Communion? What is the relationship of the Primates' Meeting to the Lambeth Conference and the Anglican Consultative Council? Do the Primates have sufficient resources for their ministry?**

V.   The Inter-relation of the Instruments of Communion

6.34 In reviewing the worldwide instruments of communion this report has at times commented on the relationship of one to the other and on their inter-connectedness with structures at other levels of the Church's life. Three instruments, the ACC, the Primates' Meeting and the Lambeth Conference have their own distinctive characteristics and potentially hold in balance and tension three aspects of the life of the Communion. Lambeth focuses the relation of bishops to bishops and therefore dioceses to dioceses. The Primates' Meeting focuses the relation of Primates to Primates, and therefore Provinces to Provinces. The ACC, which is the most comprehensive gathering, represents the voice of the inner life of the Provinces, with representatives of laity, clergy and bishops. These three instuments of interdependence are presided over by the Archbishop of Canterbury, thus focusing the unity and diversity of the Communion.

6.35 At the present time the formal structural and continuing relations between the Lambeth Conference, the Anglican Consultative council and the Primates' Meeting is the responsibility of the Secretary General and the Anglican Communion Secretariat which staffs all three bodies. Greater clarity on the relations between the instruments of communion themselves would make for creative, effective and sustainable relations within the Anglican Communion. It is urgent that ways be found to strengthen the resourcing of the ACC Secretariat if it is to serve effectively the worldwide structures of Anglican belonging.

VI.   Final Reflections

6.36 A deeper understanding of the instruments of communion at a world-level, their relationship one to another and to the other levels of the Church's life should lead to a more coherent and inclusive functioning of oversight in the service of the *koinonia* of the Church. When the ministry of oversight is exercised in a personal, collegial and communal way, imbued with the principles of subsidiarity, accountability and interdependence then the community is protected from authoritarianism, structures serve the personal and relational life of the Church and the diverse gift of all is encouraged in the service of all. The Church is thus opened up to receive the gifts of the Holy Spirit for mission and ministry and enabled to serve more effectively the unity and community of humanity.

6.37 We have necessarily concentrated in the report on the worldwide instruments of the Anglican Communion. However, by virtue of our baptism we have in a communion in the Holy Trinity and therefore with the universal Church. The long history of ecumenical involvement, both locally and internationally, has shown us that Anglican discernment and decision making must take account of the insights into truth and the Spirit-led wisdom of our ecumenical partners. Moreover, any decisions we take must be offered for the discernment of the universal Church.

Lambeth Conference 1988 Resolution 18 the Anglican Communion: Identity and Authority

This Conference:

1.   Resolves that the new Inter-Anglican Theological and Doctrinal Commission (or a specially appointed inter-Anglican commission) be asked to undertake as a matter of urgency a further exploration of the meaning and nature of communion; with particular reference to the doctrine of the Trinity, the unity and order of the Church, and the unity and community of humanity.

2.   (a) urges that encouragement be given to a developing collegial role for the Primates' Meeting under the presidency of the Archbishop of Canterbury, so that the Primates' Meeting is able to exercise an enhanced responsibility in offering guidance on doctrinal, moral and pastoral matters.

        (b) Recommends that in the appointment of any future Archbishop of Canterbury, the Crown Appointments Commission be asked to bring the Primates of the Communion into the process of consultation.

3.   Resolves that the Lambeth Conference as a conference of bishops of the Anglican Communion should continue in the future, at appropriate intervals.

4.   Recommends that regional conferences of the Anglican Communion should meet between Lambeth Conferences as and when the region concerned believes it to be appropriate; and in the event of these regional conferences being called, it should be open to the region concerned to make them representative of clergy and laity as well as bishops.

5.   Recommends that the ACC continue to fulfil the functions defined in its Constitution (developed as a consequence of Resolution 69 of the 1968 Lambeth Conference) and affirmed by the evaluation process reported to ACC-6 (see *Bonds of Affection*, pp 23-27); in particular to continue its consultative, advisory, liaison and communication roles within the Communion (and to do so in close co-operation with the Primates' Meeting).

6.   Requests the Archbishop of Canterbury, with all the Primates of the Anglican Communion, to appoint an advisory body on Prayer Books of the Anglican Communion. The body should be entrusted with the task of offering encouragement, support and advice to Churches of the Communion

in their work of liturgical revision as well as facilitating mutual consultation concerning, and review of, their Prayer Books as they are developed with a view to ensuring:

(a)   the public reading of the Scriptures in a language understood by the people and instruction of the whole people of God in the scriptural faith by means of sermons and catechisms;

(b)   the use of the two sacraments ordained by Christ, Baptism with water in the threefold name, and Holy Communion with bread and wine and explicit intention to obey our Lord's command;

(c)   the use of forms of episcopal ordination to each of the three orders by prayer with the laying-on of hands;

(d)   the public recitation and teaching of the Apostles' and Nicene Creeds; and

(e)   the use of other liturgical expressions of unity in faith and life by which the whole people of God is nurtured and upheld, with continuing awareness of ecumenical liturgical developments.

EXPLANATORY NOTE

On 1 above. If there is the possibility of ordination of women bishops in some provinces, it will throw into sharper focus the present impaired nature of communion. It is a matter of urgency that we have a further theological enquiry into and reflection on the meaning of communion in a trinitarian context for the Anglican Communion. Such an enquiry should relate to ecumenical discussions exploring similar issues. This, more than structures, will provide a theological framework in which differences can be handled.

On 2 above. We see an enhanced role for primates as a key to a growth of interdependence within the Communion. We do not see any inter-Anglican jurisdiction as possible or desirable, an inter-Anglican synodical structure would be virtually unworkable and highly expensive. A collegial role for the primates by contrast could easily be developed, and their collective judgement and advice would carry considerable weight.

If this is so, it is neither improper nor out of place to suggest that part of the consultative process prior to the appointment of a future Archbishop of Canterbury should be in consultation with the primates.

On 3 above. We are convinced that there is considerable value in the bishops of the Anglican Communion meeting as bishops, both in terms of mutual understanding and as an effective agent of interdependence.

On 4 above. Regional issues need regional solutions. Regional conferences can also provide for wider representation.

On 5 above. We value the present work of the ACC. We do not see, however, that it ought to move beyond its present advisory role.

On 6 above. Concern for how the Church celebrates the sacraments of unity and with what consequences is a central expression of episcopal care and pastoral oversight in the Church of God. As bishops of the Anglican Communion we have a particular responsibility for securing those elements in worship which nurture our identity and unity in Christ and which therefore have an authority for us as Anglicans. (A parallel but significantly different resolution has been proposed by the Anglican Consultative Council: Resolution 12 of ACC-7.)

(See further paras 113-152 of the Report on 'Dogmatic and Pastoral Concerns'.)

An Anglican Congress

1.   In considering the worldwide instruments of Anglican unity the Commission considered what role and contribution an Anglican Congress might make in the future. The Commission did not see a Congress as becoming a fifth instrument of unity for the Anglican Communion. Nevertheless, it did acknowledge the creative opportunity a Congress might, from time to time, offer the Communion, for the renewal of its life, witness and mission. At the same time the Commission was aware that, at a time of economic pressure on all institutions, the calling of a Congress would put additional financial strain upon the Communion.

2.   The following paragraphs begin to explore some of the issues that would need to be considered if it were thought the time was right for calling for an Anglican Congress.

3.   Local congregations and communities are strongest when there are regular opportunities to come together for worship, social gatherings and other festivals. The ties of friendship between individuals and families are strengthened when they share their joys and sorrows. Similar occasions offered to Anglicans on Provincial, regional and worldwide levels, could also develop and strengthen ties of affection within the Communion.

4.   A World Anglican Congress held perhaps once every ten years might provide an opportunity to bring together representatives from various vocations and spheres of life. It would provide an occasion for conversation, and for sharing of needs and opportunity for prayer and worship.

5.   In the planning of the Congress, Provinces and dioceses should be explicitly invited to propose participants who have a variety of God-given gifts to offer, and a capacity to receive the gifts of others and to be enriched by them. It would be of the essence of such a Congress that the diversity of cultural contexts in which the Anglican Church has taken root, should be visible.

6.   The Congress would need to be planned in such a way that mutual cross-cultural communication could take place. Even if there were a small number of official conference languages, attention needs to be paid to the mode and style of communication, so as to facilitate genuine giving and receiving. A premium should be set upon face-to-face contact, as distinct from amplified addresses inhibiting response and dialogue. Nor

should mutual communication be regarded as an end in itself, but as governed by and serving the goal of the universal mission of the Church, under the guidance of the Holy Spirit. A Congress should not be so tightly structured and organised as to inhibit the freedom of the Spirit and the fruit of new discovery and infectious insights and joy.

7.   The Congress would need to be attentive to particularity of context and life and an effort would be made to avoid misty generalities. The stress would be laid on quality and depth, not quantity and superficiality. The Congress would avoid global tourism, and vague or fashionable international rhetoric, and give the opportunity for the exploration of complexity in depth.

8.   If it is to be a proper reflection of the life of the Anglican Communion it would be essential that participants be full-hearted participants in the mission of the local church, and understand and accept the responsibility of accountability to that church, both in preparation for the Congress and following the Congress.

9.   Membership of the Congress should include laity, deacons, priests and bishops. The Archbishop of Canterbury would preside, and be accompanied by a number of Primates, as well as by other bishops. Efforts should be made to symbolize the personal, collegial and communal aspects of the ministry of the Archbishop. At the same time as the unity of the Church is made visible, the recognition of the diversity of God's gifts should also be expressed. There should be opportunity to show how plurality and unity are held together within the one fellowship.

10.   As an international Congress, it would not be appropriate for decisions or resolutions to be taken. A message to the Communion might be an appropriate form of communication.

Anglican Communion Office

*Renewing
the Anglican
Eucharist*

Renewing the Anglican Eucharist
Findings of the Fifth International Anglican Liturgical Consultation,
Dublin, Eire, 1995

David R Holeton (ed)
Professor of Liturgics, Trinity College, Toronto
Chair of the Fifth International
Anglican Liturgical Consultation

Courtesy of
Grove Books Limited
Ridley Hall Rd., Cambridge CB3 9HU

Contents

Introduction

The eucharist is at the very heart of Anglican life. It is both source and fulfilment of the koinonia we share as Christians and it flows from the baptismal waters from which we were born anew.

It is not surprising, therefore, that the renewal of Anglican eucharistic life has been the focus of ongoing attention in the Anglican Communion as a whole. The 1948 Lambeth Conference (Resolution 78a) affirmed that the *Book of Common Prayer* (1662) was a 'strong bond of unity throughout the whole Anglican Communion' and, accordingly, asked that 'great care... be taken to ensure that revisions of the Book... be in accordance with the doctrine and accepted liturgical worship of the Anglican Communion.' Within just a few years, the somewhat monolithic status accorded to the 1662 Prayer Book had diminished significantly as new prayer books diverged increasingly from that model both in liturgical shape and doctrine. The role played by the 1662 Prayer Book in Anglicanism eroded to such an extent that the Mission and Ministry Statement of the 1988 Lambeth Conference (§ 184) suggested that, 'its era is slipping irretrievably into the past.' Within forty years, the Prayer Book that was once held to be 'a strong bond of unity' had effectively disappeared from the ongoing life of many parts of the Communion.

As new Prayer Books appeared around the Communion, and as it became clear that they were decreasingly dependent on the 1662 Prayer Book for either liturgical shape or eucharistic doctrine, let alone the Tudor English of its language, a search began for new bonds of unity held to be so important to Anglican self-identity. Repeatedly, this involved turning to the eucharist and its liturgical expression. Thus, over the past forty years there have been at least four occasions on which the question of eucharistic renewal has been addressed on an inter-Anglican basis.

In 1958, the Lambeth Conference (Resolution 76) asked that 'the Archbishop of Canterbury... appoint an Advisory Committee to prepare recommendations for the structure of the Holy Communion service which could be taken into consideration by any Church or Province revising its eucharistic rite...' Action was taken on this resolution when a liturgical consultation held after the Toronto Anglican Congress of 1963 appointed a committee of four to draw up a document suggesting a basic shape or pattern for eucharistic liturgies.[1] In 1965, this committee produced the document *The Structure and Contents of the Eucharistic Liturgy and*

the Daily Office which contains a brief outline of the 'five phases in the celebration of the full eucharistic rite' with a brief description of the content of
each.[2] What was of great significance in this report was the movement away
from upholding a particular Prayer Book as the model for Anglican unity in
favour of a common structure of the eucharistic rite. The report was also
quite radical in its recommendations on some of the contents of each
'phase' of new Anglican eucharistic rites, and particularly in its suggestions
for what could be omitted in future provincial eucharistic revisions.[3]

Just over a decade later, the Limuru Meeting of the ACC (Resolution 26)
asked that a report on liturgical matters be made to the 1973 meeting of the
ACC.[4] This report, again identified a number of 'basic elements in the celebration [of the eucharist]' (this time eight), and provided a commentary
on what was believed to be the appropriate contents of each 'element.'[5]

Each of these reports played an important role in the life of the Anglican
Communion and their recommendations are reflected in many of the new
eucharistic rites that appeared around the Communion in the ensuing years.

Much, however, has evolved in Anglican liturgical life over the past twen-
ty years since the last of these reports was prepared and many provinces
are once again either actively revising their eucharistic rites or contem-
plating doing so in the near future. During its work on the question of
Christian Initiation done by the Fourth International Anglican Liturgical
Consultation (Toronto, 1991) it became clear to the members of that
Consultation that the eucharist should be the next area of concern to
receive the attention of the IALC.

This was done in two stages. In August 1993 a preparatory conference was
held at Untermarchtal when over forty participants addressed some of the
basic issues in eucharistic renewal in the life of the Anglican Communion.
Much of the work from this meeting was published as _Revising the
Eucharist: Groundwork for the Anglican Communion,_ a document that was
intended to enable widespread discussion in the Communion in preparation for the Fifth International Anglican Liturgical Consultation scheduled to be held in Dublin in August 1995.[6]

The Steering Committee then proposed the following headings for group
work at Dublin:

•   Eucharistic Theology. The development of a comprehensive theology
of the eucharist within the broad framework of a theology of church and
sacraments (including eschatological, paschal mystery, and ethical dimensions) within which traditional Anglican points of tension will be addressed,
e.g., the role of the Spirit, offering, consecration, sacrifice, presence.

• Ministry, Order, and the Eucharist. The ecclesiological issues, i.e., the relationship of the eucharist to both the universal and the local church and the implications of this relationship for practice, e.g., who may participate? who may minister? who may preside? how may the eucharist be extended? how may the eucharist be shared in ecumenical contexts?

• The Structure of the Eucharist. The structure of the whole rite as well as the structure of the eucharistic prayer; the function of the structure in conserving the tradition and the extent to which that tradition may responsibly be stretched; proposed common eucharistic prayers and possible models; a review of the guidelines proposed by Lambeth 1958 for Provinces revising their eucharistic liturgy.

• Ritual, Language, and Symbolism. The symbolic nature of the eucharistic assembly and the inherent symbolism of the eucharistic action; the implications of symbolism for the use of space, for iconography, inculturation, inclusivity, vesture, gesture, and other ritual actions; the essential components of the eucharist, its symbolic character, and the significance of the symbols and their relationship to cultural contexts.

• Liturgical and Eucharistic Renewal. Liturgical education for eucharistic renewal in both practice and spirituality, the resources available and required, and curricula designed for teaching programs on liturgy.

When IALC-5 met in Dublin, it drew almost eighty participants from around the Communion who, for a week, worked 'towards the development of principles which would inform the Communion during the next phase of liturgical revision and renewal.' The Principles and Recommendations of the Consultation and the Papers of the five working groups are the fruits of the preparatory work done at Untermarchtal, provincial discussions on the questions raised there, ongoing scholarly research, and this intensive period together in Dublin.

From this it is clear that the question of eucharistic renewal is of ongoing concern to the whole Communion and that the work of IALC-5 is one contribution to that process. The Principles and Recommendations which represent the considered opinion of the Consultation make some important affirmations which will help establish a context for Anglican eucharistic renewal in the coming years. Some of these are obvious consequences of earlier IALCs, notably IALC-1 on Children and the Eucharist (Boston, 1985) and IALC-4 on Christian Initiation (Toronto, 1991); others break new ground and are significant in that they represent the consensus of a large and diverse gathering of Anglican liturgists.

The Papers of the five working groups reflect varying degrees of consensus both within the groups themselves and within the Consultation as a whole. It is of considerable significance, however, that a subject like eucharistic sacrifice, which for so long has been at a stalemate in some parts of the Communion and a source of division within many provinces, has been addressed and the resulting discussion has given signs of a common way forward—thanks, in part, to a return to biblical sources and the insights of a wide variety of other churches. It is also important that the question of *epiclesis*, also a divisive issue among Anglicans, has been placed in the wider context of the Trinitarian structure of the eucharistic prayer itself, thus providing new directions for dialogue. Similarly, the question of lay presidency, which has more recently become a matter of considerable tension within the Communion, has been put in a wider theological and pastoral context creating the possibility of resolving the issue satisfactorily. Each of these areas is, however, some distance from a genuine consensus and further work on them must be done.

Because time was short and the Papers of the working groups were not put before the entire Consultation, they represent only the work of the groups themselves (modified by some input from plenary sessions during the week) and not IALC-5 as a whole. This does not diminish their importance but suggests, instead, that they represent a variety of levels of development.[7] It also leaves some work undone. For example, a suggested structure for eucharistic rites—something affirmed in the second of the Principles and Recommendations and so influential in the Communion when such outlines were presented in the 1965 and 1973 reports—would be of greater help to those Provinces engaged in eucharistic revision and renewal as a matter of consensus rather than remaining in the Paper of a working group.

IALC-5 made some significant achievements in its work. The task, however, is ongoing. As earlier reports made no claim to being a final word for the Anglican Communion, neither does this one. A variety of unresolved questions on which conversations are in a relatively early stage, as well as the rapid developments that are taking place around the eucharist throughout both Anglicanism and the churches in general will certainly see another IALC turn its attention to the task of eucharistic revision and renewal in the coming years. It is our common hope that the work of the Dublin Consultation will further encourage the ongoing renewal of our eucharistic life as Anglicans and play an important part in the ensuing theological dialogue and emerging consensus.

David R Holeton
Chair

Principles and Recommendations (Adopted by the Whole Consultation)

1   In the celebration of the eucharist, all the baptized are called to participate in the great sign of our common identity as the people of God, the body of Christ, and the community of the Holy Spirit. No baptized person should be excluded from participating in the eucharistic assembly on such grounds as age, race, gender, economic circumstance or mental capacity.

2   In the future, Anglican unity will find its liturgical expression not so much in uniform texts as in a common approach to eucharistic celebration and a structure which will ensure a balance of word, prayer, and sacrament, and which bears witness to the catholic calling of the Anglican communion.

3   The eucharistic action models the way in which God as redeemer comes into the world in the Word made flesh, to which the people of God respond by offering themselves—broken individuals—to be made one body in Christ's risen life. This continual process of transformation is enacted in each celebration.

4   The sacrificial character of all Christian life and worship must be articulated in a way that does not blur the unique atoning work of Christ. Vivid language, symbol, and metaphor engage human memory and assist the eucharistic action in forming the life of the community.

5   In the eucharist, we encounter the mystery of the triune God in the proclamation of the word and the celebration of the sacrament. The fundamental character of the eucharistic prayer is thanksgiving and the whole eucharistic prayer should be seen as consecratory. The elements of memorial and invocation are caught up within the movement of thanksgiving.

6   In, through, and with Christ, the assembly is the celebrant of the eucharist. Among other tasks it is appropriate for lay persons to play their part in proclaiming the word, leading the prayers of the people, and distributing communion. The liturgical functions of the ordained arise out of pastoral responsibility. Separating liturgical function and pastoral oversight tends to reduce liturgical presidency to an isolated ritual function.

7   The embodied character of Christian worship must be honoured in proclamation, music, symbol, and ritual. If inculturation is to be taken seriously, local culture and custom which are not in conflict with the Gospel must be reflected in the liturgy, interacting with the accumulated inculturation of the tradition.

8   The church needs leaders who are themselves open to renewal and are able to facilitate and enable it in community. This should affect the liturgical formation of laity and clergy, especially bishops as leaders of the local community. Such continuing formation is a priority and adequate resources for it should be provided in every Province.

9   Celebrating the eucharist involves both reaffirming the baptismal commitment to die to self and be raised to newness of life, and embodying that vision of the kingdom in searching for justice, reconciliation and peace in the community. The Spirit who calls us into one body in Christ equips and sends us out to live this divine life.

Membership of the Consultation
The following were members of the Consultation:

Anthony Balgrove Aarons SSF, USA, J. Neil Alexander, USA, Solomon Amusan, Nigeria, Lawrence F. Bartlett, Australia, Paul Bradshaw, USA, Colin Buchanan, England, Evan Burge, Australia, Jean Campbell OSH, USA, George Connor, New Zealand, William R. Crockett, Canada, Ian D. Darby, South Africa, Edward Darling, Ireland, Brian Davis, New Zealand, Keith M. Denison, Wales, Carol Doran, USA, Ronald L. Dowling, Australia, Richard Fabian, USA, Kevin Flynn, Canada, Daphne Fraser, England, John St.H. Gibaut, Canada, Paul Gibson, Canada, David M. Gitari, Kenya, Tom Gordon, Ireland, Martha Gray-Stack, Ireland, Robert Hagesi, Solomon Islands, Raymond W. Hartley, Australia, David Hebblethwaite, England, John W.B. Hill, Canada, David R. Holeton, Canada, Enrique Illarze, Brazil, Elson Jakazi, Zimbabwe, David J.Kennedy, England, Michael Kennedy, Ireland, Barbara Liotscos, Canada, Trevor Lloyd, England, Gordon Maitland,Canada, Richard Cornish Martin, USA, Jean Mayland, England, Brian Mayne, Ireland, Gillian Mendham, Australia, Ruth Meyers, USA, Harold Miller, Ireland, Leonel Mitchell, USA, Boyd Morgan, Canada, Clay Morris, USA, Robert Okine, Ghana, Juan M.C. Oliver, USA, John Paterson, Ireland, Ian Paton, Scotland, William Petersen, USA, David G. Peterson, Australia, H. Boone Porter, USA, Juan Quevedo-Bosch, Cuba, Ian Robertson, England, Jonathan Ruhumuliza, Rwanda, Orlando Santos de Oliveira, Brasil, Thaddeus A. Schnitker, Germany, Charles Sherlock, Australia, John Simalenga, Tanzania, David H. Smart, Canada, Bryan Spinks, England, David Stancliffe, England, Kenneth W. Stevenson, England, Ian Tarrant, Zaïre, Gianfranco Tellini, Scotland, Gordon Tikiba, Kenya, Phillip Tovey, England, Michael Vasey, England, Themba J. Vundla, South Africa, Louis Weil, USA, Carol Ann Wilkinson, England, John Baldovin SJ, USA (ecumenical partner).

The Group Statements

The five Groups worked from the headings set out in the Introduction on pages 4-5 above. Their statements, subsequently edited for publication, were presented to the Consultation but are subscribed to only by the members of the respective Groups.

I   Eucharistic Theology

A   *The Doctrine of the Trinity*

1.   Central to the Christian Faith is the revelation of the Triune God of love. All Christian worship is the work of God the Holy Trinity, who enables human beings, made in God's image, to return thanks and praise. Eucharistic theology, however, is often discussed as though it were simply a Christological, or at best, a 'binitarian' issue.

2.   Eucharistic worship reflects our status as created beings using bread and wine, fruits of God's creation, to realize our status as those redeemed, baptized in the three-fold Name and as Christ's body animated by the Holy Spirit. All three Persons of the Trinity are properly to be acknowledged throughout the eucharistic celebration. Similarly, eucharistic theology should be seen within the wider context of Trinitarian theology.

3.   The eucharist celebrates the Father's bestowing of divine grace on the community of believers in the Church through the combined ('perichoretic') interaction of the Son and the Spirit. Through the Son, the Church knows God as Father and knows God as creator and gives thanks for creation. It gives thanks for the incarnation and redemption through the Son and rejoices in its sanctification and re-creation by the Spirit.

4.   To participate in the eucharist is incarnational. It involves a bodily response, both corporately and individually. It is with our hands and mouths that we take, eat and drink the sacramental signs of the body and blood of Christ. The eucharistic bread and wine are offered to us to be eaten and drunk so that Christ may dwell in us. When Christ 'shares his bread with sinners' we praise God for the fuller revelation each new participation brings us. Our devotion and love thus engendered and nourished are evidence of the Spirit's joyful moving in us.

5.   It is the Triune God whose presence and fellowship we have when we take, eat and drink the body and blood of Christ. When in the eucharist we make the memorial (anamnesis) of the one sacrifice of Christ, it is none other than the self-giving love of the Trinity which is proclaimed and experienced.

6.   The Western eucharistic rites have not always given full expression to our Trinitarian faith. The classical forms of the eucharistic prayer in the East have an explicitly Trinitarian structure which became lost in the West. It is not found in the Roman Canon, nor was it part of the awareness of most of the Reformers. More recently, we have returned to the pre-Cappadocian custom of addressing the eucharistic prayer to the Father, through the Son, in the Spirit. But belief in the unity of being, in technical language the homoousia, of the Three Persons means that each may be addressed directly in public prayer, as much as in hymns and private prayers.

7.   There is a strong case not only for continuing the present trend of giving an explicitly Trinitarian structure to the eucharistic prayer, but for making explicit in at least some new prayers the equality of being of the three Persons. The grace as the opening greeting or the beginning of the Sursum Corda; a Trinitarian form of absolution; post-communion prayers and solemn three-fold blessings are examples of where this may be achieved.

8.   This could be further achieved by including devotional prayers and hymns which are addressed to Christ and to the Holy Spirit, such as the Veni Creator, 'Be present, be present, O Jesus...' (CSI) and the Agnus Dei. In much recent liturgical revision such devotional prayers have been discouraged. However, in many parts of the Anglican Communion the laity regard such devotions as extremely important in expressing deeply felt spiritual needs and beliefs.

9.   The restoration of a Trinitarian structure for the eucharistic prayer in historic as well as contemporary Anglican texts has included the restoration of an invocation (epiclesis) of the Holy Spirit. Modern scholarship understands the 'deep structures' of the prayer to embrace thanksgiving and supplication. In the Jewish models from which the Christian prayers grew, the supplication is for the restoration of Jerusalem or the future of Israel. In early Christian prayers this becomes prayer for the gathering of the Church into the Kingdom. The link between this eschatological perspective and the work of the Spirit is made explicit in Romans 8. In Christian prayer, therefore, the supplication became an explicit invocation of the Holy Spirit. The epiclesis later came to be interpreted as an invocation upon the elements of bread and wine or upon the communicants or both, but it is better understood in its earliest forms as invoking the Spirit upon the whole life of God's people as expressed in the

eucharistic action. Difficulties which many Anglicans have felt with an epiclesis in this part of the eucharistic prayer may be transcended if the invocation avoids a narrow focus on the elements or the communicants. The thanksgiving and proclamation section with its twin foci of God as creator and redeemer may be opened up towards supplication for the fulfilment of God's promise through the work of the Spirit. The recovery of the epiclesis thus enables the Church to enter into the full Trinitarian pattern of eucharistic praying. The assembled community is gathered into the whole sweep of the Triune God's work in creation, redemption, and promise. Thus we are given a vision of the transformation of the whole creation.

10.   To sum up, our eucharistic prayers may more explicitly express belief in the equal divinity and involvement of the Son and Spirit with the Father and make it clear that in the eucharistic mystery we encounter the mystery of the Triune God.

B   *Thanksgiving and Blessing*

1.   Thanksgiving is a fundamental concept of the Christian life and finds a special place in baptism, the eucharist, and in other rites of the Church. In relation to the holy communion we ought to see the entire rite as eucharistic; thanksgiving permeates every aspect of it. It is within this context that we see the significance of the eucharistic prayer (of thanksgiving/consecration). The scope of this thanksgiving (which itself derives from the Lord's giving of thanks at the Last Supper) is comprehensive, and embraces creation and salvation history (centred on the self-giving of Christ) as well as eucharistic consecration.

2.   We would encourage Provinces as a matter of policy to offer a range of complementary eucharistic prayers which in their very complementarity can embrace or point to the whole range and depth of eucharistic theology, without any one prayer having to bear the whole weight of meaning. Thanksgiving for Christ's saving work, centred on the cross, must find expression in all eucharistic prayers.

3.   In relation to the structure of the eucharistic prayer, we see this as consisting essentially of thanksgiving and supplication, recognizing that the one is intimately related to the other.

4.   We would draw attention to the inter-related character of the traditional parts of the eucharistic prayer inclusive of the opening dialogue (derived to some extent from Jewish sources), thanksgiving to God for his work in creation, the rehearsal of the mighty acts of God in Christ, the institution narrative, the anamnesis, the epiclesis of the Holy Spirit, petitions, and doxology.

5.   The institution narrative is part of the series of mighty acts which we remember. Rather than being a formula for consecration it is best understood as the mandate for the performance of the eucharistic action, and the promise of Christ's presence.

6.   The post-communion prayer(s) may take up the theme of thanksgiving for communion but need not necessarily be restricted to this. Together with the dismissal, for example, such prayer may articulate the sending out of the community in mission and service.

7.   We would draw attention to the value of hymns with the theme of thanksgiving for use at the eucharist. We would emphasize the devotional character of hymns in interpreting the liturgy as well as in nourishing piety.

8.   The concept of consecration by thanksgiving has a wider application than the eucharist itself. In relation to persons we see this as exemplified in ordination prayers, and in relation to material gifts in the blessing of the baptismal water.

9.   Generous quantities of the eucharistic elements should be placed upon the table to reflect the generosity of God who gave his only Son for us. Supplementary consecration should be avoided as far as possible, but if it is required, then any words used should not be seen as an independent liturgical act, but should clearly refer to the eucharistic prayer. Whatever is done and said at this point should take seriously both the nature of the sacrament and the sensibilities of the faithful.

10.   Thanksgiving for what God in Christ has accomplished once for all on the cross anticipates what God still has in store for us and for the whole creation of which the eucharist is the foretaste and pledge.

C   The Presence of Christ in the Eucharist

1.   The Lord Jesus Christ promised that whenever two or three gather in his name he would be in their midst. The risen Lord is present throughout the eucharistic celebration. Christ's presence is to be discerned in the assembly and in the proclamation of God's word. Christ's forgiveness is declared and received in faith, and his peace is proclaimed and exchanged among the people.

2.   The mystery of Christ's presence is given unique expression, to be discerned by faith, in the whole sacramental action when bread and wine are taken, 'eucharistized,' distributed, and consumed, in remembrance of him.[8] This remembrance or anamnesis is no mere mental recollection,

but effects a real encounter with the Lord in his saving acts, especially his atoning death and victorious resurrection. In appointing bread and wine as the visible and tangible means of the presence of his body and blood, the Lord affirms that participating in the sacrament allows the faithful communicant truly to feed upon his sacrificial life.

3.   In the sacrament of his body and blood, our Lord comes as saviour, brother, friend and healer. His life and his presence are to be found here, recognized by faith, and gratefully acknowledged. Through the presence of the risen Lord, the communicant is fed as a member of the family of God and strengthened by the grace of the Holy Spirit.

4.   The identification of the bread and wine with Christ's body and blood is to be understood, in his own words, as related to the acts of eating and drinking as he commanded, and to receiving by faith with thanksgiving, the benefits of his saving death and resurrection. It is desirable, therefore, that the words used in the administration of the sacrament do not reflect a static and limited view of the personal presence of Christ, but rather a recognition of an encounter in grace with the living Lord.

D   Sacrifice

The Power of Sacrifice

1.   Sacrifice is a central theme in the Bible and in Christian tradition. It points to the cost of obedience, even to death on a cross. In Christ is revealed the self-giving love of God, love which gives of God's own self. Through the Spirit, this love reaches into the heart of human living and dying, calling forth the faithful witness of those who follow Christ even to death. It is seen in the living sacrifice of dedicated self-offering which serves others. Sacrifice was an integral part of the everyday life of ancient Israel as it is of much of African life and of the life of other cultures today. Even in modern secular societies sacrificial ideas continue. For example, parents 'make sacrifices' for their children, athletes to win prizes, and soldiers in the bloody business of war. Sacrificial imagery is not nice: it entails cost, passion, blood, sweat and screams. It also calls forth extremes, whether of enthusiastic celebrations or life-giving loyalties. It can also fuel dangerous ideological extremes, and encourage abuse. Sacrifice is a concept full of power.[9]

2.   How then does sacrifice relate to Christian faith? God in Christ has done what we could not do for ourselves. Taking on our fragile form, Christ entered into the depth of our predicament to restore us to God. Freely giving up his own self, he was given over to suffering and death so

that we might live. In this passion Christians have come to see expressed the self-giving love of God, a love which took the first steps towards us. In trying to express the profound truths represented here, the scriptures take up a whole range of images from life—the battle-field, court-room, market, and household for example. Prominent among these are sacrificial concepts, drawn from both the life of Israel and the Graeco-Roman world. These concepts are often transformed in their Christian use. This rich range of imagery points clearly and decisively to Jesus Christ, crucified and risen, as the Way in and through whom sins are forgiven, relationship with God is restored, and the promise through the Spirit of a new creation is anticipated.

Sacrifice and Atonement

3.   The language of sacrifice in the scriptures covers a wide range of ideas. It cannot be brought under a single definition or concept, since it was performed with a variety of different rites and these rites express a variety of motivations.[10] None of these practices initiated relationship with God nor provided for the forgiveness of sins. They were means of furthering and deepening the covenant relationship initiated by God, which was to be lived out in a sacrificial, just life-style of obedience to God's law.

4.   The depth of what relationship with God entails is seen in the rites of the day of atonement, which provided annually for the restoration of a disobedient people.[11] What is striking about these rites is that they break out of the usual categories and customs of sacrifice. Neither of the two animals involved is burnt on the altar: the one over which Israel's sin is confessed dies in the wilderness; the one from which a few drops of blood are taken into the Holy of Holies is burnt outside the camp. There is a profound mystery indicated here. How the Holy One forgives sin remains unknown, but the reality of forgiveness is proclaimed with deep seriousness. It is these rites which Hebrews takes up in seeking to plumb the depths of Christ's atoning work. Christ takes on the role of both animals, and that of the high priest, bringing his own blood into the holy place of God's own presence (Hebrews 9-10). The language of atonement thus has a unique function in pointing to Christ, interpreting for us the meaning of his saving action in restoring us to communion with God.

5.   Other New Testament writers describe such notions of atonement in terms of 'hilasterion,' rites which in the Graeco-Roman world were thought to appease angry deities.[12] The performing of these rituals held the hope that the gods concerned would cease to take an interest in those so involved. Such ideas, dangerous and revolting as they were in the light of the revelation of God to Israel, were common in the world of the first-century church,

which dared to take them up to express the profound depth of God's act of reconciliation in Christ. In so doing, at least two transformations were made to the hilasterion concept: the initiative is spoken of as lying with God, not the worshipper (cf. Rom 3.25), and its motive is changed from one of appeasement to self-giving love. 'In this was love, not that we loved God, but that God loved us, and sent his Son to be the "hilasterion" for our sins' (1 John 4.10). Such an act of atonement has two closely related aspects: it requires a response—'beloved, if God loved us so much, we ought also to love one another'—and it was made 'not for us only, but also for the sins of the whole world' (1 John 2.2).

Eucharistic Sacrifice

6.   When the language of sacrifice is applied to the eucharist, it should be clearly distinguished from the language of atonement. What the Son of God did in his taking of our flesh, and free self-giving in death, was to make full atonement for the sins of the whole world. As the Book of Common Prayer puts it, 'he made there by his one oblation of himself once offered, a full, perfect and sufficient sacrifice, oblation and satisfaction for the sins of the whole world.' The images here may be mixed, but they make it unambiguously clear that Jesus Christ did wholly and completely for the human race what we could not do. He died for our sins, and lives to restore us to God. Any idea of 'eucharistic atonement' would detract from the completeness of Christ's atoning work. In and through the Spirit of grace, however, we are called to respond to Christ in sacrificial self-giving, a response focussed and expressed in the 'perpetual memorial of his precious death until his coming again.' It is from this perspective that the eucharist may properly be described as a 'sacrifice of praise and thanksgiving.' 'Eucharistic sacrifice' is our glad response to God in Christ.[13]

7.   The sacrificial images reflected in the scriptures are taken up in all sorts of ways in Christian life and worship. In the celebration of the eucharist sacrificial language describes our response to God's self-giving in Christ in a variety of ways:

a)   First, the language of sacrifice describes the whole rite, and includes such elements as the offering of prayers, money, food and drink and other gifts in response to the proclaimed Word of God, and offering ourselves as 'living sacrifices' in response to our feeding upon Christ.

b)   Secondly, when we not only 'say,' but 'do' as Christ commanded, taking bread and wine, offering thanks, and receiving them, we join in the actions of a sacrificial meal. We 'surrender' bread and wine for

God's use, eating and drinking at peace with God and one another in Christ's presence.

c)   Thirdly, in the great prayer of thanksgiving we associate the bread and cup with our sacrifice of praise. The particular words used will distinguish the unique atoning work of Christ from our present sacramental sacrifice which commemorates it, but no one formula is necessary. A particular pattern which commends itself to many is the idea that in the eucharist the Church continues to look to its great High Priest, the risen Lord who pleads his one perfect and completed atoning sacrifice. This links with the 'day of atonement' language of Hebrews noted earlier and with the present sacrificial dimension of the church's responsive offering of praise and thanksgiving.

8.   Historically, and in current ecumenical discussion, the use of the language of 'propitiation' in relation to the eucharist has raised significant problems. This is illustrated by the strong support for such language by Roman Catholic authorities, on the one hand, and its equally firm rejection by Christians who espouse the importance of substitutionary atonement, on the other hand. These difficulties can only be overcome by carefully distinguishing between Christ's atoning work on the one hand and the church's eucharistic response on the other hand. It is useful, therefore, to distinguish 'eucharistic atonement' from 'eucharistic sacrifice.' The former blurs the 'primary' atoning work of Christ with the church's 'secondary' appropriation of its benefits, and must be rejected. If this distinction is clearly made, the way is left open for using the language of 'eucharistic sacrifice' as a rich way in which the atoning passion of the living Christ is sacramentally remembered before God and lived out in passionate lives of self-giving love.

9.   It is recognized that in the modern world, language about sacrifice, especially when expressed in terms of self-giving, can be perceived as oppressive. Victims of abuse—one ethnic group by another, children abused by adults (physically, emotionally, and sexually), women and men by their partners—can experience the language of sacrifice as a reinforcement of their oppression and even as implying that God or the gospel requires them to endure it. For this reason, great care and sensitivity is required in the way in which we use such concepts.

E   Memorial: Memory, Time, and Redemption

1.   When Jesus commanded his disciples to 'do this in remembrance of me' (1 Cor 11.25), they responded by drawing the eucharist into their own corporate memory.[14] It is here that the Church finds its God-given

identity reaffirmed, an identity initiated by God and inaugurated at baptism.

2.   Much attention has been focussed in the human sciences on the 'collective unconscious' as the context for individual and community growth. When, in the eucharist, the church celebrates the memorial of our redemption, the community brings into consciousness the story of salvation with all its saving power. 'Memory' here is a dynamic concept which looks back to the cross and forward to the end of all things. This approach can enlarge our understanding of the eucharist as an 'anamnesis' of God's saving acts. There are several Eastern eucharistic prayers in which the Church 'remembers' both the cross and Christ's return in glory. In this way, the eucharist unlocks the memory of God before his people.

3.   There are a number of important implications which this approach provides for a renewed understanding of the eucharist.

First, it means that the Lord's Supper is both a part of time and history and also a window into eternity, because God's view on us is one that sees history whole, and not partial.

Secondly, the memorial itself, the motivation to celebrate the eucharist, is tinged with sacrifice, but always of a secondary, derivative character, because the one sacrifice is that which Christ has offered for us all. This means that our memory, scarred by human sin, can find a new wholeness at that table, as those memories are not only reconciled but redeemed— another costly triumph of Christ in human lives.

Thirdly, the eucharist has a specific ministry to human memory, in which the essential movement of sacrifice finds an important place. Local communities and individuals, indeed the whole Church, come before God to offer that memory, which is both broken and redeemed, an offering which is part of Christ's intercession at the Father's right hand. So Christians are fed as they move out of the past, through the present, into the future—God's future.

Fourthly, the meeting of time and eternity at the eucharist provides a means whereby the Christian community offer themselves (Rom 12.1) in a way that has been described as 'entering into the movement of Christ's self-offering to the Father.' What this means is that the people of God are enabled to claim for themselves the implications of Christ's unique work on the cross at every single Eucharist, no matter when, or where, or indeed in what kind of circumstances it takes place. Indeed that very universal provision is yet one more characteristic of the all-pervading grace of God himself.

F   *Creation, Re-creation, and Eschatology*

1.   The purpose of God in history is to sustain the created world and women and men made in God's image. Creation itself is the work of the Trinity; the Father creates through the Son and the Spirit.

2.   The Church at the eucharist is a microcosm of the creation as it celebrates the divine purpose both in creation and in redemption. The Church voices with creation and on behalf of creation the divine praises.

3.   As material things become the vehicles of divine grace, so we are recalled to our responsibility to the creation, to care for and exercise stewardship towards the resources of the earth. The gifts of bread, wine, water, and other offerings witness to our grateful dependence on God. In Africa, for instance, it is common for a variety of gifts to be presented as symbols of thanksgiving. While it is appropriate that a prayer should be provided for the presentation of the offerings of the people, the preparation of the gifts is preparatory to the main eucharistic action, and such prayer should not trespass on the ground of the eucharistic prayer.

4.   The eucharistic celebration manifests the worth of human beings created in God's image and redeemed by God's love. The eucharistic bread and cup are distributed equally to all as sign and symbol of the equal worth of all people in the sight of God. This demonstrates the dignity bestowed by God on all as sons and daughters, and celebrates the forgiveness, acceptance and empowering wrought through Christ's sacrifice. The missionary power of the sacrament lies in this demonstration of the free grace of God offered to all people.

5.   Although the Church witnesses to the goodness of God in creation, the disintegrating effect of rebellion against God means that, along with human enslavement to sin and death, in St Paul's words, the creation itself is in 'bondage to decay.' The gospel is cosmic in its scope, embracing the salvation of humanity but also the hope of the liberation of the creation from its bondage to share 'in the glorious liberty of the children of God' (Rom 8.21). The gift of the Spirit is a deposit guaranteeing this inheritance, the first-fruits of God's new creation in Christ. The eucharist celebrates and proclaims the victory of Christ over sin and death. The invocation of the Spirit on the action of the eucharist is a pledge of the transformation of the communicants, and also of the transformation of all creation, as gifts of God's creation become our spiritual food. The epiclesis embraces petition for the unity of the Church through the Spirit; this is both a prayer for the present and for the eschatological gathering of all the people of God in Christ.

6.   The eucharist is therefore an eschatological sign of God's new creation in Christ by the power of the Spirit. In this sense it is intimately linked
to baptism. Baptism is the primary sacrament of the making of the eschatological community. In baptism, Christians are born again and reimaged;
they become a new creation. The eucharist calls out and renews the baptized community. It celebrates the Kingdom values and demands of love,
justice and mercy and prefigures the feast of the Kingdom in which those
values find their ultimate and perfect expression. It challenges Christians
to live the present in anticipation of the future, and to respond as instruments of that future. It witnesses to the strand in the Gospel tradition that
points to the eschatological vindication of the poor and oppressed and so
presents to the Church the divine mandate for justice.

7.   The promise of the kingdom is expressed in the parables of the wed-
ding banquet and in the miraculous feedings. The reality of new and risen
life in Christ is definitely expressed in the sermon following the feeding
(John 6) and in Luke's account of Emmaus (Luke 24). These diverse features in the Gospels widen and enlarge our understanding of the eucharist.

8.   The eucharist is a proclamation of the Lord's death until he comes
(1 Cor 11.26). 'Until he comes' has an active sense, i.e., in order that he
might come.[15] The eucharist is thus the urgent plea of the Church for the
restoration of all things, a vivid expression of desire for God to achieve his
goal for the cosmos.

9.   As the eucharist renews our union with Christ, it is the pledge and
guarantee of our union with all who are in Christ, both living and departed. The eucharist thus celebrates the communion of saints, and prays for
the gathering together of all in Christ for eternity. This finds appropriate
expression both in the conclusion to the prayers of the people, the lead-
in to the Sanctus, and the supplicatory section of the eucharistic prayer.

10.   Because of these many themes, the celebration of the eucharist is
specially linked with the Lord's Day, which always celebrates creation, resurrection, and new life in the Spirit.

II   Ministry, Order, and the Eucharist

1.   As the Body of Christ, the Church of God is the primary symbol of
Christ's presence in the world, and is the celebrant of the eucharist. Even
the smallest groups of Christians embody the Church locally when they
hear God's word and celebrate the sacrament with their bishop, or one
whose presidency is acknowledged both by the group and by their bishop.
Yet in larger Christian communities, it may not be appropriate for the

eucharist to be celebrated with just two or three people present, which could encourage an individualistic rather than a communal understanding of the sacrament. When someone is prevented temporarily from joining in the worship of their local church, as for example through sickness, it would better reflect the communal nature of the eucharist for a small group of people to go directly from their Sunday eucharist to the housebound person, with elements consecrated at the celebration, sharing the word, prayers, and fellowship of liturgy with them, than to provide a celebration involving that person and a presbyter alone.

2.   Christ through the Spirit calls all humankind into the Kingdom of God, of which the Supper is a primary sign. Consequently, the Church's mission includes drawing people to hear the word of God, to pray for the salvation of the world, to offer praise and thanksgiving, to share in eucharistic fellowship, and then to go forth in the power of the Spirit to serve God in the world. All who come to our worship should be invited to participate as fully as possible in the Christian liturgical celebration of creation and redemption, and those who are unbaptized, 'should be encouraged to make their commitment to Christ in baptism, and so be incorporated within in the one body which breaks the one bread.'[16] On the other hand, there are situations where it is appropriate for communion to be withheld from those whose sinful behaviour is a source of scandal to the Christian community, until such time as they exhibit the fruits of repentance.

3.   Many revisions of prayer books throughout the Anglican Communion reflect the recovery of a plurality of ministries within the celebration of word and sacrament. Chief among these are the liturgical functions that belong to the assembly as a whole. The People of God are called to gather and greet one another in the Lord's name, to hear God's word, to pray for the world, to offer the sacrifice of praise and thanksgiving, and to share the eucharistic meal. Not only should these functions be safeguarded and developed in future revisions, but appropriate liturgical catechesis should be provided to strengthen the laity in the dignity and fullness of their baptismal priesthood.

4.   Within this eucharistic assembly different individuals exercise a variety of ministries. Some are representative, performed on behalf of the whole body (e.g., the bringing of the eucharistic elements to the table and the gathering of the alms and oblations). Other ministries arise from the particular gifts that individuals have received (e.g., singing, reading). While the former may—and should—be exercised by any of the baptized, the latter need to be recognized by the community (e.g., not every baptized Christian should play the organ!).

5.   The orders of deacon, presbyter, and bishop are distinguished from

these ministries in a special way. Their primary role is pastoral responsibility for the life and mission of the Church, and it is out of this responsibility that their liturgical functions arise, and not the other way around. Nevertheless, the liturgical formation of the ordained should be no less demanding and rigorous than their pastoral formation.

6.   Deacons serve the Church by marshalling, coordinating, and facilitating the various ministries of its members in the world. They should function in a similar way in the eucharistic assembly. While they may take a prominent part in the ministry of the word, the preparation of the table, and the distribution of communion, they should not diminish the involvement of others in these functions, but rather model them and enable others to carry them out more effectively.

7.   Bishops and presbyters also serve by leading the whole Christian community or in its priestly, prophetic, and pastoral mission to the world. Consequently eucharistic presidency belongs to them. Presiding at the eucharist includes overseeing the gathering and dismissing of the community, the ministry of the word, the prayers of the people, and the peace, as well as leading the community in its eucharistic action by taking and giving thanks over the bread and wine, and by participating in the distribution of holy communion. However, overseeing the liturgy does not mean performing every liturgical ministry. For instance, overseeing the ministry of the word does not necessarily entail reading or preaching; and others should participate in leading the prayers of the people, preparing the eucharistic gifts, and distributing holy communion.

8.   A special word needs to be said about the ministry of distributing holy communion. In some Anglican dioceses this is done by ordained ministers alone; in others lay people assist, while in yet others lay people may administer the chalice but not the bread. Furthermore, some dioceses permit lay ministers to take the consecrated elements to the sick, while others do not. In the light of the vision of the ministries of the Church—lay and ordained—outlined above, we believe that the distribution of holy communion belongs as much to the laity as to the clergy, and that there is no justification for treating the bread differently from the wine: those who distribute the sacrament are ministers of _communion_ and not of the chalice alone. While this ministry is not a charism as such, those who undertake it should receive careful training, and like those who minister the word by reading or preaching, they require the community's approbation as to their suitability. In particular, those taking the sacrament to the sick should also engage in regular pastoral care towards them, so that liturgical and pastoral ministries are not disengaged from one another.

9.   In those communities where pastoral leadership is not the ministry

of one person alone but is shared by a college of presbyters, or by a bishop with his or her presbyters, it may be thought appropriate for this collegial form of leadership to be expressed liturgically. This should be done by the other presbyters being visibly associated with the presider throughout the entire eucharistic celebration, but they should not participate in words or gestures that belong exclusively to the presider. It is also inappropriate to distribute elements of liturgical presidency among the ministers within a single celebration, since that undermines the unifying function of presidency within the rite.

10.   What should happen when a local church lacks a presbyter? In many parts of the Anglican Communion, holy communion is distributed by a deacon or a lay person from previously consecrated elements. This practice ought to be no more than an emergency measure, because it robs the assembly of its right to participate in the full eucharistic action (see #3 above). Communion from previously consecrated elements is intended for the those unable to be present at the eucharistic assembly, not for the eucharistic assembly itself.

11.   Some have proposed that in the absence of a presbyter, the bishop might instead authorize a eucharistic celebration presided over by a deacon or lay person. This solution, like the distribution of previously consecrated elements by deacons or lay people, can sever the connection between pastoral and liturgical leadership. If such persons are acting as leaders of a Christian community, they are exercising what are essentially presbyteral functions, and therefore ought to be ordained as presbyters. The authorization by a bishop of a deacon or lay person to preside at the eucharist constitutes an appointment to office, rendering 'lay presidency' a contradiction in terms. Moreover, the sign of appointment to presidential office in Anglican tradition is the laying–on–of–hands and prayer.

12.   Another option for communities that lack a presbyter for a short time is to forego eucharistic worship altogether. We need to remember that both in the past and even today in many parts of the Anglican Communion, Christians have been regularly nourished by the word in Morning and Evening Prayer, and in other non–sacramental services, with infrequent (perhaps monthly or quarterly) communion. Where, however, the absence of presbyteral leadership is extended, communities should be encouraged to seek out persons from among them who might be ordained as presbyters.

III   The Structure of the Eucharist

Introduction: The Value of Structure

The Church is shaped by the way it prays. This includes, but is not limited to, the shape provided by the church's liturgical structures. These structures exist inter-dependently with the full range of the church's prayer actions (i.e. the use of texts, music, movement, time, and space) by:

- providing the framework for the people of God to exercise their individual gifts;

- providing a given framework in which flexibility, local identity and variation can be experienced;

- giving context so that the various aspects of worship may be experienced and offered;

- ensuring that the components of worship are included in a way which gives appropriate balance and establishes the relationship between the elements;

- promoting unity in the worshipping community;

- providing a basis of unity from one community to another;

- helping to explicate God's relationship with humans through Jesus Christ in the power of the Holy Spirit.

From early Christian times basic structures of liturgical worship in the eucharistic assembly have existed. In recent years, Anglican provinces, informed by these common patterns of post-apostolic worship, the insights of the liturgical movement, and the emerging ecumenical consensus, have sought to clarify and adopt a common pattern. We therefore recommend recognition of the following basic structure for the Sunday assembly:

1.   Gathering of God's People. The people of God gather as an assembly to draw near to God and to celebrate new life in Jesus Christ.

2.   Proclaiming and Receiving the Word of God. The scriptures are read and the word of God is celebrated in song and silence, reflection, preaching, and response.

3.   Prayers of the People. The people of God, as the royal priesthood, intercede for the world, the church, the local community, and all in need.

4. Celebrating at the Lord's Table. The assembly offers praise and thanksgiving over the bread and wine and partakes in the body and blood of Christ.

5. Going out as God's People. The assembly disperses for a life of faith and service in the world.

The Structure Described

1   The Gathering of God's People

The opening rite should unite the assembled people as a community, prepare them to listen to God's word, to intercede as a priestly people, and to enter into the eucharistic celebration. The gathering rite should include at least the following:

> Greeting
> Song or Act of Praise
> Opening Prayer preceded by silence

To this essential structure various components may be added. Attention should be paid to the normal way of gathering and greeting in the local culture and the space in which the community gathers. The season of the liturgical year may also provide variations in the shape of the gathering rite. The gathering rite may also reflect the baptismal identity of the celebrating community.

2   Proclaiming and Receiving the Word of God

The ordered reading of Scripture, expressed in the use of an agreed lectionary and including the use of psalms as corporate prayer and praise, is an important part of the tradition. There should be two or three readings of which one, normally the last, is always from a Gospel. Regular use of the Old Testament is also recommended. The *Revised Common Lectionary* models these concerns.[17] Scripture should be presented in ways that are appropriate to the genre of the text and enable the community to hear and receive the reading as, 'The Word of the Lord.' Preaching viewed as proclamation and response is a normative element of this part of the liturgy.

Various other patterns of response are appropriate, including silence or spoken reflection, song, discussion, and prayer. Another appropriate response to the proclamation of the Word is the use of the Nicene or Apostles' Creed or other authorized statement of faith.

3   The Prayers of the People

The intercessions, which follow the proclamation, are not merely a response to the ministry of the word, but are an essential aspect of the priestly service of the Body of Christ. Leadership of the prayers is a responsibility of members of the community other than the presider. A variety of forms may be used so that the congregation clearly participates by litany, extempore prayer, or in some other way. Prayers are normally to be offered for the world and the created order, the church and its mission, the local community and all in need. These prayers commonly conclude with commemoration of the faithful departed and thanksgiving for the communion of saints. While traditionally the Lord's Prayer has been said before or after communion, it is particularly appropriate to use the Lord's Prayer to introduce or gather up the intentions of the intercessions. It should be used only once in a service.

If a corporate absolution takes place at this point, it follows the Prayers of the People and precedes the Peace.

The Peace is a sign of reconciliation between God and the community and among the members of the community. It appropriately follows the Prayers of the People and, within the movement of the rite, reaffirms that we are members of one another as we prepare to come to the table. It may also be placed elsewhere, for example, during the gathering or the going.

4   Celebrating at the Lord's Table

Preparation of the Table

Celebrating at the Lord's table begins with preparation of the table. The symbolism of one bread and one cup/flagon on the table during the prayer of thanksgiving points to the corporate nature of the eucharistic celebration of the People of God.

Priority should be given to the action of setting the table. This appropriately includes silence and should be performed by deacons and/or lay people. Care must be taken to prepare an adequate amount of bread and wine to suffice fully for the communion of the people. It may be desirable for the congregation to move and gather around the table.

Where additional prayer, song, or ritual action is desired, care should be taken not to introduce extraneous material or anticipate or overwhelm the great prayer of thanksgiving. Suitable themes include affirming the goodness of creation, solidarity with the hungry and the poor, penitential awe in approach, and expectation of the kingdom.

Bringing forward gifts of money for the poor and the work of the church may be associated with the preparation of the table, or may take place during the gathering of the assembly or after the communion.

The Eucharistic Prayer

The eucharistic prayer is composed of two fundamental elements, thanksgiving and supplication. Over time, the church has developed this essential structure by including additional components of prayer that enrich and intensify the prayer.

The precise ordering of these components in the eucharistic prayer has been a matter of considerable debate throughout the Communion and local pastoral and theological issues will no doubt continue to have impact upon further revisions. At the same time, some of these components are customarily joined together, e.g., the dialogue and the opening prayer which follows it, thanksgiving for creation and the Sanctus, the institution narrative and the anamnesis. When the structure links the thanksgiving for creation with the Sanctus and the thanksgiving for redemption with the institution narrative as its proclamatory climax, and they are followed by supplication for the work of the Holy Spirit that includes epicletic prayer for the assembly's celebration and the church's continuing mission, the prayer has a distinctively trinitarian shape.

Such a structure has been used in a number of Provinces for some time and it is becoming increasingly common in much of the Communion, which commends it as a unifying feature of eucharistic praying. Structures with similar elements have received wide scholarly and ecumenical consensus. A common arrangement of these elements is,

> Dialogue
> Thanksgiving
>> Creation
>> Redemption (as recorded by both the Old and New
>>> Testaments)
>> The Work of the Spirit
>> Sanctus
> Narrative/anamnesis
> Supplication
>> Epiclesis
>> Doxology and Amen

Other developed forms might include:

> Dialogue
> Thanksgiving for Creation
>> Sanctus
> Thanksgiving for Redemption
>> Institution Narrative
>> Anamnesis
> Thanksgiving for Work of the Spirit
>> Epiclesis
>> Supplication for the Assembly and the Mission of the Church
>> Doxology and Amen

or

> Dialogue
> Thanksgiving for Creation
>> Sanctus
> Thanksgiving for Redemption
>> Institution Narrative
>> Anamnesis
> Supplication
>> Epiclesis
>> The Work of the Spirit in the Assembly and the Mission of the Church
>> Doxology and Amen

However the components are arranged, we affirm the structural unity of the eucharistic prayer. This unity is emphasized if there are no changes in posture of either the congregation or presider. Gestures which draw attention to the institution narrative or any other component may undermine the essential unity of the prayer.

This structure makes the term 'preface' unnecessary, although there may be season and thematic variation in the eucharistic prayer.

The eucharistic prayer should be constructed to encourage the engagement of the whole assembly in the main action of thanksgiving and supplication, by clarity in the main elements of the action, evocative language which engages people in relating the death and resurrection of Christ to human experience of pain, desolation, and joy, and by memorable responses, which may be either a short repeated phrase or one which contributes to the action of the prayer. Such responses work best if they are sung, known by heart, or repeated after cantor or presider. If responses are used, they should appear between sections of the prayer and not in the middle of sections.

Anglicans have followed the ancient practice of incorporating the institution narrative within the prayer. In light of this tradition, and noting the Lambeth Quadrilateral's commitment to, 'the unfailing use of Christ's words of institution and of the elements ordained by him,' we recommend that the institution narrative should be included in the prayer. This serves to link the celebration with the reconciling death of Christ, Christ's institution of the eucharist, and with God's proffered gift of salvation.

When the narrative is part of the thanksgiving and forms the climax of the proclamation, it emphasizes the link between the eucharist and the death and resurrection of Christ. But when the narrative is part of the supplication, it risks being understood as a formula of consecration. Undue focus on the narrative risks suggesting that the eucharist is a repetition of the Last Supper rather than a proclamation of the death and resurrection of Christ.

The place of the narrative as part of the movement of the prayer may be obscured when it is isolated from its context by posture or gesture, by a change in tone of the presider, or by a shift to a dramatic recital directed towards the congregation. The role of the narrative emerges more clearly when the congregational acclamation follows the anamnesis rather than the narrative.

In order to provide for a variety of circumstances and structures, Provinces may authorize a number of eucharistic prayers. Care should be taken to ensure that all should be usable by the whole province and not designed for groups defined by age or theological point-of-view. Provinces may wish to consider whether any eucharistic prayers of other Provinces, after suitable adaptation, may be authorized for use within their own Province.

Sharing Bread and Wine

As our communion is with God and with one another, the corporate nature of what is done is important. This may be expressed by the use of words at the breaking of bread which reflect the corporate nature of the sacrament, by ministers, as part of the body, receiving after the invitation to the assembly as a whole, or even last, and by the people communicating one another on some occasions.

The people should be invited to receive communion when the elements have been prepared for distribution. During the distribution words should be said to each person, who should respond.

5   Going Out as God's People

When the feast is over, the People of God give thanks for the gift received and pray that they may bear its fruits. They are dismissed into the world for a life of mission and service.

• We encourage a *space for silence* after all have communicated. This is a time for reflection.

• *Ablutions:* The remaining consecrated elements should normally be consumed after the service or in the sacristy. If this is done in the church, it should be as unobtrusive as possible.

• *Hymns and Songs:* If there are hymns and songs after communion, they should normally precede the Prayer after Communion.

• *Prayers after Communion:* These should be brief and include a sense of mission. There is a place for well-known corporate prayers, but these should not be lengthy, and it is best to have only one post-communion prayer. On occasion, it may be suitable for informal prayers of thanksgiving or commissioning to take place at this point.

• A *Blessing* is optional.

• *The Dismissal* should always be the last words of the service. When there is a blessing and dismissal, they should be together.

A Note on Penitence and Reconciliation

There is no celebration of the eucharist without penitence and reconciliation. In an age with little consciousness of the holiness of God, as well as sin and forgiveness, members of the community of the baptized gather, conscious of their own failure to love God and neighbour, but also conscious of the fact that they are forgiven and washed from sin. Each element and seasonal reference in the liturgical celebration may evoke consciousness of sin, the need for repentance and forgiveness, and the grace and joy of justification. Such expressions include:

1.   the eucharistic action with its sharing of the 'blood of the covenant which is poured out for many for the remission of sins;'

2.   the Lord's Prayer with its petition 'forgive us our sins as we forgive those who sin against us;'

3.   the exchange of the sign of peace;

4.   a penitential petition in the prayers of the people;

5.   a corporate confession and absolution, either (i) in a separate rite before the Gathering of God's People, or (ii) during the Gathering of God's People, or (iii) after the Prayers of the People;

6.   a penitential devotion before the reception of communion;

7.   Kyrie as a response to penitential petitions during the gathering;

8.   a sprinkling with water during the gathering recalling our need for repentance and the grace of the baptismal covenant;

9.   the Ten Commandments or our Lord's Summary with response.

There are some who want to see a corporate confession and absolution in every eucharistic rite. Where such a corporate confession and absolution is used, it is important to remember that the sign of forgiveness in the rite is in the reception of the eucharist itself. Forms of absolution that emphasize that the liturgy is celebrated by the entire assembly and not by the presider alone are to be encouraged.

Additional Notes

We welcome and encourage the use of the ELLC, CIFT, and other common language texts. Commonly shared cue lines for such elements as the acclamations would be helpful.

Where an alternative form of the liturgy of the word is provided for children, they should return to the assembly no later than the preparation of the table.

In places where catechumens are dismissed this should take place before the Prayers of the People.

Music is integral to liturgical celebration and should be used to enhance and not disrupt the structures and movement of the rite.

The use of silence is an important element in the celebration. The following points in the liturgy are suggested as a minimum:

•   before the opening prayer/collect—to allow the people to offer their own prayer intentions;

- during the Proclaiming and Receiving of the Word, after the readings and/or sermon—for reflection;

- during the Prayers of the People

- within the penitential rite

- after the communion—for reflection.

What is Important?

The following scheme, suggested for the Sunday celebration of the eucharist, should be varied in keeping with liturgical seasons and special seasons and occasions.

The following table indicates the relative importance of the various elements in the eucharistic rite.

1 =   indispensable

2 =   integral, but not indispensable

3 =   would not be omitted in principle, may be limited or varied in accordance with liturgical seasons or special occasions;

4 =   not necessary but may be desirable at times.

An asterisk indicates elements of the liturgy which may appear at one point or another in the rite. Their placement, however, has significant implications and requires careful attention.

I.   The Gathering of God's People

Greeting	1
*Penitential Rite	3
Song/Act of Praise	1
Opening Prayer (Collect)	1

II.   Proclaiming and Receiving the Word

First Reading	1
Psalm	2

Second Reading	2
Gospel	1
Sermon	1
Creed	3
*Silence, songs and other responses	2

III. Prayers of the People

Prayers	1
*Lord's Prayer	1
*Penitential Rite	3
Peace	1

IV. Celebrating at the Lord's Table

Preparing the Table	1
Prayer over the gifts	4
Eucharistic Prayer	1
*Lord's Prayer	1
Silence	1
Breaking of the Bread	1
Invitation	2
Communion	1

V. Going out as God's People

Silence	1
Hymn	4
Prayer after Communion	2
Blessing	4
Dismissal	1

IV   Eucharist: Ritual, Language, and Symbolism

1   *Introduction*

The eucharist has been celebrated by the people of God throughout history in ongoing response to our Lord's command to 'do this in remembrance' of him, and in grateful reception of his continual gift of himself to us in his Supper. The eucharistic liturgy by which we 'do' what he commands is a function of all the people of God there gathered. Every local worshipping community is a fellowship of people who belong to each other in Christ. Their bonding in Christ is both expressed and strengthened in the eucharist; and the sharing of the bread and cup requires them to be responsive to him, active in participation in the rite and inter-active with each other in love and support, encouraging each other in devotion and life. The purposes of the liturgy include both the offering of true worship to God in response to God's self-giving and the building up of the people of God, so that we are bread for the world. It is the task of those who lead the liturgy to do so as pastors seeking to build up the congregation in the knowledge and love of God.

Ritual expresses and shapes the identity of institutions. The identity of the church is constituted and manifested as its members gather for worship. Pursuing our mission in the world, we are joined together by the Spirit of God in the regular celebration of the Supper of the Lord. This is the essential rhythm of Christian life: as the body of Christ we share in the one bread in order to be Christ for the world. We encounter each other and build each other up not simply by being under the same roof at the same time for the same event, but also by communicating God's truth and love in the eucharistic assembly. This we do in response to God's coming amongst us.

Celebration of the eucharist is incarnational. Through the language and symbolism of the rite and by the power of the Holy Spirit, God communicates with us and we with one another. In part this communication is by word: given to us normatively in Scripture; formed into doctrine; read in the lectionary; applied in preaching; informing our prayers; guiding our celebration; interpreting our sacramental practice; enriching our self-understanding; and undergirding all our relationships. In part this communication derives from our created humanity: we are embodied beings inhabiting the physical world within which all our lives, including our Christian gatherings, are set. In worship we have faces and speech, we make eye-contact and use other body language, we express emotions and use gestures.

Another aspect of our communication is by symbol: in the physical realities of worship, ordinary actions and objects become instruments of divine grace. As embodied people we engage with ordinary physical elements, and through this interaction the physical world becomes the vehicle of God's transforming power. Symbols communicate in ways that are pregnant with further meaning, and work within our lives by constantly imparting more than would be apprehended at first sight or by initial participation. The primary symbols in eucharistic celebration are the gathering of the community and the eating and drinking of bread and wine, a sacramental action which God invests with salvific meaning. These stand alongside the word as means of God's grace. There follows a great host of secondary symbols and signs from the physical world, symbols and signs which also communicate the truth, mercy and love of God. Our use of buildings, ornamentation, music, art, choreography, vesture and ceremonial communicates. These latter differ from the dominical sacrament in being more contingent: that is, they are more open to the church's discretion as to how the physical world is to be employed in arranging the worship of the congregation. The church's part is to recognize that this physical world is not only the inevitable setting of our worship, but is to be used positively and valued highly in its potential as a channel of God's grace to build up the corporate and individual Christian lives of that community.

From the general principle of the bonding and life-giving character of this wide-angled understanding of communication within the liturgy, we turn to address specific areas of that communication.

2   Encounter with the Word

Our encounter with God in the eucharistic celebration comes through both word and sacrament. Within the whole rite the place of the word is to be respected and never diminished. In places where there is a solemn entry with the book (Bible, or book of readings) and it is placed in a prominent place (the lectern or the table), this expresses the coming of Christ among the people. The use of a large book from which the Scripture is read gives appropriate dignity to the proclamation of the word.

It is particularly important that the scriptures be read clearly and effectively. Lay people should play their part in this ministry, and those chosen should be ready to accept training in order to do it well. Those listening to the word should do so actively and with a positive desire to encounter God through their listening. Silence observed after the readings provides time for reflection.

The exposition of the word helps to build up the people of God who in turn should be encouraged to play their part in that exposition. While we affirm the traditional sermon, we also recommend a variety of approaches to the exposition of the word, as, for example, dialogue sermon, question-and-answer sermon, interview technique, visual aids.

3   The Eucharist as Meal

The eucharistic feast has its origins in the last supper Jesus shared with his disciples. This is to be understood in the larger framework of Jesus' previous meals with disciples and others, and of the risen Christ breaking bread with his disciples on the first day of the week. As Jesus' table fellowship with all sorts and conditions of humanity was a sign of the inbreaking of the reign of God, so too eating and drinking in the fellowship of the community is a sign of the contemporary community's participation in this reign of God.

Historically, the bread and wine have been the elements of the meal. Breaking bread together and drinking from the common cup signify the community's participation in Christ. Thus the elements should be used in a manner which allows everyone to recognize that they are sharing a common meal.

When the table is prepared, bread and wine sufficient to feed the entire community should be placed on the table, and be arranged so as to facilitate the people's awareness of the common bread and wine. The size of the gathered community may require more than a single loaf of bread and more wine than can be contained in a single cup. Yet the symbol of one cup invites the community to focus on its unity as thanksgiving is rendered over that cup, and drinking from a common cup further expresses communal participation in the eucharistic action. Likewise, bread which must be broken to be shared expresses participation in a meal, and the use of ordinary bread (such as that eaten by the people in everyday life) illustrates this particularly well. The Kanamai Consultation in 1993 encouraged local people 'to produce the eucharistic bread.'

Because the presider serves the community, it may be appropriate for the presider, along with other ministers of communion, to receive the bread and cup after the rest of the community and to do so by receiving the elements from the hands of others. On occasion, in view of the nature of the eucharistic community, it may be appropriate for the elements to be passed around the congregation under the oversight of the presider, rather than for all to have to receive from a specially authorized minister.

The symbols of bread and wine express continuity with the tradition of the church and a unity of use pointing to our sharing 'one bread and one cup' throughout the world. As Christianity has spread to regions of the world where bread and wine are not local staples, questions have arisen about the use of local food and drink as eucharistic species. The Kanamai Consultation asked that 'Provinces consider whether they should permit the use of local staple food and drink for the eucharistic elements.' This should be seen as a decision to be considered at the Provincial level rather than by individual congregations. Because the use of a different eucharistic species has implications for the worldwide Anglican Communion as well as ecumenical implications, before implementing such a decision Provinces are encouraged to consult with the worldwide Communion through such bodies as the IALC, the Anglican Consultative Council, and the Lambeth Conference.

4   *Space*

In the Anglican Communion there is a great diversity in places of worship. This diversity includes worship in outdoor settings and the use of both new and old buildings. A great proportion of these were built for worship, though some also serve purposes other than worship, and some have been adapted for worship from other uses for which they were originally built. In the liturgical ordering of buildings, we are faced with two major types of projects: the adaptation of existing buildings to the needs of contemporary worship, and the creation of entirely new buildings. In the former case the existing structure will often impose limitations on liturgical ordering, and these may be difficult to overcome without considerable creativity. In the latter case, new buildings may be ordered according to our principles. Whatever their form, buildings shape the experience of worship. For this reason they inevitably express an ecclesiology, and, for good or ill, that easily becomes the self-understanding of the congregation.

Appropriately ordered, buildings express an understanding of the church as a community which shares in the celebration as a foretaste of the kingdom. Such an understanding emerges when the worship space or spaces enable people to relate fruitfully to God and to one another. For this reason congregations should reflect on the message their buildings are giving and on the way their buildings are shaping their corporate life, over and above the message the text of the liturgy itself is providing. The liturgy is logically prior to the layout of the building and its space; and the Sunday eucharist, with its components of teaching and reflecting, of transformation and encounter, should be the basis for ordering the liturgical space.

There are basic elements in the structure of the eucharist which need to be addressed in the ordering of liturgical space. The solutions adopted will be different in different contexts. The people need a place to assemble. In some churches, this may be a narthex, porch, or courtyard; in others it will be in the main body of the church. In this latter case, then they may also share in the opening rite and the liturgy of the word in that same place; but, where space permits, the use of a separate place of gathering enables the opening rite to be conducted there, with a movement into the main body of the church to celebrate the liturgy of the word.

The liturgy of the word requires that there be a place for the assembly, including a place for the presider who is part of the assembly, as well as a place for proclamation. Sometimes the word is read and preached from the same place; in some places the presider's chair is the place for preaching. The space should be so arranged that as many of the people as possible will be able to see and hear the proclamation of the word.

After the proclamation of the word and the prayers of the people, the focus of the eucharistic community shifts to the table. In some church buildings it may be possible to have the liturgy of the table in a separate space, and for the people to move there as the table is prepared. It is also often possible within a single-room building for the focus to shift to a different area where the table is located, without the congregation actually moving.

The location and shape of the table is very important. Within the church there should clearly be one main table at which the congregation gathers for the central celebration of a Sunday. The character of the table and the use of any congregational seating should further the people's understanding of the eucharist, and not be at odds with it. Thus the more the table appears as a festal table with the people round it, the more they will understand that this is both a meal shared by the people and a foretaste of the heavenly banquet. The location of the table has varied through history, but, as with its shape, the solution adopted must stem from the understanding of the eucharist in the local church. The presider may well preside from behind the table, but a gathering round it by the people is in harmony with our understanding of the rite.

Also of importance is the place of the font. The IALC's Toronto statement, Walk in Newness of Life, emphasized the symbolic significance of the abundant use of water in the baptismal liturgy. The size and shape of the font may encourage or impede this. This will require the use of a larger font than is usually found, and, given the renewed communal character of baptism, and the fact that the usual context for its celebration will be the full assembly, there also needs to be provision for the people to see, and, if possible, to gather round the font. The font therefore requires a space of its own which both reflects its significance and takes into account practical requirements of the baptismal liturgy. Merely placing it at the back of the church building if there is no room for the people, or placing it at the front to make it visible without asking the people to move, are inadequate solutions.

In the space where the people assemble, there are three primary liturgical furnishings: the place of proclamation, the table, and the font. Although these foci are of great importance, they as well as all the furniture in the church building may be such that they may conveniently be moved so that the congregation is not permanently committed to specific locations for these objects. All other foci, such as decorations, images, and, if in use, the place of reservation of the sacramental elements, are unqualifiedly subsidiary to the primary liturgical foci which take their significance from their role in the Sunday liturgy. Such decorations and other foci should not be so placed as to distract people's attention or to impinge visually upon the main furniture and spaces in liturgical use.

The experience of worship, however, is to some degree found by the use of art, decoration, and light, as well as by the arrangement of the church. Art expresses the incarnational nature of the Christian faith and allows for elements of the local culture to be brought into the church building. These elements are important to the liturgical experience of the people. Artists, architects and craftspeople all have gifts to contribute to our liturgical life.

5   *The Body in Worship*

Our encounter with God and with each other in worship engages the whole person, the body with its senses as well as the mind. Celebrations of the eucharist vary in their degrees of festivity and solemnity and in the scale and mood of their setting. All decisions about movement, gesture, posture and vesture should relate appropriately to these varying circumstances and to the local culture.

a)   Movement

Celebration of the eucharist involves movement. The presider and other ministers move to and away from their respective foci; where practicable the whole assembly may move in the course of a celebration—e.g., from a gathering near the door or font to seating near to the place of reading and exposition of the word, and then to the table. Such movement is not merely practical, it expresses the assembly's progression stage by stage through the rite. It may also be appropriate to involve the movement of dance. The arrangement of liturgical space should, as far as possible, facilitate movement and ensure clear and unimpeded sight-lines, in such a way that the assembly participates rather than being mere spectators.

b)   Gesture

Full and active participation in the celebration of the eucharist involves bodily movement as well as the hearing, reading and saying of liturgical texts. This will include personal devotional gestures; in some places particular gestures of devotion will be in general use, which are not used in other places. Such matters of personal devotion should be left to individual choice.

Those who preside or exercise other leading roles in the celebration will need to ensure that their actions and gestures are seen, perceived and understood by others, and they should take thought as to how they carry out their roles. Natural, simple and fluid gestures are more appropriate than contrived and drilled actions.

Gestures by the presider during the eucharistic prayer should underscore the unity of the prayer. The traditional manual acts which draw attention to the institution narrative or other portions of the prayer serve to locate consecration within a narrow portion of the text and may contradict a more contemporary understanding of eucharistic consecration.

c)   Posture

Local custom in matters of posture will vary in different cultures. Nonetheless, such longstanding customs as standing for the Gospel reading will often be followed. Both kneeling and standing have a place in the tradition as postures for prayer. Whereas Anglican Prayer Books have in the past required kneeling as the posture for prayer, many communities have more recently been exploring other possibilities.

Standing may be expressive of our common action in prayer, and this is permitted by current liturgical texts. Because the eucharistic prayer is an act of praise and thanksgiving offered by the whole congregation, standing throughout is considered by many to be the most appropriate posture. Standing also has great value in that it enables the assembly to identify itself with the action of the presider and helps express our risen life in Christ. There is scope for freedom in deciding the posture to be adopted for receiving communion.

d)   Vesture

Questions of dress and vesture need to be considered by all individuals taking part in the liturgy, and not only by the ordained ministers. There is a custom in some cultures of people attending Sunday worship wearing their 'best' clothes, and, provided that this does not seem to exclude those not so dressed, the custom has some value in enhancing the festal character of eucharistic celebrations. In some cultures this may be expressed in other ways, e.g., by the removal of shoes or by the decorative wearing of flowers.

Distinguishing vesture for those exercising particular roles in the liturgy may be appropriate, provided that it clarifies and supports the action being undertaken and does not impede or distract from appropriate gesture and movement. There is no necessity for everyone exercising a particular role in the liturgy to be distinctively clothed.

Customary forms of distinctive vesture emphasize historical and geographical connections between the celebrations of many ages and places; and they bring an appropriate celebratory note to each local celebration. Many see value in continuing within the received tradition of special vesture, while others may wish to be free to depart from traditional use.

6   Music

Music is an important dimension of our communication. In itself it can be a form of proclamation. It has the power to heighten the meaning of words and the capacity to intensify the human affections in liturgical prayer: to express the joy of thanksgiving, the sorrow of sin acknowledged, and the confidence of praise. It is one of the primary ways in which aspects of local culture can be dedicated in the assembly, with no single style being necessarily more appropriate than another. Music should not uncritically be allowed to settle into a single unchanging mould, but the range of song used should be always expanding; creativity should be encouraged and the harnessing of the music-making resources of the congregation pursued.

The criteria for the use of music in the liturgy are related rather to matters of craft, liturgical context, and pastoral care. There is no fixed model as to which elements should be sung or said, save that the Psalter and hymns such as Gloria in Excelsis and Sanctus, because of their musical character as songs, incline naturally toward a musical setting.

Joining in song is an important feature of the uniting of the congregation. Whatever music is used should normally be within the capacity of the people to perform rather than be delegated predominantly to a special group.

Musical leadership requires that persons with training in music be actively involved in the selection of works which are well-crafted and also are appropriate to the overall character of the celebration, including the liturgical season, the appointed readings and the structure of the rite. Such persons also need the skills and sensitivity to introduce new music while continuing to draw from the familiar music of the local community.

7   Words and Silence in the Liturgy

In the account of creation in Genesis 1, God creates by the power of the word: 'God said, "Let there be light," and there was light.' By the word of God human beings were created in the divine image to have relationship with God and one another.

The words of the liturgy express and shape our concept of God and our attitudes toward one another and all creation. The Reformation principle that worship is to be in the language of the people suggests that the texts are to be accessible in the local vernacular.

a)   Language about Humanity

The words used in the eucharist to describe members of the worshipping congregation affect the way in which we encounter one another and need to reflect the truth that we all bear God's image within us. In the English language, the use of words of masculine gender, such as 'man,' 'men,' 'mankind,' and 'forefathers,' to refer to both male and female makes women 'linguistically invisible.' Similar problems may arise in other languages used in our Communion.

In some provinces it has been recognized that such language marginalizes women and is offensive to both women and men. Recent revisions have avoided the use of male generic terms and their dependent pronouns. We encourage all Provinces who have not yet taken such action to give it serious consideration.

Care should also be taken not to offend other sections of the worshipping community by ill-chosen adjectives or metaphors.

b)   Language about God

The worshipping community encounters God through the words of the liturgy. The language we use to describe God is of crucial importance because it is formative in the devotional life of the people. Through the totality of the language of the liturgy and its progress there should be presented a fully-rounded picture of God.

Much of the language of the liturgy addresses God in terms of power, majesty and glory. God is, however, to be encountered in suffering and brokenness as well as in power and glory. The language of the liturgy needs to reflect this by using the full range of biblical imagery concerning God, and should include, for example, words which convey the immanence, vulnerability and agonizing of God, as well as the transcendence, the power and the victory.

In particular we recommend a more widespread use of 'feminine' images of God—alongside the more well-known 'masculine' ones. Some of these may be drawn from Scripture—but others from the prayer and writings of the early Fathers or the mystics and still others from contemporary life. In doing this with sensitivity it may, for example, be more helpful to describe God acting as or like a mother rather than directly as 'Mother.'

While supporting the importance of biblical imagery in general, we would nevertheless also encourage the use of images for God drawn from contemporary life. These new images may need to be tested before being taken into the body of texts for use by the whole church. A possible way forward may be to have some skeletal printed prayers—even eucharistic prayers—into which sections drawing on images from the life of the local community may be inserted. Such insertions might well be agreed after discussion in that community in advance of the service. These images may be very 'concrete' and should be encouraged in a whole variety of languages.

c)   The Language of Silence

The deepest encounter with God is often experienced within the silence which can enable a relationship which is beyond the power of words to achieve. Life is often so busy and noisy and it is not helpful if the liturgy is the same. Silence should be written into the service—at least by rubric—and both presider and congregation encouraged to use it well. In the context of the liturgy the sharing of silence is a corporate activity and ways of affirming its corporate nature need to be explored.

8   The Eucharist and the World

The ritual celebration does not exhaust the meaning of the eucharist. The celebration of the eucharist signifies the reconciliation of humanity in Christ. All receive the same gift from the same table, whether they are powerful or weak, rich or poor. In our human fallibility and sinfulness we tame the sign and pervert it into an act of personal consolation and individual pardon; yet, through the grace of God, the integrity of the sign endures and continues to call us back and remind us that, through it, God calls us to be bread for the world. Those who have been fed at God's table must go forth to serve and to work for justice in the local community and throughout the world.

V   Liturgical and Eucharistic Renewal

Preamble

The Church at worship is that body of people who have been baptized into Christ's death and resurrection and who now, in the power of the Spirit, give praise and thanks to God. All are welcome to join this body. Its vocation is to restore all people to unity with God and each other in Christ. The chief day of Christian celebration is Sunday, the day of the new creation brought about in the Paschal Mystery. In the eucharistic assembly, Christians give thanks to God for their creation, preservation and redemption. Jesus, the bread of life, is made available to all who come hungry to the table of the Lord. They in turn are called to feed others.

If faithfulness in mission is the church's response to the gospel, its gathering for eucharist is both the symbolic expression of God's reign and the means through which the community is nurtured and empowered to fulfil its calling.

The Christian community betrays the gospel when it focuses on itself and forgets who it is as the Body of Christ and does not attend to God's mission. Thus, the Church is always in need of renewal. The agent of renewal is the Holy Spirit working within the specific human circumstances of each culture.

'The incarnation is God's self-inculturation in this world and in a particular cultural context. Jesus' ministry on earth includes both the acceptance of a particular culture, and also a confrontation of elements in that culture… which is contrary to the good news or to God's righteousness.'[18]

It is with this constant need for renewal in mind that the following principles are articulated.

1   Past and Present: The Unity of Anglican Worship.

The renewal of the eucharistic liturgy in the Church will honour the tradition which is rooted in the Gospel. That tradition has taken various forms over time in different cultures. Our inheritance from the past must be reflected upon in the light of the present community's response to the Gospel.

As Anglicans we have until recently identified our liturgical unity in a more or less uniform set of texts derived from historic Books of Common Prayer. Today that unity is to be found in a common structure of eucharistic celebration. Unity among Anglicans is also expressed and furthered by a number of bodies and organizations by which we meet and work with each other.

While Anglicans have always had a variety of means to appropriate the faith of the Church on a personal basis, Anglican spirituality is characteristically a liturgical spirituality. We are formed and shaped by the experience of corporate worship. The renewal of the liturgy, then, is a privileged means by which the faithful may become more fully who they are called to be. Renewal in our day honours the witness of those who have gone before us while drawing new things out of old.

2   The Liturgical Assembly

We never arrive at a perfect Church, but the following may be regarded as a vision of a renewed liturgical assembly.

* It will be an assembly aware of itself as the body of Christ and corporately the minister of its eucharistic worship.

* All persons, both lay and ordained, will understand themselves to be part of the whole people of God who in baptism have put on Christ.

* All the varied ministries within the assembly will joyfully serve the whole community and honour and utilize the gifts of God's people.

* The eucharistic assembly will incorporate the baptized of all ages. It will see baptism as 'complete sacramental initiation leading to communion' as the IALC's 1991 Toronto statement affirms.[19]

* Those who are as yet unbaptized, whether catechumens or other seekers after truth, are welcomed, accepted, cared for and invited to hear the proclamation of God's word and to learn of the community's way of life.

* The worship of the assembly will engage the whole human body with all its senses through the full and robust use of symbolic actions.

* The words spoken and sung and the symbolic actions of the worship will be relevant and accessible to the participants—food for their journeys of faith.

* The worship will be rooted deeply in the culture of the people. In multi-cultural congregations the different cultural gifts will be valued, accepted and employed.

* The principal, though not necessarily sole, act of worship on Sunday will be the eucharist. The eucharistic celebration will include the breaking open of the biblical word in preaching and teaching as well as the sharing of the bread of life and the cup of salvation.

- The people will be so built up, consoled, challenged and encouraged, that they may leave the assembly joyfully to be Christ's salt and light to the world.

3   Liturgy, Formation and Mission

The Christian community gathers weekly at eucharist to remember the promise and celebrate Christ's vision of God's coming rule of justice, love and peace. The celebration inspires the attitudes, feelings and thoughts of Christians, and motivates them to fulfil their mission of proclaiming and working for God's reign.

An intentional process of formation (e.g., a catechumenal process) beyond the liturgy, but also integral to it, will incorporate newcomers to the community and renew the commitment of all the faithful to the church's mission.

The liturgy itself must be crafted so that the meaning of its symbolic action is communicated to the participants, and thus nourishes their life in Christ, and empowers them for witness and service.

Thus, a healthy Christian spirituality emerges from the congregation's commitment to worship and to the mission of God which involves nothing less than the renewal and healing of the entire creation.

The worshipping and teaching fellowship is the place of formation in Christ. Formation is the process of accompanying and guiding persons by attending to their hearts, minds and wills as they are transformed by the Spirit. The whole community of faith is involved in this process. In order to support and further such a process, provinces, dioceses, and congregations will need to plan and provide adequate resources.

4   Processes for Provincial Liturgical Renewal

a)   Congregational Renewal

The effective proclamation of Good News to the world depends upon a congregation's living out its baptismal ministry.

Strategies for congregational renewal include the development of forums for discussion, particularly those based on the 'experience-reflection' model of learning. Such a model is integral to the catechumenal process but may be adapted to the needs of the baptized as well. Crucial elements in such a process include the following.

- opportunities to discover and engage deeply in the record of salvation history in order to relate it to daily life.

- participation in the liturgy and reflection upon the experience of the liturgy.

- apprenticeship in prayer, especially intercessory prayer.

- encouragement and mutual support for ministry to the world.

Pastoral preparation and dialogue are essential to liturgical renewal within congregations. While resistance to renewal will likely arise, this can be seen as a pastoral opportunity. In particular, when people are asked to give up something they have valued they will grieve and, indeed, are entitled to do so. The course of liturgical change does not necessarily move forward evenly and consistently. Congregations or groups within congregations are likely to be involved in both old and new practices simultaneously. Leaders and people need to live with the untidiness of such situations.

b)   Leadership and Renewal

The church needs leaders, both lay and ordained, who are able to facilitate and enable renewal and who understand the nature of renewal in community. Moreover, they must experience renewal themselves. Thus, renewal is a collaborative effort between leadership and people. To be effective, it should be an expression of the life of the people.

Education and formation for ministry, involving varieties of academic and practice-based modes of learning, should be available for all leaders, lay and ordained.

The communities in which education and formation for ministry occur will engage in regular corporate worship. They will participate in patterns of self-governance and liturgical worship which are appropriate for healthy congregations and communities.

In theological education, a participatory model is recommended for use in planning and preparing liturgy within the learning community. Seminaries and other theological training centres need to be encouraged to treat liturgical study as a discipline in its own right, fundamental to both Anglican theology and spirituality.

By virtue of the episcopal office, the bishop has the opportunity to renew the vision of the diocese and to affirm liturgical renewal, together with the responsibility to shape and model renewal. We commend to all bishops the creation of standing diocesan liturgical committees composed of lay people and clergy, some of whom will be specialists in liturgy. In some places it may be more effective to establish such a committee at a provincial or national level. Continuing education resources to facilitate renewal will need to be made available. This would include, for example, the provision of diocesan or provincial training programmes in liturgy for musicians. Diocesan workshops can be helpful in establishing and sustaining parish worship committees. At whatever level, such committees would work to enable praying communities to renew the quality of their worship through attention to architecture, music, gesture, art, and vesture, as well as texts.

Further copies of this text are available in booklet form from Grove Books Limited, Ridley Hall Road, Cambridge CB3 9HU Tel: 01223-464748, Fax: 01223-464849

Notes

1   Archbishop H H Clarke, Primate of Canada, Bishop C K Sansbury of Singapore, Archbishop L W Brown of Uganda and the Reverend Professor Massey H Shepherd of the United States.

2   (London: Church Information Office, nd [1965]). Reproduced in Colin O Buchanan (ed), *Modern Anglican Liturgies 1958-1968* (London: Oxford University Press, 1968) pp 31-32.

3   The development from the 1958 Lambeth Conference to the Pan-Anglican Document is traced in detail in Buchanan, op cit, pp 8-32.

4   'Liturgy 1968-1973' in *Partners in Mission*, [Report of the Second Meeting of the Anglican Consultative Council (Dublin, 1973)] (London: ACC, 1973) pp 70-86. Prepared by Bishop Leslie Brown (by then Bishop of St. Edmundsbury and Ipswich) and Canon Ronald Jasper of Westminster Abbey.

5   'Liturgy 1968-1973,' pp 71-73.

6   David R Holeton (ed), subtitled: *Papers in Preparation for the Dublin Consultation,* (Alcuin/GROW Joint Liturgical Study No 27, Nottingham: Grove Books, 1994).

7   This is not uncommon in consensus documents. In working on the World Council of Churches document *Baptism, Eucharist and Ministry,* for example, it was commonly agreed that the three parts of the text reflected different levels of development.

8   In the words of Richard Hooker, 'What these elements are in themselves, it skilleth not, it is enough that to me which take them they are the body and blood of Christ,' and 'Christ assisting this heavenly banquet with his personal and true presence doth by his own divine power add to the natural substance thereof supernatural efficacy, which addition to the nature of those consecrated elements changeth them and maketh them that to us which otherwise they could not be.' (Eccl. Pol. v.lxvii, 12, 11)

9   See Ian Bradley, *The Power of Sacrifice,* (London: Darton, Longman & Todd, 1995).

10   In the Hebrew scriptures there were two kinds of gift-sacrifices: holocausts ('olah), and vegetable or cereal offerings (minhah). To make a 'whole burnt offering' ('olah) was to dedicate oneself to God at significant cost, an idea taken up by Paul in speaking of Christians as 'living sacrifices' (Rom 12.1-2). The gift of God's well-being was celebrated in the 'peace meal' (sh'lamim) of a community, while 'cereal offerings' (minhah) were made in grateful thanks for the bounty of harvest. In order that the people might approach God with confidence, 'sin' (hatta'th) and 'guilt' ('asham) offerings dealt with unwitting religious and civil wrongs. Israel's identity as a people was commemorated in the annual passover rites, involving a range of sacrificial acts.

11   Yom kippur (Leviticus 16).

12   The term 'hilasterion' is difficult to translate. 'Expiation,' the removal of an offence, does not bring out the change of personal relationships involved. 'Propitiation,' on the other hand, while describing a relationship, is so tied up with ideas of appeasement as to be distorting. Moreover, neither word conveys much to many English speakers today. 'Atoning sacrifice' is perhaps the best modern equivalent, picking up the use of hilasterion to refer to the 'mercy seat' in Hebrews 9.5.

13   This distinction can also be illustrated from the experience of societies where sacrifice continues as a regular part of daily life. For example, in Nigeria some tribes practise two basic types of sacrifice: acts of appeasement, and feasts of thanksgiving for the successful outcome of the act. This carries analogies with the rites of Israel and is useful for distinguishing between the finished work of Christ and our celebration of it in a sacrificial thanksgiving meal. See Solomon Amusan, 'Sacrifice in African

Traditional Religion as a means of Understanding Eucharistic Theology,' in *Our Thanks and Praise* (forthcoming). Background paper prepared for IALC-5.

14   See Augustine, *On the Trinity,* 14.

15   J Jeremias, *The Eucharistic Words of Jesus,* (London: SCM Press, 1966) p 254.

16   *Walk in Newness of Life: The Findings of the Fourth International Anglican Liturgical Consultation,* Toronto 1991, I 14.

17   The Consultation on Common Texts, *The Revised Common Lectionary,* (Canada: Wood Lake Books/United States: Abingdon Press/Great Britain, Norwich: Canterbury Press, 1992).

18   'Down to Earth Worship: Findings of the Third International Anglican Liturgical Consultation, York, England, 1989,' 4, in David R. Holeton, ed., *Liturgical Inculturation in the Anglican Communion,* (Alcuin/GROW Liturgical Study 15, Nottingham: Grove Books Limited, 1990) p 9.

19   Walk in Newness of Life, Principles of Christian Initiation, c.

Anglican Communion Office

THE JERUSALEM DOCUMENT

Memorandum of Their Beatitudes
The Patriarchs and of the Heads
of Christian Communities in Jerusalem

on

The Significance of Jerusalem for Christians

The Significance of Jerusalem for Christians

Preamble

1.   On Monday, the 14th of November, 1994, the heads of Christian Communities in Jerusalem met in solemn conclave to discuss the status of the holy city and the situation of Christians there, at the conclusion of which, they issued the following declaration:

Jerusalem, Holy City

2.   Jerusalem is a holy city for the people of the three monotheistic religions: Judaism, Christianity and Islam. Its unique nature of sanctity endows it with a special vocation of calling for reconciliation and harmony among people, whether citizens, pilgrims or visitors. And because of its symbolic and emotive value, Jerusalem has been a rallying cry for different revived nationalistic and fundamentalist stirrings in the region and elsewhere. And, unfortunately, the city has become a source of conflict and disharmony. It is at the heart of the Israeli-Palestinian and Israeli-Arab disputes. While the mystical call of the city attracts believers, its present unenviable situation scandalises many.

The Peace Process

3.   The current Arab-Israeli peace process is on its way towards resolution of the Middle East conflict. Some new facts have already been established, and some concrete signs posted. But in the process Jerusalem has again been side-stepped because its status and especially its sovereignty over the city are the most difficult questions to resolve in future negotiations. Nevertheless, one must already begin to reflect on the questions and do whatever is necessary to be able to approach them in the most favourable conditions when the moment arrives.

Present Positions

4.   When the different sides involved now speak of Jerusalem, they often assume exclusivist positions. Their claims are very divergent, and are indeed conflicting. The Israeli position is that Jerusalem should remain

the unified and eternal capital of the State of Israel, under the absolute sovereignty of Israel alone. The Palestinians, on the other hand, insist that Jerusalem should become the capital of a future State of Palestine, although they do not lay claim to the entire modern city, but envisage only the eastern, Arab part.

Lessons of History

5.   Jerusalem has had a long, eventful history. It has known numerous wars and conquests, and has been destroyed time and again, only to be reborn anew and rise from its ashes, like the mythical phoenix. Religious motivation has always gone hand in hand with political and cultural aspirations, and has often played a preponderant role. This motivation has often led to exclusivism or, at least, to the supremacy of one people over the others. But every exclusivity of every human supremacy is against the prophetic character of Jerusalem. Its universal vocation and appeal is to be a city of peace and harmony among all who dwell therein.

Jerusalem, like the entire Holy Land, has witnessed throughout its history the successive advent of numerous new people; they came from the desert, from the sea, from the north, and from the East. Most often, the newcomers were gradually integrated into the local population. This was a rather constant characteristic. But when the newcomers tried to claim exclusive possession of the city and the land, or refused to integrate themselves, then the others rejected them.

Indeed, the experience of history teaches us that in order for Jerusalem to be a city of peace, no longer lusted after from the outside and thus a bone of contention between warring sides, it cannot belong exclusively to one people of to only one religion. Jerusalem should be open to all, shared by all. Those who govern the city should make it "The Capital of Humankind." This universal vision of Jerusalem would help those who exercise power there to open it to others who also are fondly attached to it and to accept sharing it with them.

The Christian Vision of Jerusalem

6.   Through the prayerful reading of the Bible, Christians recognise in faith that the long history of the people of God, with Jerusalem as its centre, is the history of salvation which fulfils God's design in and through Jesus of Nazareth, the Christ.

The one God has chosen Jerusalem to be the place where His name alone will dwell in the midst of His people, so that they may offer to Him accept-able worship. The prophets look up to Jerusalem, especially after the purification of the exile; Jerusalem will be called "the city of justice, faith-ful city" (Is 1,26-27) where the Lord dwells in holiness as in Sinai (cf Ps 68,18). The Lord will place the city in the middle of the nations (Ez 5,5), where the Second Temple will become a house of prayer for all people (Is 2,2, 56,6-7). Jerusalem, aglow with the presence of God (Is 60,1), ought to be a city whose gates are always open (Is 11), with Peace as magistrate and Justice as government (Is 17).

In the vision of their faith, Christians believe the Jerusalem of the Prophets to be the foreseen place of the salvation in and through Jesus Christ. In the Gospels, Jerusalem rejects the Sent-One, the Saviour; and He weeps over it because this city of the prophets that is also the city of the essential salvific events—the death and resurrection of Jesus—has completely lost sight of the path to peace (ch Lk 19,42).

In the Acts of the Apostles, Jerusalem is the place of the gift of the Spirit, and the birth of the Church, which is the community of the disciples of Jesus who are to be his witnesses not only in Jerusalem but even to the ends of the earth (1,8). In Jerusalem, the first Christian community incarnated the ecclesiastical ideal, and thus it remains a continuing reference point.

The Book of Revelation proclaims the anticipation of the new, heavenly Jerusalem (Gal 4,26: Heb 12,22). This holy city is the image of the new creation and the aspi-rations of all peoples, where God will wipe away all tears, and "there shall be no more death or mourning, crying out or pain, for the former world has passed away" (21,4).

7.   The earthly Jerusalem, in the Christian tradition, prefigures the heavenly Jerusalem as "the vision of peace." In the Liturgy, the Church itself receives the name of Jerusalem and relives all of that city's anguish, joys and hopes. Furthermore, during the first centuries the liturgy of Jerusalem became the foundation of all liturgies everywhere, and later deeply influenced the development of diverse liturgical traditions, because of the many pilgrimages to Jerusalem and the symbolic meaning of the Holy City.

8.   The pilgrimages slowly developed an understanding of the need to unify the sanctification of space through celebrations at the Holy Places, with the sanctification in time through the calendared celebration of the Holy events of salvation (Egeria, Cyril of Jerusalem). Jerusalem soon occu-pied a unique place in the heart of Christianity everywhere. A theology and spirituality of pilgrimage developed. It was an ascetic time of biblical refreshment at the sources, and a time of testing, during which Christians

recalled that they are strangers and pilgrims on earth (cf Heb 1 1,13) and their personal and community vocation, always and everywhere, is to take up the cross and follow Jesus.

The Continuing Presence of a Christian Community

9.   For Christianity, Jerusalem is the place of roots, ever living and nourishing. In Jerusalem is born every Christian. To be in Jerusalem is for every Christian to be at home.

For almost two thousand years, through so many hardships and the succession of so many powers, the local Church, with its faithful, has always been actively present in Jerusalem. Across the centuries, the local Church has been witnessing to the life and preaching, the death and resurrection of Jesus Christ upon the same Holy Places, and its faithful have been receiving other brothers and sisters in the faith, as pilgrims, resident or in transit, inviting them to be reimmersed into the refreshing, ever living ecclesiastical sources. That continuing presence of a living Christian community is inseparable from the historical sites. Through the "living stones" the holy archaeological sites take on "life."

The City as Holy and as Other Cities

10.   The significance of Jerusalem for Christians thus has two inseparable, fundamental dimensions:

1)   a Holy City with holy places most precious to Christians because of their link with the history of salvation fulfilled in and through Jesus Christ;

2)   a city with a community of Christians which has been living continually there since its origins.

Thus for local Christian, as well as for local Jews and Muslims, Jerusalem is not only a Holy City, but also their native city where they live, whence their right to continue to live there freely, with all the rights which come from that.

Legitimate Demands of Christians for Jerusalem

11.   In so far as Jerusalem is the quintessential Holy City, it above all ought to enjoy full freedom of access to its holy places and freedom of

worship. Those rights of property ownership, custody and worship, which the different Churches have acquired throughout history, should continue to be retained by the same communities. *These rights which are already protected in the Status Quo of the Holy Places, according to historical "Firmans" and other documents, should continue to be recognised and respected.*

The Christians of the entire world, Western or Eastern, should have the right to come on pilgrimage to Jerusalem. They ought to be able to find there all that is necessary to carry out their pilgrimage in the spirit of their authentic tradition: freedom to visit and to move around, to pray at holy sites, to embark into spiritual attendance and respectful practice of their faith, to enjoy the possibility of a prolonged stay and the benefits of hospitality and dignified lodgings.

12.   The local Christian communities should enjoy all those rights to enable them to continue their active presence in freedom and to fulfil their responsibilities towards both their own local members and the Christian pilgrims throughout the world.

Local Christians, not only in their capacity as Christians per se, but like all other citizens, religious or not, should enjoy the same fundamental rights for all: social, cultural, political and national.

Among these rights are:

- the human right of freedom of worship and of conscience, both as individuals and as religious communities;

- civil and historical rights which allow them to carry out their religious, educational, medical and other duties of charity;

- the right to have their own institutions, such as hospices for pilgrims, institutes for the study of the Bible and the Traditions, centres for encounters with believers of other religions, monasteries, churches, cemeteries, and so forth, and the right to have their own personnel to run these institutions.

13.   In claiming these rights for themselves, Christians recognise and respect similar and parallel rights of Jewish and Muslim believers and their communities. Christians declare themselves disposed to search with Jews and Muslims for a mutually respectful application of these rights and a harmonious coexistence, in the perspective of the universal spiritual vocation of Jerusalem.

Special Statute for Jerusalem

14.   All this presupposes a special judicial and political stature for Jerusalem which reflects the universal importance and significance of the city.

1)   In order to satisfy the national aspirations of all its inhabitants, and in order that Jews, Christians and Muslims can be "at home" in Jerusalem and at peace with one another, representatives from the three monotheistic religions, in addition to local political powers, ought to be associated in the elaboration and application of such a special statute.

2)   Because of the universal significance of Jerusalem, the international community ought to be engaged in the stability and permanence of this statute. Jerusalem is too precious to be dependent solely on municipal or national political authorities, whoever they may be. Experience shows that an international guarantee is necessary.

Experience shows that such local authorities, for political reasons or the claims of security, sometimes are required to violate the rights of free access to the Holy Places. Therefore, it is necessary to accord Jerusalem a special statute which will allow Jerusalem not to be victimised by laws imposed as a result of hostilities or wars but to be an open city which transcends local, regional or world political troubles. This statute, established in common by local political and religious authorities, should also be guaranteed by the international community.

Conclusion

Jerusalem is a symbol and a promise of the presence of God and the fraternity and peace for humankind, in particular for the children of Abraham, who include the Jews, Christians and Muslims. We call upon all parties concerned to comprehend and accept the nature and deep significance of Jerusalem, City of God. None can appropriate it in exclusivist ways. We invite each party to go beyond all exclusivist visions or actions, and without discrimination, to consider the religious and national aspirations of others, in order to give back to Jerusalem its true universal character and to make the city a holy place of reconciliation for humankind.

Anglican Communion Office

THE PORVÖO DECLARATION

The Porvöo Declaration

We, the Church of Denmark, the Church of England, the Estonian Evangelical-Lutheran Church, the Evangelical-Lutheran Church of Finland, the Evangelical-Lutheran Church of Iceland, the Church of Ireland, the Evangelical-Lutheran Church of Latvia, the Evangelical-Lutheran Church of Lithuania, the Church of Norway, the Scottish Episcopal Church, the Church of Sweden, and the Church in Wales, on the basis of our common understanding of the nature and purpose of the Church, fundamental agreement in faith and our agreement on episcopacy in the service of the apostolicity of the Church, contained in Chapters II-IV of *The Porvöo Common Statement,* make the following acknowledgements and commitments

a (i) we acknowledge one another's churches as churches belonging to the One, Holy, Catholic and Apostolic Church of Jesus Christ and truly participating in the apostolic mission of the whole people of God;

(ii) we acknowledge that in all our churches the Word of God is authentically preached, and the sacraments of baptism and the eucharist are duly administered;

(iii) we acknowledge that all our churches share in the common confession of the apostolic faith;

(iv) we acknowledge that one another's ordained ministries are given by God as instruments of his grace and as possessing not only the inward call of the Spirit, but also Christ's commission through his body, the Church;

(v) we acknowledge that personal, collegial and communal oversight *(episcopé)* is embodied and exercised in all our churches in a variety of forms, in continuity of apostolic life, mission and ministry;

(vi) we acknowledge that the episcopal office is valued and maintained in all our churches as a visible sign expressing and serving the Church's unity and continuity in apostolic life, mission and ministry.

b   We commit ourselves

(i) to share a common life in mission and service, to pray for and with one another, and to share resources;

(ii) to welcome one another's members to receive sacramental and other pastoral ministrations;

(iii) to regard baptised members of all our churches as members of our own;

(iv) to welcome diaspora congregations into the life of the indigenous churches, to their mutual enrichment;

(v) to welcome persons episcopally ordained in any of our churches to the office of bishop, priest or deacon to serve, by invitation and in accordance with any regulations which may from time to time be in force, in that ministry in the receiving church without re-ordination;

(vi) to invite one another's bishops normally to participate in the laying on of hands at the ordination of bishops, as a sign of the unity and continuity of the Church;

(vii) to work towards a common understanding of diaconal ministry;

(viii) to establish appropriate forms of collegial and conciliar consultation on significant matters of faith and order, life and work;

(ix) to encourage consultations of representatives of our churches, and to facilitate learning and exchange of ideas and information in theological and pastoral matters;

(x) to establish a contact group to nurture our growth in communion and to co-ordinate the implementation of this agreement.

Anglican Communion Office

PETITION ON CLIMATE CHANGE

World Council of Churches Petition on Climate Change

150 Route De Ferney
P.O. Box 21001211
Geneva 2 Switzerland

Telephone 022-791 61 11
Telefax 022-791 03 61
Telex 415 730 OIK CH
Cable OIKOUMENE GENEVA

To Member Churches and National Councils in Industrialised Countries

Re: Petition Campaign on Climate Change

Dear Friends,

For some years, the World Council of Churches has been concerned with climate change and its implications for the future of humanity. You remember the statement the Central Committee issued at its meeting in Johannesburg (January 1994) and the study of the paper which was shared with you. The following describes the broad range of current WCC initiatives on climate change which are coordinated by the committee chaired by Dr. David Hallman.

Unfortunately, governments are slow in taking the measures needed to meet the threat. In March/April last year delegations of the countries that have ratified the Climate Change Convention met in Berlin. Mindful of our ecumenical relationships, the WCC supported the urgent appeal from countries most exposed to the consequences of climate change (see the statement by the Pacific Conference of Churches on pp. 20-23 of the enclosed booklet). However, the governments did not adopt binding reduction targets of greenhouse gas emissions. They only decided to engage in a new round of negotiations, in the hope that new results can be reached by Autumn 1997 when the UN-General Assembly will evaluate the follow up of the United Nations Conference on Environment and Development (1992).

Often, government representatives explained their inability or unwillingness to act by referring to the perceived lack of support by the population. Clearly, further progress is only possible if the level of consciousness about the urgency of the issue can be raised. To contribute to this goal, the World Council of Churches proposes to the member churches in the industrialised governments, through this petition, to take more determined actions. This petition would be circulated simultaneously in industrialised countries. We are concentrating on industrialised greenhouse gas emissions and largely have resisted taking adequate steps to address the magnitude of the problem, in our view.

The petition campaign is being launched between April and June of 1996, depending upon the country, and will run through January 1997. The signatures then will be first submitted to national governments and later, in an appropriate way, to the UN. We enclose the text of the petition. Obviously, the wording will need to be adapted to the context of each country.

Some details about climate change and its impact on society can be found in the WCC study paper of which we include another copy. Meanwhile, a new report of the Intergovernmental Panel on Climate Change (IPCC), a representative UN body of scientists has been published (December 1995). It confirms earlier findings and further affirms that actions of humankind are contributing to the problem. Therefore, it urges governments not to further delay action.

In preparing for our campaign, we have made contact with various international church organisations. We are happy to report that the following have greed to support the campaign: Ecumenical Patriarchate of Constantinople, Lutheran World Federation, World Alliance of Reformed Churches, General Conference of Seventh-Day Adventists, World YMCA and World YWCA. Others have indicated that they will take up the matter through their decision making bodies in due time. From initial contacts, we are also confident that various environmental organisations will be supportive of the campaign. Therefore, we encourage you to be in contact with the organisations in your country affiliated with these bodies.

I draw your attention to the attachment which provides details about the climate change petition campaign in your country. If you need further information from the WCC, please contact Dr David Hallman in care of Ms Marise Pegat-Toquet, World Council of Churches, Unit III, Justice, Peace and Creation, 150 route de Ferney, P.O. Box 2100, 1211 Geneva 2, Switzerland, Tel: 022-791 6551 or 022-791 6121, Fax: 022-791 03 61, Telex: 415 730 OIKCH or by e-mail: mpt@wcc-coe.org.

Revd. Dr. Konrad Raiser
General Secretary
World Council of Churches

**CLIMATE CHANGE
URGENT ACTION NEEDED!**

International Petition to Governments of Industrialised Countries

There is now strong scientific consensus that the atmosphere is warming as a result of human activity, and that this is likely to have far-reaching environmental, social and economic consequences. Climate change is a serious threat to the well-being of creation.

The effects of climate change are predicted to include more intense storms, more floods, more droughts and more disease. To keep climate change within bearable limits, the emissions of greenhouse gases, especially carbon dioxide (CO_2), must be significantly reduced.

Industrialised countries are the main source of these emissions, while the first victims will be the small island states such as in the Pacific and low-lying coastal countries like Bangladesh.

Despite the clear risks, governments are slow to act.

In solidarity with those most likely to suffer from climate change, the signatories of this petition ask their government to take steps required to meet the danger:

• by fulfilling their promise made in the context of the Rio Earth Summit to reduce greenhouse gas emissions to 1990 levels by the year 2000;

• by establishing firm polity measures and adopting a binding international agreement which will achieve greater reductions in emissions after the year 2000, primarily through renewable energy sources, energy efficiency, reforming market incentives and new consumption patterns (without relying on an increase in nuclear power generation); and

• by initiating more forcefully the public debate on climate change issues, and increasing the citizens' active participation in finding solutions.

By signing this petition, we declare our commitment to accept the consequences of reductions for society, economy and our personal lives. We are prepared to take responsible steps in our own lives to reduce our energy consumption and greenhouse gas emissions. We believe that such changes would improve the long-term quality of life for all.

NAME	ADDRESS	SIGNATURE

1. _____
2. _____
3. _____
4. _____
5. _____
6. _____
7. _____
8. _____
9. _____
10. _____

PETITION BACKGROUND

This petition is being circulated throughout industrialised countries. It has been initiated by the World Council of Churches and has the support of the following organisations so far: Ecumenical Patriarchate of Constantinople, Lutheran World Federation, World Alliance of Reformed Churches, World Alliance of Young Men's Christian Associations (YMCA), World Alliance of Young Women's Christian Associations (YWCA), Friends of the Earth, International Society of Doctors for the Environment, and General Conference of Seventh-Day Adventists. More endorsements are anticipated.

Climate Change

The UN's Inter-governmental Panel on Climate Change (IPCC) has recently confirmed in its Second Assessment Report that the climate changes we observe today are due to human activity. The IPCC includes scientists from around the world working on climate change.

These changes are caused by the emission of greenhouse gases which leads to a gradual warming of the atmosphere. Carbon dioxide, the most significant of these gases, is released in large quantities into the atmosphere through the burning of fossil fuels, e.g., through industry, heating, the increasing number of cars and other vehicles. In the past, and at present, the industrialised countries are the main source of these emissions. If the total amount over the last century is taken into account, they are responsible for over 80 percent. Therefore, it is imperative that the consumption of energy from fossil fuels be dramatically reduced in these countries.

At the Earth Summit in Rio de Janeiro (1992), our government signed the

Convention on Climate Change and accepts, as a first step, the obligation to stabilise greenhouse gas emissions by the year 2000 at 1990 levels. From the beginning, it was clear that further reductions had to be achieved after the year 2000. However, measures to date are insufficient. Projections show that emissions will increase considerably after 2000. This danger must be prevented.

We will all suffer from the consequences of climate change, but the first victims of rising sea levels and more intense storms will be small island states and low-lying coastal zones such as Bangladesh.

In international negotiations they press for swift action. The Alliance of Small Island States (AOSIS) has submitted to the international community a proposal to strengthen the Convention on Climate Change, i.e., to reduce emissions from industrialised countries by 20% by the year 2005.

The IPCC Reports show that a reduction of at least half of the present level will have to be achieved in the next 50 years, in order to prevent dramatically destructive effects. In order to avert the loss of small island nations and other serious climate change consequences for us all, the faster we take the necessary measures, the less drastic they will need to be in the future.

Significant reductions can occur though increased energy efficiency and use of renewable energy resources. Yet deeper reductions in industrialised country emissions, needed in the longer term, will require more far-reaching changes. Morally, there is no other choice. The signatories of the petition call on both the government and the public to move forward on the needed reductions. We are further convinced that, in the long run, the decisions required will enhance the quality of life for present and future generations, both in our own country and around the world.

The signatories believe that taking action to reduce the threat of climate change is an important contribution to the struggle for justice, peace and the well-being of all creation.

A Final Thought

The Anglican Communion story is one of sorrow and challenge, of joy and thanksgiving. It is a way of life for Christians who honour Scripture, Tradition, and Reason as foundations for their faith and who look for God the Holy Spirit for guidance and empowerment as God's purposes continue to be revealed more and more. The Via Media is an exciting place to be as it allows Anglicans to have confidence in the inheritance of the apostolic and catholic faith and an openness to the Spirit leading us to fullness of life in Jesus.

The Editors